'The authors are amongst the most experienced clinician-researchers in the field of eating disorders. With the publication of *A Cognitive Interpersonal Therapy Workbook for Treating Anorexia Nervosa: The Maudsley Model*, they bring their treatment for anorexia nervosa to you. Whether you work through the workbook on your own or together with a therapist, you will be benefiting from the wisdom that can only come from decades of clinical experience.

The treatment approach and workbook emerged from listening carefully to patients and carers in order to understand their perspective and their needs for a successful treatment. The book carefully walks you down a path of recovery, richly augmenting text with exercises and illustrations to engage you in the process of achieving wellness. By including true stories from people who have recovered, the authors invite you to enter the recovery space of those who have successfully overcome the burden of anorexia nervosa.

They will help you transform your vicious flower of illness into a virtuous flower of recovery and help you to write your own story of who you can and will be once you leave anorexia nervosa behind. You will experience their empathy and understanding in every chapter of this book. *A Cognitive Interpersonal Therapy Workbook for Treating Anorexia Nervosa: The Maudsley Model* is an important evidence-based tool that is indispensable to your recovery journey.'

Professor Cynthia Bulik, PhD, FAED, Distinguished Professor of Eating Disorders, University of North Carolina at Chapel Hill, Professor, Karolinska Institutet, Stockholm, Sweden.

'It gives me great pleasure to provide this endorsement of the MANTRA workbook. Working with people who are simultaneously embracing and battling anorexia nervosa is one of the hardest types of therapy I have encountered in thirty years of practice as a clinical psychologist across a number of clinical settings and conditions. When I first came across the emerging MANTRA approach in 2003, it was like a breath of fresh and invigorating air. It provided a validating and respectful approach, utilized the principles of motivational interviewing in the way material was presented, contained clear connections between the evidence and inclusion of a range of modules, and was associated with creative and engaging exercises that allowed for inclusion of collaborative work with a therapist.

Many years have now passed, and a body of solid evidence for the usefulness of MANTRA with anorexia nervosa has accumulated, such that it is now one of three recommended adult outpatient treatments in the 2017 NICE guidelines. This published workbook now gives people with lived experience of anorexia nervosa and therapists alike easy access to MANTRA by providing: Logically sequenced creative and self-reflective exercises that encourage the person with anorexia nervosa to develop an observer's point of view and see the bigger picture, thus freeing them up to make different choices about how they respond to the anorexia nervosa; Clear advice and tips based on best-practice and informed by emerging research; Illustrative examples from people's experiences with feeling confused by, and overwhelmed with, anorexia nervosa, and making inroads against this destructive disease.

It is certainly my clinical experience with this workbook that people with anorexia nervosa find it engaging, challenging, and promoting self-efficacy and optimism for a future that involves a healthier and richer life that has expanded well beyond the confines of control over food and weight. It should certainly be on every clinician's shelf if they working with this group of people.'

Professor Tracey Wade, Matthew Flinders Distinguished Professor of Psychology, Flinders University, Adelaide, Australia

A Cognitive Interpersonal Therapy Workbook for Treating Anorexia Nervosa

Based on the authors' pioneering work and up-to-date research at London's Maudsley hospital, *A Cognitive Interpersonal Therapy Workbook for Treating Anorexia Nervosa: The Maudsley Model* provides adults with anorexia nervosa and the professionals working alongside them with a practical resource to work through together.

The treatment approach described here, which is called the Maudsley Model of Anorexia Treatment for Adults (MANTRA), is recommended by the National Institute of Clinical and Care Excellence (NICE) as a first-line, evidence-based treatment for adults with anorexia nervosa. *Workbook* provides adults with anorexia nervosa and the professionals working alongside them with a practical resource to work through together.

The manual is divided into accessible modules, providing a co-ordinated, step-by-step guide to recovery. Modules cover e.g.:

- Nutrition
- Developing treatment goals
- Exploring thinking styles
- Developing an identity beyond anorexia.

A Cognitive Interpersonal Therapy Workbook for Treating Anorexia Nervosa is a highly beneficial aid to recovery for those with the condition, their families and mental health professionals.

Ulrike Schmidt is Professor of Eating Disorders at King's College London and a Consultant Psychiatrist in Eating Disorders at the South London and Maudsley NHS Foundation Trust.

Helen Startup is a Consultant Clinical Psychologist and Senior Research Fellow at the Sussex Partnership NHS Foundation Trust.

Janet Treasure is Professor of Psychiatry at King's College London and a Consultant Psychiatrist in Eating Disorders at the South London and Maudsley NHS Foundation Trust.

A Cognitive Interpersonal Therapy Workbook for Treating Anorexia Nervosa

- The Maudsley Model

Ulrike Schmidt, Helen Startup and Janet Treasure

Routledge
Taylor & Francis Group

LONDON AND NEW YORK

First published 2019
by Routledge
2 Park Square, Milton Park, Abingdon, Oxon OX14 4RN

and by Routledge
711 Third Avenue, New York, NY 10017

Routledge is an imprint of the Taylor & Francis Group, an informa business

British Library Cataloguing-in-Publication Data
A catalogue record for this book is available from the British Library

Library of Congress Cataloging-in-Publication Data
A catalog record for this book has been requested

ISBN: 978-1-138-83193-3 (hbk)
ISBN: 978-1-138-83289-3 (pbk)
ISBN: 978-1-315-72848-3 (ebk)

Typeset in Stone Serif
by Apex CoVantage, LLC

Contents

Acknowledgements

A big thank you goes to all our colleagues in the Eating Disorders Unit at the Maudsley Hospital who have shared with us their clinical wisdom, creativity and passionate belief in helping their patients to get bigger lives. They have seen this manual through successive versions and have questioned, critiqued, inspired and immensely improved what is the present version.

Our heartfelt thanks also go to our patients and families who inspired some of the stories presented here, road-tested this book and treatment approach and generously commented on their experience of working with this manual. The carers' worksheets were written with the help of people who had their own experience of an eating disorder. Many thanks to Dr Pam MacDonald, Dr Emmakate Buchanan and Dr Anne Crane.

We are also very grateful to Kate Williams, the chief dietician at the Maudsley Hospital, who successfully dragged the nutrition chapter into the 21st century at a time when she had many other things to think about, most notably her retirement and her grandchildren. And finally thank you, Holly Holman, for your motivating and timely feedback on all the chapters.

Introduction

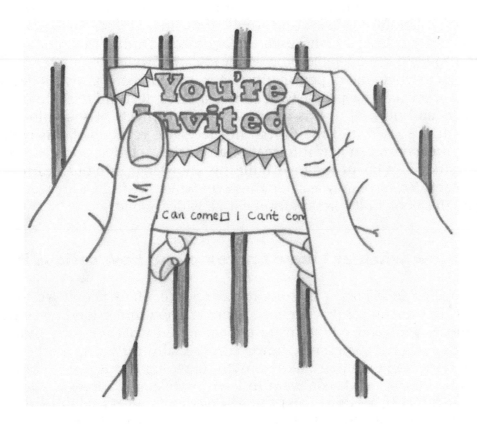

This workbook is for people who have anorexia nervosa (hereafter referred to as 'anorexia') and who want to work on their recovery or are considering it. Yes, even if you haven't yet made up your mind or are terrified of the prospect of change or recovery, this book is definitely for you, helping you to consider the pros and cons of seeking help and making changes. It is also a book for families, partners and friends, describing how they can support the person with anorexia. Finally, it may be useful for any therapists working with people with anorexia, to help them structure their work.

The birthplace of the book and the approach on which it is based is the Eating Disorders Unit at the Maudsley Hospital in London, which has a strong track record in developing new treatments and services for people with eating disorders and their families. Several of these treatments have been adopted all over the world and are recommended by the National Institute of Clinical and Care Excellence (NICE) in its guidelines. Therefore, we decided to call our approach the Maudsley Model of Anorexia Nervosa Treatment for Adults, or MANTRA for short. MANTRA has been tried and tested in several clinical trials and is recommended by the (2017) NICE guidelines[1] as a first-line treatment for anorexia nervosa.

Our motivation in developing MANTRA stemmed from our frustration that many of the existing treatments weren't sufficiently tailored to the needs of people with anorexia. Over a period of more than 10 years, we have drafted and re-drafted improved versions of this workbook based on helpful feedback and input from many of our patients and from many colleagues who used the approach. During this time there has also been considerable progress in research, trying to answer questions as to what kind of personality factors put someone at risk of developing anorexia; how people with anorexia think, feel and relate to other people; and how all of this interacts with the effects of starvation, to keep them locked into the illness. In successive versions of this workbook, we have taken new information from these clinical and neuroscience studies on board and have built this knowledge into our treatment approach. We have now reached the point where we feel we are ready to share this book in its present form with a wider public.

I don't know whether I have anorexia and how serious it is

Diagnosing anorexia per se is not rocket science. Many people we come across in our clinical practice have a pretty good understanding of the common signs and symptoms of anorexia, and what are early indicators of concern. Sometimes, however, especially early on, the person themselves can't see that there is anything wrong and it is close others who are concerned. If you want to learn more about anorexia, the UK National Health Service (NHS) Choices website[2] and the website of the charity Beat[3] contain solid information for people with anorexia and other eating disorders to help them understand their condition. Alternatively, there are a number of easily accessible books out there.[4] And if you are really keen on the latest research information on all aspects of anorexia, there are also a couple of detailed review papers in high-quality journals.[5, 6]

However, we are not advocating self-diagnosis here. Occasionally, other medical conditions can mimic anorexia or contribute to weight loss. It is also really hard for people with anorexia to judge how severe their condition is, what are the associated risks and when and how much to worry. Often anorexia leads to or occurs together with other psychological or physical problems. These may need treatment in their own right, and if addressed may allow the person to move forward much more swiftly. It is therefore always advisable to have a thorough medical assessment, to get a clear diagnosis of the main problem and any linked problems, an assessment of risks and recommendations about what kind and level of professional support and treatment is needed for you to move forward.

I want to go it alone – is that possible?

Anorexia often isolates people and cuts them off from vital supports. It can also make the person rather wary of close others who may want to give support but inadvertently take over. Similarly, experiences with health professionals – sad though this may seem – are not always optimally helpful and supportive and are sometimes outright unhelpful. So it is entirely understandable that you might want to go it alone with this book. However, anorexia plays many tricks on the person, and without some form of external feedback and support it is much harder to notice and resist these. So our firm advice is that you do think again and try to find an understanding and helpful professional or close other to get you started and support you.

If that seems scary, have another look at the National Health Service (NHS) Choices and Beat websites (notes 2 and 3) which we have already mentioned. These have links and resources available to support help seeking. For example, Beat has produced a guide about how to talk to your general practitioner and what help is available in different areas. In other countries, similar charities exist that may be a useful starting point when you are unsure about whether and where to seek help and what to ask for.

Destination 'bigger life'

It has become a bit of a cliché to think of recovery from an illness such as anorexia as a journey. Having said that, the image of a journey is a useful cliché. Talking with clinicians in our team, depending on their background they see recovery from anorexia either as a journey across treacherous seas, as a climb up a steep mountain, as a wander through deep dark forests or alternatively as a trip up a giant sand dune (where in order to get to the top you'll need to keep momentum going or you'll slide back). Or sometimes it is seen as an arduous journey across all these different terrains.

However, for many of our patients the prospect of recovery from anorexia feels a bit like a journey into outer space, i.e. a journey from which there may be no return and where the destination is uncertain, open-ended and potentially fraught with encounters with nasty aliens and other unimaginable challenges.

We firmly believe that recovery from anorexia is a journey with a definite destination, one which – if it was a train station – would be called 'bigger life', with greater possibilities for flourishing and fulfilling your potential, greater connection to other people, greater stamina and better health. Unlike an *actual* journey to a place, arriving at destination 'bigger life' means you will continue to face many challenges but are now better equipped to deal with them.

So working with this book requires a bit of a leap of faith, that there really is anything worthwhile at the end of the journey. Patients often contact us several years after treatment to tell us how much their lives have changed for the better, with them enjoying relationships, having families and flourishing in their studies and work. What they also often say is how hard it was for them to make a start, to build up momentum and to keep going with rebuilding their lives. But they all agree that it has been very worthwhile. So do please get stuck in.

How to use this book

Chapter 1 gives a bit of an overview over our MANTRA treatment model and puts this into the context of the promises and problems of anorexia. We also describe what other treatments are out there. If you are the sort of person who likes to have an overview before getting 'stuck in', do have a look at Chapter 1. However, especially if you are working through this book with a therapist, you can skip straight to Chapter 2 and get started. You can then decide which of the following chapters are most relevant to you and in which order. Whilst not every chapter is equally relevant to everybody, we do recommend that everybody works through Chapters 5 and 6 because they are key to understanding what keeps your anorexia going and planning which chapters to focus on thereafter. Two key sections of the book concern emotions and relationships (Chapter 7) and thinking style (Chapter 8). We agonised over which order to present them in. Many people working through this book will have identified difficulties in both areas as contributing to their anorexia (Chapter 5). The thinking style chapter (Chapter 8) on the surface probably seems less challenging to many people, whereas the chapter on your emotional and social mind (Chapter 7) may lead you into much hotter water. Nonetheless we chose to present the more challenging chapter first simply because strong feelings tend to bubble up whenever people try to make changes, and here we present you with tools for dealing with these. However, if you prefer, it is perfectly alright to reverse the order and go to thinking styles first. The chapter on identity (Chapter 9) comes near the end because we thought that for many people the issue of who they are without anorexia would arise once they had made considerable changes, i.e. towards the end of their therapeutic journey. However, we have had some patients who have found it very useful to go to this chapter early on, to help motivate themselves to make changes to their anorexia. So you can see, there is no right or wrong here and you can follow your instincts.

And finally. . .

Here is how one of our patients summed up the MANTRA workbook for her:

> For me MANTRA has acted like an anchor on the bad days . . . use it as guidance, because everyone will connect with the areas in different ways. . . . do not feel stupid or childish when drawing pictures, or filling out a chart. MANTRA is not there to patronise, it is there to aid; in fact once you start to fill in sections it actually helps you to come to terms with your own thoughts and feelings reflectively at your own pace. Also I would suggest giving yourself freedom to write, scribble and doodle on each page if you feel the need to – there is no right or wrong.

Notes

1 National Institute for Health and Care Excellence. Eating disorders: recognition and treatment. 23 May 2017. http://nice.org.uk/guidance/ng69.
2 www.nhs.uk/conditions/Anorexia-nervosa/Pages/Introduction.aspx.
3 www.b-eat.co.uk/?gclid=CMbPntP0gNQCFW4R0wodINkPeg.
4 Treasure, J. & Alexander, J. (2013). *Anorexia Nervosa: A Recovery Guide for Sufferers, Families and Friends*. 2nd edition. Routledge. London and New York.
5 Zipfel, S., Giel, K.E., Bulik, C.M., Hay, P., & Schmidt, U. Anorexia nervosa: aetiology, assessment, and treatment. *Lancet Psychiatry*. 2015 Dec; 2(12):1099–111.
6 Treasure, J., Zipfel, S., Micali, N., Wade, T., Stice, E., Claudino, A., . . . Wentz, E. Anorexia nervosa. *Nature Reviews Disease Primers*. 2015 Nov; 26(1):15074.

Chapter 1

The background to MANTRA

The promises and problems of anorexia

Anorexia nervosa is a puzzling illness. At the heart of it are symptoms which to the casual observer are hard to understand. Persistent food restriction, driven by intense fears of fatness, fullness and eating certain foods leads to significant weight loss. A range of other behaviours designed to aid weight loss may also be used. As the illness gathers momentum, it increasingly takes a toll on the person's brain, body and mind. Thinking becomes preoccupied with food and how to avoid it, decision making and concentration become impaired, the ability to read one's own and others' emotions becomes limited, anxiety and depression increase, and myriad physical problems arise affecting all major organs from the heart to the bones. In parallel, the illness becomes ever more visible to others, who in turn become increasingly concerned and may be alarmed by the person's obliviousness to growing concerns and danger.

One rarely speaks of a 'mild' case of anorexia. The problem with anorexia is that for a sensitive individual facing a period of life stress, it does a lot of things very well: it promptly and efficiently numbs the person's emotions; it consumes their thoughts by setting itself as the priority; it narrows the person's interpersonal world; and it acts as a buffer to the demands of loved ones. In the short term, anorexia offers something of a cocoon from the demands of life and the social world, but in a relatively short space of time it takes hold as symptoms become rewarding, compulsive or habitual. It represents a quandary: it is a serious psychiatric condition with a high mortality rate, yet from the perspective of the person with anorexia it is often considered a 'valued' part of their identity.

Most clinicians dedicated to work in eating disorders are united in the acknowledgement that this is a tricky and at times anxiety-provoking area of clinical work. Whether you are a person with anorexia, a loved one wanting to be of help or a therapist supporting your patient toward recovery, the journey to overcoming anorexia requires a great deal of patience and endurance along with a genuine curiosity to get to know the specifics and subtleties of the illness. We have developed a treatment approach that has been directly informed by the views of people with anorexia and their families, by our clinical work and our research in this field. The modules stem from growing research data, highlighting that individuals with anorexia have particular struggles managing their social and emotional world and a particular thinking style and that the effects of starvation have a big role to play in the 'stuckness' endured by individuals with anorexia. The aim of the treatment is to encourage the individual with anorexia to get to know their anorexia as fully as possible, to be conscious and curious about its role in all spheres of life so that they can make decisions about whether to remain with anorexia or whether to take steps to live in a different way.

In this chapter we will begin with an overview of available psychological treatments for anorexia; we will present our MANTRA model and then some evidence for its effectiveness. Finally, we will present some evidence outlining what patients and therapists think of MANTRA.

Available treatments: is the glass half empty or half full?

Most experts, including those on the NICE guidelines (2017),[1] agree that psychological therapies, which include a focus on eating and weight and related thoughts and feelings, are the treatment of choice for people with anorexia. For most people with anorexia, this can be delivered in community settings. In the UK only a small proportion of people with a very severe form of the illness get treated in specialist inpatient units. So how well are we doing with those psychological therapies, and is the glass half empty or half full? Until recently, we would definitely have said that in relation to anorexia treatments the glass was half empty. Now we think that the glass is at least half full, if not more so. What is the reason for this change in opinion? First, until about five years ago only a trickle of mainly small clinical trials focused on treatments for anorexia nervosa. This is reflected in the fact that the first set of eating disorder guidelines by NICE published in 2004[2] did not give a single 'grade A' recommendation about the treatment of anorexia nervosa. (NICE only gives grade A recommendations for treatments that are supported by several high-quality large clinical trials.) Since then the evidence base has much improved, and over the last five years in particular large-scale trials of anorexia treatments have emerged which give us much clearer answers as to what works. We can now say with considerable confidence that for children and adolescents with anorexia, family-based treatments work better than individual treatment. Different forms of effective family-based treatments are available, ranging from anorexia-focused family therapy (where everyone is included and seen together) to multi-family group treatments (where several families with youngsters with anorexia are seen together and can learn from each other) and separate treatment of parents and the young person. For adults with anorexia, three different individual psychological therapies have an evidence base and are recommended by NICE (2017) as a first choice. These are cognitive behavioural therapy (CBT), MANTRA and specialist supportive clinical management. A fourth treatment, focal psychodynamic therapy, can be considered as an alternative. As yet there is no clear front runner and it is hard to know which of these treatments works best for whom.

So what are the strengths and characteristics of MANTRA? Importantly, in contrast to some of the other anorexia treatments which have been adapted from treatments for other disorders, MANTRA is unique in that it has been designed with the needs, characteristics and illness-maintaining factors of anorexia in mind.

In our development of MANTRA we started off trying to map out the key factors that may 'drive' a person into anorexia and those that keep them 'stuck' with anorexia. We did this based on a thorough review of the research literature.[3] This model has since been revised based on further research evidence.[4] Our treatment programme is based on this model and is organised into modules that seek to directly tackle each of the factors that we know keep anorexia going. As every person with anorexia will vary, there is flexibility in the treatment programme. There are certain 'core' modules (Chapters 2 to 6), which most people with anorexia tell us are useful and important, and we would recommend that these are worked through in order. Then there are various other modules, some of which will suit some people and not others. As we go along, we will try to guide you to devise a treatment plan that suits you or the person you are trying to support. We will begin by sharing our model of anorexia; see what you think.

The MANTRA model

MANTRA (the Maudsley Model of Anorexia Nervosa Treatment in Adults) is a cognitive-interpersonal[5] treatment for adults with anorexia that considers both the biology and psychology of the disorder and how these factors interact to keep anorexia going.[3, 4, 6] MANTRA is a stand-alone treatment for anorexia that when delivered weekly can take between 20 to 30 one-hour sessions, depending on illness severity and the degree of support you have along the way. So far, MANTRA has been applied mainly within clinic settings and guided by therapists. However, an adapted version of MANTRA was recently piloted by our team in an internet-delivered relapse prevention study for individuals with severe anorexia.[7] In this study individuals with severe anorexia who had been treated as inpatients and were leaving hospital completed the modules at home with weekly email support from a therapist. The study showed that patients benefited from MANTRA, suggesting that this treatment package can be completed with good outcome and with minimal professional guidance. However, we did encourage all the patients in the study to have some monitoring of physical risk from their general practitioner (GP) or eating disorder team. So if you are not working through MANTRA with a therapist, we would recommend that as a minimum you let your GP know that you are engaged in self-help treatment so that they can help you monitor your progress. We also suggest that you aim to choose at least one person you trust (either family or friend or professional) to share in your journey. This is someone you can call on for support and share in the highs and lows of recovery. What we did learn from the internet relapse prevention study is that minimal support (such as weekly emails from a sensitive professional) is very much more helpful than just going it alone.

The MANTRA model proposes that anorexia typically arises in people with a certain type of personality including anxious, sensitive and/ or perfectionist, obsessional traits. Maybe you can recognise these traits? The model suggests that anorexia is maintained by four broad factors, all of which are intensified by the biological effects of starvation. Thus an unhelpful feedback loop is formed between the consequences of starvation and these maintenance factors. At the heart of the treatment manual is an individualised formulation depicted as a 'vicious flower' which maps out the 'petals' or factors that keep an individual's illness going. These factors include, first, an inflexible, detail-focused and perfectionist way of approaching life tasks (such as needing to be absolutely certain a piece of work is 'perfect' before handing it in); second, difficulties in the domain of emotions and relationships (such as difficulties allowing, 'being with', managing and showing emotions, particularly in the context of relationships, feeling sensitive to rejection or the possibility of failure); third, in keeping with these characteristics, affected individuals typically develop beliefs about the positives of anorexia in their lives (such as anorexia keeps me safe, in control and admired by others); lastly, family members and partners may unwittingly maintain anorexia by bending their behaviours to the illness, enabling anorexia behaviours and/or getting very emotional about things. Low motivation or not being ready to change is common among those with anorexia. It is important to say that MANTRA assumes that this is the starting point for many people, and we will work with ambivalence associated with change. Early modules incorporate techniques to assess and work with issues of low or fluctuating motivation or limited confidence in one's ability to change.

Anorexia is a notoriously relapsing condition, and therefore holding on to, maintaining and building on any gains that have been made in the face of life changes and stressors is considered crucial. The final module is focused on the 'pulling together' and consolidation of gains and also on relapse prevention. A 'staying well plan' is devised in the form of a 'virtuous flower' of health and wellbeing with petals that represent factors, for that individual, that promote positive mental health.

Does MANTRA work, and what do patients and therapists tell us about it?

The 'gold standard' method of evaluating whether a therapy works or not is to compare it directly with the next best treatment and to allocate patients randomly between these two treatments. So far, using this method, there have been three such clinical trials[8-12] comparing MANTRA against specialist supportive clinical management (SSCM)[8-11] and with CBT.[12] In all these trials, these psychological therapies were delivered as outpatient treatments. Whilst overall there was no clear front runner, and patients in all three treatments improved similarly, there were some differences between the treatment conditions. Findings suggest that compared to SSCM, which focuses mainly on improving poor nutrition and low weight, MANTRA had a number of advantages. First, MANTRA was thought by patients to be significantly more acceptable and credible than SSCM.[13] Second, for those with a more severe form of the illness (i.e. greater weight loss at the start of treatment), MANTRA seemed to get better outcomes in terms of making greater strides towards recovery. Finally, while a small number of patients allocated to SSCM experienced adverse effects (such as increasing their weight through binge eating), no such negative effects were noted for MANTRA. Several of our patients who took part in our most recent large-scale trial testing MANTRA versus SSCM told us they wished they had had MANTRA early on in their illness, i.e. as their first treatment. Therefore, we separately looked at outcomes in those patients who had presented to us with their first episode of illness. Of those patients receiving MANTRA, 50% had made a complete recovery at two years after starting treatment compared to only 14% of patients receiving SSCM – a major and significant difference.

In our trials, both therapists and patients were very positive about the MANTRA programme.[13-15] Interviews exploring therapists' views of using the approach and manual described it as affording a good balance of structure and flexibility, along with offering a breadth of 'tools' to flexibly and successfully weave into a time-limited treatment. Patients' reports of working collaboratively through the manual with their therapist also highlight the benefits of the structured approach, the value of gaining new perspectives on their difficulties, and of acquiring skills to manage their eating disorder as well as to enhance confidence and overall quality of life. Thus results from studies using this manual strongly support the case for the treatment approach being appealing and manageable for individuals with anorexia, and above all we hope will mean that individuals with anorexia feel 'held' enough by the treatment approach to stick with it and see it through. This is very important given the tendency of individuals with anorexia, noted in many clinical trials, to begin a treatment and drop out. The aim of this manual is to help individuals recover from anorexia but to do this in a way that feels manageable and safe and that leads to long-lasting change. As clinicians with many years of experience working with this patient group, we remain encouraged by the enormous strengths that individuals with anorexia bring to their treatment. As people with anorexia are often gifted, insightful and sensitive souls, there is so much of value to harness and foster even when the road to recovery seems less than straightforward. Once they have overcome the trauma of the illness, with recovery these people really come into their own and grow and flourish, express their creativity and also are able to reach out and help others and contribute to society.[16–18]

Summary

In this opening chapter we have introduced you to the problem of anorexia and considered how MANTRA aims to help you understand and tackle the illness. We have been clear that the evidence basis for any one treatment is not definitive, yet MANTRA shows considerable promise for individuals who are particularly unwell with the illness and it is a treatment that can be completed with minimal professional input (although we would always recommend having as much support as is possible as this will make recovery more likely). Furthermore, therapists and people with anorexia tell us that they value and can relate to MANTRA as an approach. We have explained that the treatment will be based around a formulation or individualised 'vicious' flower of factors that keep anorexia going. This will help individuals with anorexia get familiar with the specifics and subtleties of their illness. Following this, treatment will be organised around modules that map onto factors we know keep anorexia going, gradually unpicking unhelpful ways of managing and exploring alternatives. As we progress there will be helpful hints and suggestions to help get the most out of each module and to foster curiosity and motivation.

Notes

1 National Institute for Health and Care Excellence. Eating disorders: recognition and treatment. May 2017. www.nice.org.uk/guidance/ng69.

2 National Institute for Health and Care Excellence. Eating disorders in over 8s: management. January 2004. www.nice.org.uk/guidance/cg9.

3 Schmidt, U., & Treasure, J. Anorexia nervosa: valued and visible. A cognitive-interpersonal maintenance model and its implications for research and practice. *British Journal of Clinical Psychology*. 2006 Sep; 45(Pt 3):343–66.

4 Treasure, J., & Schmidt, U. The cognitive-interpersonal maintenance model of anorexia nervosa revisited: a summary of the evidence for cognitive, socio-emotional and interpersonal predisposing and perpetuating factors. *Journal of Eating Disorders*. 2013 Apr; 15(1):13.

5 We talk about MANTRA being a cognitive-interpersonal treatment because it focuses on thinking style and on relationships and emotions, as key factors contributing to keeping people stuck with anorexia.

6 Schmidt, U., Wade, T.D., & Treasure, J. The Maudsley model of anorexia nervosa treatment for adults (MANTRA): development, key features and preliminary evidence. *Journal of Cognitive Psychotherapy*. 2014; 28:48–71. This paper is useful for therapists wanting to start off working with MANTRA.

7 Sternheim, L. (2017). Randomised controlled feasibility trial of an email guided manual based self-care intervention programme based on the Maudsley model of anorexia treatment for adults. In *Treatment of Anorexia Nervosa: A Multi-Method Investigation Translating Experimental Neuroscience into Clinical Practice* (ed. Schmidt, U., Sharpe, H., Bartholdy, S., Bonin, E.M., Davies, H., Easter, A., . . . Treasure, J.). www.journalslibrary.nihr.ac.uk/pgfar/pgfar05160/#/abstract.

8 Schmidt, U., Oldershaw, A., Jichi, F., Sternheim, L., Startup, H., McIntosh, V., . . . Treasure, J. Out-patient psychological therapies for adults with anorexia nervosa: randomised controlled trial. *British Journal of Psychiatry*. 2012 Nov; 201(5):392–9.

9 Schmidt, U., Renwick, B., Lose, A., Kenyon, M., Dejong, H., Broadbent, H., . . . Landau, S. The MOSAIC study – comparison of the Maudsley model of treatment for adults with anorexia nervosa (MANTRA) with specialist supportive clinical management (SSCM) in outpatients with anorexia nervosa or eating disorder not otherwise specified, anorexia nervosa type: study protocol for a randomized controlled trial. *Trials*. 2013 May 30; 14:160.

10 Schmidt, U., Magill, N., Renwick, B., Keyes, A., Kenyon, M., Dejong, H., . . . Landau, S. The Maudsley outpatient study of treatments for anorexia nervosa and related conditions (MOSAIC): comparison of the Maudsley model of anorexia nervosa treatment for adults (MANTRA) with specialist supportive clinical management (SSCM) in

outpatients with broadly defined anorexia nervosa: A randomized controlled trial. *Journal of Consulting and Clinical Psychology*. 2015 Aug; 83(4):796–807.

11 Schmidt, U., Ryan, E.G., Bartholdy, S., Renwick, B., Keyes, A., O'Hara, C., . . . Treasure, J. Two-year follow-up of the MOSAIC trial: a multicenter randomized controlled trial comparing two psychological treatments in adult outpatients with broadly defined anorexia nervosa. *International Journal of Eating Disorders*. 2016 Aug; 49(8):793–800.

12 Byrne, S., Wade, T., Hay, P., Touyz, S., Fairburn, C.G., Treasure, J., . . . Crosby, R.D. A randomised controlled trial of three psychological treatments for anorexia nervosa. *Psychological Medicine*. 2017 May 29: 1–11. Epub ahead of print.

13 Zainal, K.A., Renwick, B., Keyes, A., Lose, A., Kenyon, M., DeJong, H., . . . MOSAIC Trial Group. Process evaluation of the MOSAIC trial: treatment experience of two psychological therapies for out-patient treatment of anorexia nervosa. *Journal of Eating Disorders*. 2016 Feb; 9(4):2.

14 Waterman-Collins, D., Renwick, B., Lose, A., Kenyon, M., Serpell, L., Richards, L., . . . MOSAIC Trial Group. Process evaluation of the MOSAIC trial, part I: therapist experiences of delivering two psychological therapies for treatment of anorexia nervosa. *European Eating Disorders Review*. 2014 Mar; 22(2):122–30.

15 Lose, A., Davies, C., Renwick, B., Kenyon, M., Treasure, J., Schmidt, U., & MOSAIC Trial Group. Process evaluation of the Maudsley model for treatment of adults with anorexia nervosa trial. Part II: Patient experiences of two psychological therapies for treatment of anorexia nervosa. *European Eating Disorders Review*. 2014 Mar; 22(2):131–9.

16 http://tabithafarrar.com/. This is the recovery website of Tabitha Farrar, specifically for adults with the illness.

17 www.youtube.com/watch?v=zkTDLR-Glyk. This is the TED Talk of the artist Elise Pacquette, who recovered from anorexia.

18 www.thediaryhealer.com/. This is the website of the author June Alexander, who recovered from anorexia.

Chapter 2

Getting started

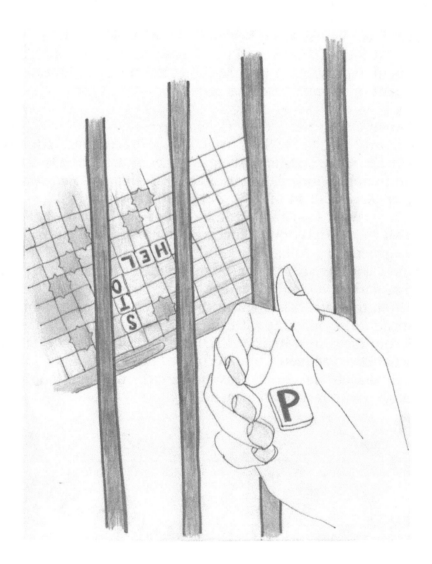

Beginning my journey: taking off the blinkers

At these early stages in your therapeutic journey we suggest you allow yourself time to 'step back' and reflect on your relationship with anorexia.

In our experience, getting well from anorexia involves a process of developing the ability to 'look on' at your anorexia in a slightly removed, yet curious and reflective manner. Abigail, who was only recently told she had anorexia learned to ask herself *what is my anorexia demanding of me right now and what are her motives?* as a way of keeping perspective and not automatically being pulled in to the demands of just one part of herself. Kate, who had anorexia for over two decades, described this process as rather like calling on the advice of a wise and trusted friend to help her carry out a bit of a life review. In our clinical work, we have witnessed many times the ways in which anorexia can embed itself deeper and deeper into a person's life such that months, years, even decades can pass without basic reflective questions being asked, such as *what does my anorexia do for me and what does it take away? What might my life look like without anorexia? And dare I ask*: *what indeed will life hold for me in the future if anorexia is still with me?* It's important to take the time to self-reflect in this way and to do your very best to tolerate the mixed feelings and uncertainty that may come from this.

Whether this is the first time you have suffered with anorexia or you have had anorexia for many years, we want you to make a deal with us: commit to thoroughly considering what your anorexia is all about, what it gives you and what it takes away. Commit to looking into the future and picturing yourself, your life, and your relationships both with and without anorexia. Take off the blinkers for a short while, arm yourself with your wise, reflective 'friend' and let's see what we can discover about you and about your anorexia and about your vision for your future. In this chapter we will ask you to:

- Consider your relationship with change. Are you actually ready for change? Do you see change as important/possible?
- Reflect on your anorexia and also on your non-anorexic parts. This is because recovery from anorexia first involves facing your anorexia 'head on' and getting to know it.
- We will then ask you to think about your relationship with anorexia, both what it offers you right now and also what it takes away. Also how you picture a future for yourself both with and without anorexia.
- This chapter will end with helping you consider your core principles. We hope that the core principles closest to your heart can guide your decision making throughout your therapeutic journey.

First steps: ready, willing and able?

We can learn a lot from people who go on to recover from anorexia. They may have had only a brief encounter with anorexia or they may have been to a really dark place. One way or another, they know how bad it can be and they also know all about the allure of starvation. People recovered from anorexia can almost always recall a time when nothing in the world seemed more important to them than their anorexia. They remember a time when change seemed completely out of the question and their commitment to anorexia was absolute. We understand this. Anorexia can involve a tendency toward a 'black and white' thinking style, or the tendency to think in absolutes (i.e. *anorexia is everything to me and I will never let go of it*). However, what we find is that when these individuals are encouraged to 'step out' from their anorexia and 'look on' at this part of themselves (by calling on their wise, reflective friend), there is usually a little more flexibility in their thinking than first glance suggested. For example, the very fact that you are reading this means that at least a small part of you is curious about the possibility of change. We know that any decision about change is not easy as it involves juggling mixed feelings. All we ask at this stage is that you *consider* the possibility of change. The following rulers can help you reflect on this process.

1 Importance to change

Ask yourself the following questions and make a mark on the ruler below:

How important is it for you to change? What score would you give yourself out of 10?

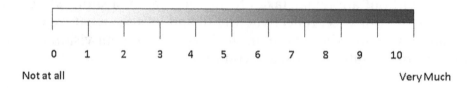

Can you write a few sentences about your desires, reasons and needs for change?

2 Ability to change

Ask yourself the following question:

How confident are you in your ability to change? What score would you give yourself out of 10?

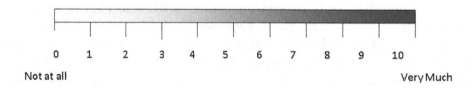

REFLECTION

Once you have done this for each ruler, reflect on the following.

- Why have you given yourself this score, rather than 0 or 10?
- What could enable you to have a higher score?
- What would you notice about yourself if you had a higher score?
- What resources would you have to draw on to get to a higher score?
- Would other people be able to help you get to a higher score?

TOP TIP: GIVING YOURSELF TIME TO REFLECT

A key part of each exercise is to give yourself time at the end to reflect about it. What is the take home message here? What have I learned about myself, my relationship with anorexia and/or with other people? Are there any action points following from the exercise?

My relationship with my anorexia

In this section we want you to get to know your anorexia so that you can make an informed choice about whether to stick on this path or whether to consider alternatives.

TOP TIP

There are a lot of different exercises here to get you started. Not all of these will appeal to you. Some may need adapting to personalise them to you and your circumstances. Remember, this is not a textbook and you should feel free to ditch or adapt exercises. Where you do decide against doing certain exercises, be clear about your motivation for this.

OK, now read the description below of a relationship that a patient of ours, Mary, once described to us. To give a little background, Mary is a woman in her mid-twenties with two small children; she described a key relationship in her life in the following way:

Although my body suffers because of my relationship with Charlie because of how he treats me and how cross he can become, although I can see he puts me down, I still need Charlie, I know where I am with him and importantly I know he will protect me from the scary world outside, he tells me so. Somehow he makes me feel that at least someone loves me and will be there for me. I know that he will never leave me, even if he does hurt me and prevent me from having other friends, even if he has started to say I should stop being a teacher because I don't need anyone but him, I just cannot imagine him not being there. Over the years I have lost track of who I am away from Charlie. Better the devil you know.

Now read the following description of a relationship that Olive, a woman in her mid-thirties also with two children, once described to us. Olive is a postgraduate student.

Every morning I struggle to leave the house because Anna tells me I look fat and because I have started to really struggle first thing in the morning when my energy levels are low and my legs ache. I find I am only 'half there' with my little daughter. Anna demands all my attention and my body is really starting to pay the price. Despite this, I wouldn't want it any other way. You see, Anna is my best friend, she has always been there for me, and she is both familiar and comforting. Whilst everyone else I cared about has walked away, she hasn't gone anywhere. Somehow she seems steady and reassuring and the more time I spend with her, the more I cannot picture a life without her. Yes, I know, I struggle to concentrate at Uni and I don't have the energy to socialise with people on my course, and my mothering is not what it could be, but Anna wouldn't want it any other way.

You have probably guessed by now that the second description is from someone describing their relationship with anorexia, the toll it takes but also the companionship and steadiness it offers. Mary's situation was a bit different. She had spent considerable time in and out of a woman's refuge because of an abusive relationship she became entangled in with a female partner. Eventually she left this relationship, but above she describes what this relationship meant to her. It's hard not to hear the physical and emotional suffering both these women endure, yet also to be confronted by their commitment to these relationships. People tend to appreciate how difficult it is to 'see the wood for the trees' for a sufferer of domestic violence but it was eye-opening to see the parallels with anorexia. Even though you may be far from seeing your anorexia as an abusive partner, you owe it to yourself to use your wise, reflective 'friend' to take a balanced look at where you are at. In our experience, it's ever so common for people to experience their anorexia as *both* a friend and an enemy. How do you see your anorexia?

Externalising anorexia

One thing we know for sure is that you are more than someone with anorexia! You were not born with anorexia and much of what makes you who you are is beyond the influence of anorexia: your genes, your early life relationships, your spirit, your core values, your gut feelings. You are an individual with your own personality, values, ideas and experiences.

In the quest to remove the blinkers and to 'look on' at your anorexia, we suggest that you try to develop a mental image of your anorexia and even name it (minx, monster or whatever). You might already have an image in your mind and it could be helpful to think about sharing this with your trusted therapy companion or with your therapist.

Spend a few minutes thinking about this:

My image of my anorexia is. . .

- What does my image of my anorexia tell me about myself, my relationship with the anorexia, and the challenges and difficulties I will encounter if I decide to change?
- What does it look like? What are the characteristics, attributes, personality of my image of my anorexia (e.g. is it cold, warm, spiky, soft)?

Once you have spent some time gathering this image, please describe your anorexia in a couple of sentences, as though you were describing it to a close friend. For example, Anne described her anorexia as follows:

A cheeky looking version of me called 'Trixie' with big eyes and a prominent grin, red in colour and prickly to anyone who touches her. She values perfection and achievement above all else and is motivated to make Anne thin, thin thin . . . whatever the costs.

Now spend a few minutes thinking about the non-anorexic part of you

Now spend a few minutes thinking about the rest of you, the 'you' that is underneath the anorexia. Close your eyes and gather a picture of this side of you, the side free of anorexia. Use the following prompts to guide you:

- When you think of your non-anorexic self, what image/memories do you see?
- What are the goals and motives of your non-anorexic self?
- What are its characteristics, attributes, personality?

My non-anorexia part. . .

Now please describe your non-anorexic part in a couple of sentences, again as though you were describing this aspect of yourself to a close friend.

Lydia saw her core self as like the centre of a closed flower, she was aware of lots of potential which was closed off and cocooned by the petals. She even had an image of herself laughing spontaneously when out with a group of friends which reminded her what fun she used to have. She values her loving relationships above all else and considers this side of herself as a loyal friend.

One of the aims of treatment is to strengthen your non-anorexic parts. As a first step in this process, you might find it helpful to compare and contrast the two parts of you: the anorexia part and the non-anorexia part. Keep the images from above in mind and think about how these different sides of you behave in different areas of your life.

Comparing the different parts of me

In the following table, we have identified some different life domains and made a start with comparing your non-anorexic and anorexic parts in different domains by putting in a few examples. Why not complete the table by adding your own experiences and feelings relating to each domain?

Life Domains	Anorexic Part	Non-anorexic Part
Nutrition/Self-Care	e.g. Following rules and directives, calorie counting, scrutinising food labels, anxiety, worry, guilt.	e.g. Choosing from a broad spectrum of foods. Sharing meals with others. Fit, strong and well nourished. Free, calm, content and energised.
Physical health		
Psychological health		
Work/study		

Life Domains	Anorexic Part	Non-anorexic Part
Relationships with family and friends		
Romantic relationships		
Leisure Activities		

Understanding my relationship with anorexia

Anorexia, my friend

People who have recovered from anorexia often tell us that anorexia came at a time in their lives when things were tough. Some people describe to us times of real hardship; of loss of loved ones, of relationship stress, of educational demands. Whereas sometimes people describe lots of smaller worries that might span issues such as relationship worries, life changes (such as changing school; starting university) or worries about whether they fit in or not. Whatever the triggers, people often recall a time when they experienced anorexia as a solution to life's problems. However, what's interesting is that as individuals approach recovery, they begin to share with us some of the downsides of anorexia, the bits that are less friend-like! We shall come on to these bits, but for now we would like you to think about what has been positive in your experience with anorexia. Many people we talk to describe positive aspects of anorexia, and these are important to acknowledge in our quest to remove the blinkers and for you to see anorexia for what it is.

In the following table, we have given some of the positive statements we hear. For each statement think of how this may apply to your life and provide an example. Then rate the importance of this for you at present on a scale of 0 to 10 (0 = not at all, 10 = extremely). Do feel free to add plenty of your own!

Statements	Give an example	Importance (Rating 0–10)
AN makes me safe		
AN deadens my feeling		
AN makes me feel powerful		
AN communicates to others		
AN is an escape route		
Any others? Add your own statements here		

To really get in touch with the sense of friendship that anorexia can offer, we want you to have a go at the following exercise. Write a letter to 'anorexia, my friend', describe in detail what this friendship means to you, what it gives you, and what it protects you from. Try to be as open and free as possible when you write this letter. Dig deep and speak from your heart; let your vulnerable self speak.

TOP TIP: INCREASING EMOTIONAL 'HEAT'

In this section we have suggested first a preparatory exercise which is based on writing a list of things, and then we ask you to write some letters. You may think that doing both is unnecessary and stop after the list. In our experience, the letters definitely add something. Anorexia has a tendency to make people a bit numb and cut off from their feelings. Letters are usually good at connecting thoughts and feelings. It can therefore make things feel much more real and adds a bit of 'emotional heat'. If you are ready for even greater 'heat' you can read the letters out aloud to yourself, you can imagine a close other listening to this to add further heat or you can read them out to your supporter or therapist. This may sound a bit scary, and you will be the best judge as to what works for you. It is a way of taking safe risks to help you move forward.

> Write a letter to 'anorexia, my friend' using some of the ideas from the preceding table.

Below is an example from Carrie, an 18-year-old A-level student who has had anorexia for just over a year.

Dear Anorexia, my friend,

I am so lucky to have you as my friend, thank you so much for always being there for me and for not letting me down. When I started my new school I struggled to make good friends and the loneliness nearly engulfed me. Also the anxiety of not fitting in was just too much and having you to focus on, made all this manageable. You give me something I can be good at, something I can master. You enable me to stop caring about whether I am liked or not, or whether my grades are the best. If I'm truly honest you also help me let my mum know that everything isn't so wonderful for me. She always wants me to be happy and to just smile and get on with it and I think you being here makes her take note and get real about my rubbish life. Thank you for being here and for doing so much for me at a time when I really feel like I am sinking.

With love,
Carrie

Anorexia, my enemy

In this section, we would like you to think about what has been not so good in your experience with anorexia, the ways it has been unhelpful to you in your life and held you back. If you have had anorexia for a long time, try to step outside the everydayness of anorexia and look on at it with some objectivity. If you have only just encountered anorexia, don't allow yourself to be blinkered: what are the downsides of where you are at right now?

Again, for each domain, think of how this may apply to your life and provide an example. Then rate the relevance of this for you at present on a scale of 0 to 10 (0 = not at all, 10 = extremely).

Domains	Example from you	Importance (Rating 0–10)
Relationships		
Health		

Domains	Example from you	Importance (Rating 0–10)
Work/education		
Finances		
Any others? Add your own here		

Now have a go at writing a letter to 'anorexia, my enemy'. Try to be as free, open and honest with yourself as you can. People we have worked with us tell us over and over how important these letters were in getting in touch with their relationship with their anorexia. Dare to look deep and confront all that anorexia is for you right now.

Below is an example from Ben, who had anorexia off and on for over six years:

Dear Anorexia, my enemy,

I don't even know where to begin. The past years seem like a blur of tiredness and hunger and just getting through each day. You have taken away my health but also my dream to become a vet. I was smart at school, really smart, but you make my head a fuzzy blur and my passion has died now to ever make it to university. I have one friend left, one poor soul who visits me at home because I no longer like to leave the house during winter because I am freezing all the time. I also have osteoporosis and have been told by my doctor that I should no longer do the sports I used to enjoy, such as climbing and skiing. I sometimes feel angry towards you, anorexia, for all the misery you cause, but at the same time I cannot imagine life without you. I feel trapped and bad about myself for not being able to see a way out of this heel. You have ruined my life and you will continue to do so if I don't stop you. Can you believe I am only 30 . . . ? Anorexia, you have taken away my young years, you have made me an old and anxious man too soon.

With sadness,
Ben

Now you have a go.

Write a letter to 'anorexia, my enemy' using some of the ideas from the preceding table.

TOP TIP: SUSPENDING HIGH STANDARDS

Especially if you are a bit of a perfectionist, you may find letter-writing daunting and time-consuming. To make the process less daunting:

- Try to write something that comes from the heart, i.e. without over-thinking it, and something that is good enough rather than perfect.
- Write by hand, rather than on your computer.
- Don't spend hours. Set aside 10–15 minutes for each letter, and then switch to the opposite letter. If necessary set an alarm clock.
- Always be sure to give equal amounts of time to both letters, i.e. friend and enemy or future with or without anorexia.

REFLECTION

After doing this task, you might want to reflect on what you have learned from this task:

- Return to the first worksheet in this chapter (page 16) and consider again how important change is and how confident about change you are. What score would you give yourself now?

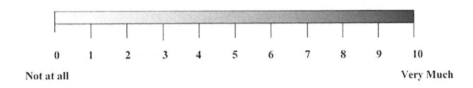

| 0 | 1 | 2 | 3 | 4 | 5 | 6 | 7 | 8 | 9 | 10 |

Not at all   Very Much

- Has this task stirred up any emotions in you?

How has anorexia changed my life?

Particularly if you have had anorexia for a long time, it may be that you have come to expect little from life and that you are used to accepting whatever anorexia allows you. Dare to step back and consider in what ways having anorexia has changed your life. Even if you are relatively new to anorexia, there will have been some changes. It is important to be aware of them. The following questionnaire identifies several life areas and aims to help you map out how content you are with each part.

- Think about how happy you are with each of the life areas listed. Take a coloured pen or pencil and score in the first column how happy you are in each area of your life **now**, using a scale of 0 (very unhappy) to 10 (very happy). Then in the second column, score how happy you were in this area **before** the anorexia nervosa began.

- Now, look at the scores you have given for your current and past happiness and in the third column write down the **reason** for any changes in your happiness.
- Reflect on your current and past happiness ratings. Keeping these in mind, score how important an improvement in each area is to you using a scale of 0 to 10 (0 = not at all important and 10 = very important). For example, if improving your relationship with friends is of primary importance, give it a 10. If an area does not apply to you, e.g. you do not have a partner or you are 10/10 happy with the area, put N/A.

My happiness with:	Rate current happiness (0–10)	In the past (0–10)	Reasons for change in happiness	Importance of improvement (0–10)
My physical health				
My social life				
My job				
My school and/or education				
How I manage money, finances and legal issues				
My relationship with food				
My emotional health				
How much exercise I get				
My relationship with my spouse/partner				

My happiness with:	Rate current happiness (0–10)	In the past (0–10)	Reasons for change in happiness	Importance of improvement (0–10)
My relationship with my children				
My relationship with my parents				
My relationship with my closest friends				
My relationship with the world and environment and/or with God				

Back to the future

Remember that nothing stays the same; the 'you' with anorexia today will not look or feel or be doing the same as the 'you' with anorexia five years in the future. For a start, your body will start to react to the cumulative effects of low weight, your social life will have taken a prolonged bashing and your career will be whatever your anorexia allowed it to be. It's worth being clear what your future could look like both with and without anorexia and being sure it's what you want to sign up for.

A helpful way to attain different perspectives is to think about how things might be for you five years into the future. Have a go at completing the following table:

1 If you still have anorexia
2 If you have recovered from anorexia

1 Five years, still with anorexia	In five years time still with anorexia, the following will have happened in these areas:
My physical health	
My social life	

1 Five years, still with anorexia	In five years time still with anorexia, the following will have happened in these areas:
My job	
My school and or education	
How I manage my money, finances and legal issues	
My relationship with food	
My emotional health	
How much exercise I get	
My relationship with my spouse/ partner	
My relationship with my children	
My relationship with my parents	
My relationship with my closest friends	
My relationship with the world and environment and/or with God	
My happiness generally	

2 Five years without anorexia	In five years, after recovering from anorexia, the following will have happened in these areas:
My physical health	
My social life	
My job	
My school and or education	
How I manage my money, finances and legal issues	
My relationship with food	
My emotional health	
How much exercise I get	
My relationship with my spouse/ partner	
My relationship with my children	
My relationship with my parents	
My relationship with my closest friends	

2 Five years without anorexia	*In five years, after recovering from anorexia, the following will have happened in these areas:*
My relationship with the world and environment and/or with God	
My happiness generally	

REFLECTION

- How do you see the future now?
- What, specifically, would you like to be different?
- What, specifically, could you do to get started?
- If the first step is successful, then what?
- Who else (if anyone) could you ask for support and assistance? What could you ask them for?
- What would be the signs that things are going well?
- How would you know if you were off-track?
- What would you do if you got off-track?

We now suggest that you do the following exercise: years have gone by. You continue to have anorexia. Everything has gone wrong. All the negative consequences that you considered have come true. You feel alone, powerless and at the end of your tether. You decide to write to your one close friend, whom you haven't seen for a while, as she (assuming your friend is a woman) has been abroad. You know that she cares about you and will not be deceived by superficial news, and that when you meet her on her return, she will see it all anyway. You have found in the past that she has been able to provide emotional and practical support when you have needed help. You know you can trust her, and must be completely open in describing your present difficulties.

Here are a few guidelines to consider in writing to your friend:

- What weight will you be?
- What medical complications will you have?
- What career/job will you be pursuing?
- Where and with whom will you be living?
- Who will be your friends?
- Will you be in a relationship? Married? Have children?

TOP TIP: ADAPTING EXERCISES TO GET THE MOST OUT OF THEM

- If you find that five years into the future seems a long time off, think about one year into the future.
- A variant of the future exercise that some people enjoy is to write back from the future explaining to a friend what the steps were that you took to get yourself well.

Now be as realistic as possible, and talk in the present tense. Here is an example of a letter from Lola, a young woman with anorexia, who is preparing herself to undertake the journey of recovery:

Dear Gemma,

I look forward to catching up when you return home next month. I thought I would tell you all about my current situation so that we can pick up where we left off when you went away five years ago. I'm afraid my story is quite sad and upsetting to have to share, but I know I can trust you, and have faith that something good will come out of sharing honestly with you, as happened in the past.

My anorexia has continued, which means I have been battling it for 15 years now. My weight is at its lowest, yet I am more unhappy now than I have ever been. I really thought that reaching such a low weight would bring me such wonders, although all I feel is desperate and stuck and sad.

I severely restrict my food every single day and 'bad' foods are completely off limits. This means that anything you might see as a treat, I see as the enemy and I will do anything to avoid these foods. Preparing my food consumes my day. I keep a semblance of control by sucking on sugar free lollipops to distract my head from my aching stomach. I cannot sleep at night because I am starving and I wake to my stomach rumbling. But, of course, I cannot and will not give in to this. Will this desperate situation ever end?? Sometimes I fear it never will . . .

This illness has taken a severe toll on my health, way more than I have thought it would. I am bony and cannot drive my car for long periods as my limbs ache, I am cold all the time (even in summer!), and I have osteoporosis which meant that I broke my leg last winter by a slight fall in the street. I have hair on my back which is hideous and I could never allow anyone to see my naked body, so you can imagine there have been zero sexual relationships in my life since I saw you last. I cannot even walk to the local shop without feeling dizzy. Perhaps my biggest regret is that whilst my mind has been obsessed with weight loss, with getting thinner, with wearing tiny clothes and with complete control, the big goals I once had have passed me by; as you know, I was always desperate to be a mum one day and to live quite a simple life in a nice house with a nice family. This seems completely out of the question now. Such sadness I feel when I dwell on this and how desperately lonely I feel.

I have not worked or painted for over three years now. Do you remember how I loved to paint? I can barely stand for long enough to sketch an outline any more. I live with my parents. Our relationship has changed. They fluctuate between clingy and terrified I will die and anger at what I have done to myself and to the family. John – the love of my life – left me eight years ago. He said he could no longer bear to see someone he loved abuse themselves so. He also said that he didn't want to be with someone who had a child's body and who was so dependent on their parents for basic care. This hurt me to hear, but I know it's all true. Gosh as I write this the tears are falling as I can see how anorexia has destroyed everything around me. Dear friend, I hope you can even bear to even look at me when we meet next!

Despite all of this, I cling to a glimmer of hope. I remember that moment, five years ago, when you offered to help me overcome my illness, sharing your wisdom and love. Back then, the challenges of change seemed too difficult and risky. However, I now clearly see that there is no other way forward, and I want to accept that offer of help that you so generously made before. I know that you will be pleased that I have made this first step and have mustered the courage to write to you.

With love from Lola.

Now write your own letter to your own friend. Read it through carefully. Don't kid yourself. Be honest and open. Do you really want to spend another five years shackled to your eating disorder while your friends are out having fun and getting on with life? Read your letter out loud to yourself. How does hearing these predictions make you feel? What take-home message has it left you with?

Refer back to the guidelines at the start of this section. Now write a second letter. Imagine your situation in five years. This time, you have successfully overcome your anorexia because you are starting recovery work right now. Casting your mind back to the present, what steps have helped you to get well? Whose support has been invaluable? How have you managed to build momentum? What obstacles have you overcome and how? What does your future without anorexia look like? Is this the sort of future you want to aim for? That is, a future where you are the choreographer of what you do and say?

Now read your letter aloud to yourself. What does it feel like to consider that this future is in your reach, it could be yours? All you need to do is shake off the anorexia and free your spirit up to grasp the goodies of life. Why should everyone else have them and not you?! What take-home message has this left you with?

TOP TIP: OVERCOMING CHALLENGES AND STUMBLING BLOCKS

- Anorexia has a tendency to make people want to stay active and on the move. For some people, completing exercise sheets can be a way of 'keeping busy' in a rather mindless way. If you notice this tendency in yourself, try to slow down, and make sure you spend as much time on the reflection as on the exercise itself.

- Some people find letter-writing silly, childish or weird. We agree it is a somewhat unusual thing to ask you to do. However, in our experience we find it works. Can you suspend judgement till you have tried it?
- Some people find they cannot think about their future with or without anorexia at all at this stage it is simply too hard. That is OK at this stage. It is just important to be aware of what makes it so impossible. Perhaps there is some other big problem in your life and if anorexia was gone this other problem would suddenly loom ultra-large.

Making your decision to go

Only you can decide to work at change now or to continue with anorexia. Probably this will not be simply one decision but numerous smaller decisions that you will make over the following days, months and years. Strong forces will try to suck you back. Expect, like others venturing on this journey, to make many mistakes. However, don't feel disheartened because we will help you acquire skills to turn any mistakes into helpful lessons.

Guiding principles

We want to encourage you to put your anorexic part to the side for a moment and to allow your non-anorexic parts to speak, to tell us about your underlying values and principles. These tend to be constants. They may well have been pushed to the side or overshadowed by the commands of anorexia for a while, but if you dig deep we shall find them! You see, some people tell us that leaving anorexia is hard because they are terrified of what is left. It's as though they are so used to following the commands of anorexia, it feels terrifying to step out alone and deal with life. We want to reassure you. Although moving away from anorexia may well feel scary and unsteady for a time, you always have something to fall back on to help you move forward: your core principles. As part of thinking about your life, your anorexia and where you are currently at, as well as where you want to be, the kind of person you'd like to be and how you'd like to live your life, it can be very helpful to map out the guiding principles and core values in your life. You can take these everywhere you go and even though anorexia may have overshadowed them; they are still in there, we promise. Now, let's do some work digging them out!

- Look at the whole list of principles/values shown on page 35 and pick out the **five values** that are **least important** for you and never have been. Mark these in yellow. Rank these in order with least important as number 1.
- Now pick out the **five values** that are **most important** to you as **guiding principles** in your life and mark them in green. Rank them in order of their importance to you, 1 being the most important.
- Now cast your mind back to the time before your anorexia began, what were the values that seemed most important then?

Least Important	Most Important
1	1
2	2
3	3
4	4
5	5

REFLECTION

- Which values are most strongly linked with your anorexia side?
- Which values are most strongly linked with your non-anorexic side?
- Can you think of someone you know of, such as a character from history, a novel, TV, who most lives by the guiding principles you aspire to? (Note: do not choose anyone just because of their looks.)
- Have any of your values become ignored, side-lined or exaggerated because of your anorexia? Or does anorexia interfere with your values in any other way?
- Can any of your values help you fight your anorexic part?

TOP TIP

Anorexia can wreak havoc with your values. For example, many of our patients value truthfulness, honesty and trust, yet anorexia may make them untrusting, secretive and sometimes even lie, so close others end up seeing the person as not trustworthy and the person with anorexia themselves is conflicted over this. This is often done seemingly to protect another value the person holds, i.e. being independent. However, anorexia has a tendency to strengthen and exaggerate values such as independence, autonomy, and control that keep you alone and disconnected from the love and support of others. So if you feel very torn between different values, try to listen, be guided by and act in accordance with those that are aligned with your non-anorexic side.

Finally, here's what one of our patients told us about her experience of using this module to guide her recovery:

The stepping stones which the 'Getting Started' section provided, were of great aid, giving me a gentle approach to recovery. The scale chart (from 0–10) gave me an idea of where my mind was at, which allowed me to become more aware of what mind set I had been functioning in for a very long time. It gave guidance into how to set out realistic goals from the start of the recovery process, and allowed me to realise how much it was affecting the whole of my life.

Acceptance
To fit in with others

Accuracy
To be correct in my opinions & actions

Achievement
To accomplish & achieve

Adventure
To have new & exciting experiences

Attractiveness
To be physically attractive

Authority
To be in charge of others

Beauty
To appreciate beauty around me

Caring
To take care of others

Certainty

Comfort
To have a pleasant, enjoyable life

Compassion
To feel concern for others

Complexity
To have a life full of variety & change

Contribution
To make a contribution that endures

Control

Courtesy
To be polite & considerate to others

Creativity
To have new & original ideas

Dependability
To be reliable and trustworthy

Ecology
To live in harmony with the environment

Faithfulness
To be loyal & reliable in relationships

Fame
To be known and recognised

Family
To have a happy, loving family

Flexibility
To adjust to new or unusual situations easily

Forgiveness
To be forgiving of others

Friends
To have close & supportive friends

Fun
To play & have fun

Generosity
To give what I have to others

God's will
To seek & obey the will of God

Growth
To keep changing & growing

Health
To be physically well & healthy

Helpfulness
To be helpful to others

Honesty
To be truthful & genuine

Hope
To maintain a positive & optimistic attitude

Humility
To be modest & unassuming

Humour
To see the humorous side of myself & the world

Independence
To be free from dependence on others

Industry
To work & well at my life tasks

Inner peace
To experience personal peace

Intimacy
To share my innermost feelings with others

Justice
To promote equal & fair treatment to all

Knowledge
To learn & possess valuable knowledge

Leisure
To take time to relax & enjoy

Logic
To live rationally & sensibly

Loved
To be loved by those close to me

Loving
To give love to others

Moderation
To avoid excesses & find a middle ground

Monogamy
To have one close, loving relationship

Orderliness
To have a life that is well-ordered & organised

Pleasure
To feel good

Popularity
To be well liked by many people

Power
To have control over others

Realism
To see & act realistically and practically

Responsibility
To make & carry out important decisions

Risk
To take risks & chances

Romance
To have an intense, exciting love relationship

Safety
To be safe & secure

Self-control
To be disciplined & govern my own actions

Self-esteem
To like myself just as I am

Self-knowledge
To have a deep, honest understanding of myself

Service
To be of service to others

Sexuality
To have an active & satisfying sex life

Simplicity
To live life simply, with minimal needs

Special

Spirituality
To grow spiritually

Stability
To have a life that stays fairly consistent

Strength
To be physically strong

Success

Tolerance
To accept & respect those different from me

Tradition
To follow set patterns of the past

Virtue
To live a morally pure & excellent life

Wealth
To have plenty of money

World peace
To work to promote peace in the world

Furthermore by immediately being guided to externalise the anorexia it was easier to stop blaming and punishing myself for the problems and instead I was able to personify the illness into an image/title. By rating my happiness about different areas of life on paper, (in written and numerical form), I understood more about where my mind set was then, is now and where it could be in the future (once again the neat layout of the chart made it easier to see and formulate ideas).

Chapter 3

No (wo)man is an island – working with support

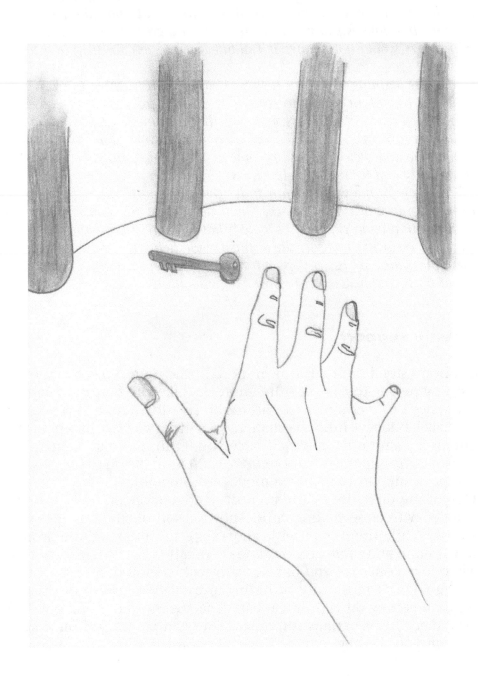

One of our patients shared the following:

When I was ill . . . I mean really ill with anorexia, I had no idea what I really needed let alone how to ask for help. It was like I had fallen down this dark pit and everyone was shouting down the pit at me to 'get (myself) sorted' and to 'just listen for once' but I was too far away to hear them and I was way too caught up in managing being down a pit to really care what they had to say anyway. After a number of attempts at getting well and many slides backwards I decided to see a therapist, she was an expert in eating disorders and actually really approachable. With her help I climbed part way out up that dark pit and then I learned something critical, I learned that anorexia doesn't have my best interests at heart, it's really isn't a great pal of mine and that things would not change if I didn't learn to ask for help and to receive it.

For me learning to ask for help was easier than learning to receive it. It was important for me to start seeing things from the perspective of my loved ones. What I realise now is that that my anorexia kind of traumatised them . . . it made them anxious and worried about me all of the time and their days had become about sleepless nights and constant worry and feelings of helplessness.

The key for me was to learn to let them in and to allow them to influence me and not to let the anorexia dictate my relationships. I learned that anorexia makes people behave in ways that made things worse for me. Once I was aware of this I could help them better to help me. Things are a bit better these days and when they are not . . . we talk about it . . . and just sometimes we laugh about it!

Working with support

It has always stood out to us how important the right type of support is in assisting people to recover from anorexia. Like any harmful relationship, anorexia thrives under conditions of isolation, and this is because anorexic behaviours cannot be challenged if other views, influences and potentials are shut out. However, once you let in new experiences and good people, its grip starts to loosen. We want to help you to identify the right type of support to help you move on from anorexia.

One of the difficulties with anorexia is that anorexic ways of being get tangled with close relationships. Anorexia sort of contaminates relationships. While the person with anorexia gets thinner, those around them get more and more anxious and desperate – how could they not? So when loved ones see you obsessing over the detail of a tiny meal or weighing yourself repeatedly or hiding away in your room exercising, rather than getting on with life, it can generate enormous anxiety. This anxiety then drives various responses. For example, others may withdraw from you or they may become preoccupied with your state and somewhat over involved, neither of which are helpful for your recovery. In addition, anorexia messes with your ability to read your own and others' emotions and intentions and impairs your ability to signal emotions and needs to others. Thus while you may experience intense emotions on the inside, your face may appear expressionless. Others may wrongly read this as you being arrogant or an 'ice queen'. These anorexia induced difficulties in reading and expressing emotions, produce a fertile soil for arguments and tensions between the person with anorexia and their close others.

Also, starvation puts you in a high stress state and flight, fright and freeze responses are easily triggered. You will be highly attuned to signs of threat but inattentive to care and compassion. Close others can become paralysed with fear and self-blame and withdraw.

There are many other panic, tension and anger-induced responses that anorexia can pull and unfortunately most are not conducive to recovery. Therefore, we stress the importance of identifying the *right* type of support, from the *right* people and critically of arming your supporters with information and guidance that can help them to *step back* from the pulls of anorexia and learn to help you. Remember that professionals are trained not to get pulled into the damaging relational patterns that anorexia promotes, but your loved ones are not. Most supportive others have only the very best intentions at heart, however, they are only human and under conditions of enormous stress they may not naturally provide the best care. In fact, we know that looking after someone with anorexia causes clinical levels of anxiety and depression. Therefore, they need information, guidance and ideally the input of experts to arm themselves with lots of tips to help you.

We hope this chapter will help you to identify the right supportive others for you. We also hope this chapter can be a resource for those supporting you. We strongly advise that your loved ones read this chapter and that you and they have a conversation about what it brings up for you all.

A Mind Exercise

It is well documented within parenting texts that some young children hold their breath when they become very angry or frustrated. Perhaps this is to muster some degree of control in their little life, to make a protest or to show how angry and trapped they feel. Children are by definition more powerless than adults. Picture that for a moment, a small child holding their breath right there in front of you? Indeed, some toddlers, in particular, can be remarkably efficient at doing this for just long enough to cause panic in the adults around them. If a child you knew held their breath to the point where they went blue in the face, and even started to lose balance and go wobbly and dizzy or even pass out, what behaviours might you engage in to try to stop them? Below is a list of things parents say they do when faced with their own child holding their breath:

- Shake them
- Shout at them
- Pour water over them
- Walk away and ignore them
- Get angry and critical.

So parents in this position are driven to engage in behaviours they don't typically associate with good parenting! But they do whatever their panic instructs them to do and whatever they need to do to end the alarming situation with their child.

It's clearly not the same, but there are a few parallels here with watching your loved one deteriorate with anorexia. Eating is a basic need, just like breathing. All of us have to do these things and none of us has special privilege or power to avoid them. So, to sit back and watch someone you love stop/curtail their eating and destroy their body and wellbeing right there in front of you is a lot to ask. Plus, the anorexic body and anorexic behaviours are highly visible and highly provocative and they induce enormous panic and helplessness in loved ones and therefore extreme responses. So, please don't be surprised if those around you don't respond to your anorexia in what you might consider 'ideal' ways.

One aim of this chapter is to try to help the person with anorexia appreciate why the responses of their carers might not always be what they feel they need and to help the person who is doing the supporting to step back from the anorexia and the panic it induces and to have greater awareness of the responses it may pull in them.

TOP TIP

How do you choose the best supportive other(s) for you? The person(s) most likely to support you to better health may not be the person closest to you. Although having parents and partners involved in your journey towards wellness is important, it may be that a sibling, friend, another trusted person or a therapist is actually better placed to 'hold steady' in regard to their own emotional reactions in order to support you. Does anyone come to mind?

Isolation versus intrusion

One of the paradoxes of anorexia is that the individual often feels extremely isolated and cut off from other people, but at the same time, close others see the suffering and are drawn in to want to help. Unfortunately, well-meaning attempts to help can hinder. Do others close to you feel confident that they are giving you the best form of support? What do you think? Are you keeping others at a distance because you have made a healthy choice for you? Or are there many secret parts of yourself that you cannot share with others? Are you terrified of rejection? Is it difficult to connect with warmth, trust and compassion? However, this is not just about you. What about the needs of those close to you? How does your illness impact on them? Getting the balance between isolation versus intrusion is not easy.

Close others looking on

In this section we ask you to step back and consider the perspectives of your family, partner and close others. Anorexia is a very visible illness – it is not a confidential affair, others are drawn in, even if they try to pull back. We have found that family members and partners find this position very difficult and have high levels of stress with clinical levels of anxiety and depression. They recognise that they need help. We have found that simple help and guidance for close others reduces their stress levels and enables them to be less anxious and depressed. Also, close others can and do provide more help and less harm if they are given the opportunity to know more about the illness. This can produce secondary benefits for you. Therefore, considering people close to you has two potential benefits. Help for them and possible help for you.

Carers' rights and responsibilities

The guidelines for good practice from NICE, the National Institute for Health and Care Excellence (2017), indicate that clinicians should offer resources and advice about the illness to close others, and consider their needs. Therefore, in line with this protocol, we have developed a short written resource for carers which can be found as an appendix at the end of this book. More detail is contained in a book written by an eating disorder expert, a recovered patient and an experienced carer.[1]

Meeting with close others

If you are in treatment, ideally your supportive other will be offered at least two sessions to support them to support you. In the meetings with close others, the clinician would answer any questions they may have about the illness in general. It is not possible to keep the anorexia nervosa a secret; the effects of the illness are clear for all to see. We find that close others often want to know how to help keep you safe and are highly anxious about the medical risk.

However, if you are not linked in with clinical services, there are ways of thinking about support that may be helpful for you and your loved ones to think about together.

We will touch on some of the relational patterns of behaviour (using animal metaphors – see later on in this chapter) and other forms of interaction that commonly develop between the supporter and the person with anorexia that are less helpful. We have found that families or close others usually understand that what they are doing now may not be the best way of helping. Once carers are given help, we find they are willing to try a different approach. They may need extra support to do this. We know that this form of help is working if you are able to make progress with the programme.

Let's start to think about you and the people close to you. Perhaps you can fill in the following form.

It can be invaluable to work with someone to help you on your journey to change. However, it is worth spending time to consider who this person might be. The following questionnaire may help you decide how well placed your possible support persons might be to help.

Name of possible support person:

	4	3	2	1	0
How easy is it to talk to this person about your problem?	Very easy	Quite easy	Not sure	Quite difficult	Very difficult
Is this person critical or easily upset about your eating? Does this person take your eating personally?	Never	Rarely	Sometimes	Often	Always
Could you talk to this person even if you weren't making progress with your eating?	Definitely	Probably	Maybe	Probably not	Definitely not
Can you trust this person to always be there when you need someone? No strings attached? No moral blackmail?	Definitely	Probably	Maybe	Probably not	Definitely not
If you overcame your anorexia nervosa, what would this person's likely response be?	Very pleased with me	Fairly Happy	I haven't a clue	Would feel lost and slightly jealous that I'm more independent and successful in my life	Would feel threatened and need to find a new role and a new way of living
How often are you in contact with this person?	At least once a week	At least once every two weeks		At least once a month	Less than once a month

Now add up the total number of points.
Total number of points:

- 16–20: you are in the lucky position of having a very good supporter near you. You should definitely ask this person to help you in your efforts to overcome your eating disorder. You may want to timetable some regular meetings with this key individual to spend time reflecting on change. You could use these meetings to share some of the findings from your experiments, to think about how they can join forces with you in the battle to shake off anorexic habits, or to help you plan and construct ways to implement non-anorexic behaviour.
- 11–15: at the moment it is uncertain whether this person is able to support you as effectively as possible. If you read appendix 1 at the end of this book you may have an idea of what makes it difficult. Analysing where a problem may lie is the first step.
- 0–10: it is possible that at the moment this person may hinder change. On the other hand, they are tied to you by blood or law. We have found that family members or close others who lie on the extreme of 'animal behaviours' benefit most from being given information. So do not reject them out of hand. Indeed these are the people to invite to the joint sessions with your therapist. Remember it is important for you as them not to be an ostrich and try to avoid a challenge. You learn something by approach – maybe it will be that they or you are not ready yet.

Taking the carer perspective

One of the key ways anorexia traps you is that it cuts off your connection with close others. Isolation and loneliness will creep up on you and kill your spirit. Involving close others is the first step towards progress.

Have a read of the appendix for close others at the end of this book. Does it seem relevant to your experience? Step back. Look at the animal metaphors and the behaviour patterns that they describe below. Do close others adopt these patterns of behaviour in their relationship with you and your anorexia? Maybe they also occur in your relationship with different parts of yourself?

Perhaps you can get inside the heads of people close to you and think about what triggers the sorts of behaviour we briefly describe below.

The animals

'Jellyfish'. This means being transparently very sad, anxious and/or mad and so much 'in' the emotion so that it is difficult to see the bigger picture of life, with a tendency to be adrift within the currents and tides of the emotional sea. Do close others overwhelm you with their displays of full-on emotion?

'Ostrich'. This means avoiding dealing with things that are painful or challenging. Do others ignore your anorexia, by burying themselves in work or never being around, pretending they haven't noticed the tiny portion on your plate or heard you being sick? Perhaps you yourself are an ostrich in your relationship with your body?

'Kangaroo'. This means being overly protective by keeping the other person in the pouch, or if you are the baby kangaroo, it means staying in the pouch. Are you safe or are you being stifled? Is your anorexia putting you in a position whereby other people take decisions and start to take over control of your life? Does anorexia stop you standing on your own two feet?

'Rhinoceros'. Are other people (close others, tutors, occupational health) becoming overly directive and imperative towards you? Does anorexia fight back with its own weapons?

'Terrier'. Are you surrounded with a constant barrage of criticism and nagging? Is this just from other people or is it your own anorexic voice?

TOP TIP

Don't get stuck on trying to work out which one animal metaphor fits your loved one perfectly. It doesn't really work like this! Think in terms of people having parts of the self which ebb and flow at times of stress. So your loved one may be calm and reflective much of the time, but as soon as you lose weight, their terrier mode kicks in, or you might find that your dad has always been the strong type and always puts on a strong front outside the house, but when it comes to mealtimes, it's like he can't take it anymore and just disintegrates into jellyfish mode.

Equally try to think in terms of which parts of you fit these metaphors. Jennifer embraced all challenges within her professional career and was known as a real problem solver and 'go-getter', yet when it came to her ever-evident anorexia, she remained the ostrich. Similarly, Rick would remain cut off and ostrich-like right up until the point of admission where finally the reality would sink in and send him lurching between jellyfish and terrier.

The relationship of anorexia to close others

It is common for the anxiety, rule-driven behaviour and focus on detail that are part of anorexia to also spread out into family life. Ask yourself the following questions.

1 Do you call on others to give you reassurance, and help with checking or involve them in other ways to make you feel safe?
2 Do other family members have to fit in with your schedules and procedures?
3 Do you influence what close others can eat and do?
4 Does your problem impinge on others (by limiting available food, making rubbish or mess, etc.)?
5 Has pleasant communication with others come to a full stop?

If you can relate to any of these questions, then you can begin to see how anorexia contaminates relationships. It infiltrates the very core of family life.

Aspirational animals

We encourage close others to aspire to emulate some of the qualities of a dolphin and a St. Bernard dog.

Supporting with wisdom like a 'dolphin'. Giving a 'hands-off' form of support, maybe keeping you afloat with gentle nudging.

Being with you through your danger with warmth and compassion, like a St. Bernard. Perhaps waiting for more help to come or until you gather strength.

Like you, your family and close others will find it hard to change. They will make mistakes – that is part of learning. However, we have found that if families are able to work together, they say that they value having gone through the anorexia nervosa experience as it has brought them closer.

Being open to other perspectives

People who are able to recover from anorexia are often open and flexible enough to examine decisions about change from the perspectives of others. You may find it helpful to think about how a family member or your best friend might set about filling in decisional rulers about you.

- *How important is it for them that you change – could you mark it on the 1 to 10 scale?*
- *How important is it for you that you change – could you mark it on the 1 to 10 scale?*
- *How painful and how unsafe does it feel to have the discrepancy in these scores?*
- *What would need to happen for you to get scores in a similar range?*

- How confident are others that they could help you?
- How confident are you that they could help you?
- How painful and how unsafe does it feel to have the discrepancy in these scores?
- What would need to happen to get the scores on an even footing?

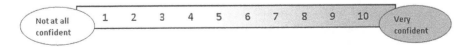

45

REFLECTION

If you step back from anorexia using the eyes of someone who can see the bigger picture, what do you learn?

So in our experience, letting the right people in, in the right way, can make recovery from anorexia both more likely and more manageable. It's just not easy to fully recover from anything let alone anorexia if you keep yourself isolated and alone. In an ideal world, you and your supportive other would sit down with a clinician who has experience in working with eating disorders so they can support you both to make the most of your personal qualities in order to beat anorexia. But where this isn't possible, we urge you to arm yourself and your loved ones with all of these available resources so that you can be mindful of each other and each other's ways of being at times of stress during your journey towards recovery.

TOP TIP

- Giving other people the opportunity to help is a marker of trust and a strong relationship.
- Building a strong relationship with others is the first step in building a strong relationship with yourself.

Note

1 Treasure, J., Smith, G., & Crane, A. (2007). *Skills-Based Learning for Caring for a Loved One with an Eating Disorder: The New Maudsley Method.* Routledge. London and New York.

Chapter 4

Improving your nutritional health

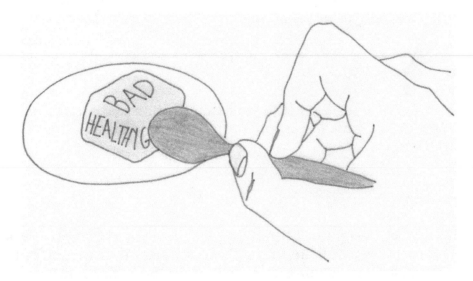

The aim of this part of the workbook is to focus on your nutritional health. If you are seen within a specialist eating disorder team, your therapist and team will assess and monitor your nutritional health, and work with you to make changes to improve it. If you are 'going it alone', we recommend that you ask your general practitioner for help in monitoring your health. The time and attention you need to give to this chapter depends on the level of your medical risk.

TOP TIP: CONSIDER YOUR APPROACH TO THIS CHAPTER WITH CAUTION!

In our experience of working with people with anorexia, we know that we simply cannot ignore the topic of nutrition; however, we urge you to consider the following before you begin working through this chapter:

- If you know you are someone who obsesses about detail then please, as you read, try to zoom out, focus on getting the gist and aim to come away with three or four key messages that can be your personal nutritional goals. Skim any sections that you know will only fuel your anorexia.

- If you are a bit of an ostrich in regard to your nutritional health, with a tendency to bury your head in the sand, commit to at least learning the facts about nutrition and wellbeing. Perhaps you are someone who needs to read this chapter fairly thoroughly so that you can at least make informed choices about how you live.

Understanding your nutritional health and risk

We begin by looking at as much information as possible about all aspects of your nutrition. This is done by using a standard assessment form, to make sure nothing is missed, and so that other people, perhaps your GP, can check your risk in the same way.

What do we check?

See pages 49 to 50 for a guide to your examination and the things that contribute to risk. Your doctor will also use a more global physical review and examination.

Weight and height

Your weight and height will be used to calculate your body mass index (BMI). This shows if you are in the healthy range. Your weight will be checked regularly to monitor gain or loss. See body mass index (BMI) chart at the end of this chapter to estimate your own BMI.

Heart and circulation

Your pulse rate and blood pressure show if your heart is strong enough to pump blood around your body normally. Blood pressure will be taken when you are sitting and standing, to check how well your heart adjusts when you stand up which makes more demands on your heart.

Your skin will be checked for signs of a red or purple rash that indicates the blood vessels are weak and leaking a little blood into the surrounding tissue.

An ECG (electrocardiogram) shows if the electrical activity driving your heart muscle is normal.

Muscle strength

You will be asked to stand up from a squat, to observe how well your core muscles work.

Temperature

Your temperature shows if your body has enough fuel to keep you warm.

Blood tests

A number of tests will be made on your blood, in particular to indicate whether:

- There is an adequate fuel supply (glucose) in your blood
- There is enough iron in your blood cells
- The salts in your blood (sodium, potassium and phosphate) are depleted
- Protein is low (urea)
- Bone nutrients are low (calcium and vitamin D)
- Liver function is impaired
- Bone marrow function (immune system) is impaired.

If you are in treatment, all of these tests would be done at the beginning, after 10 sessions, and at the end. You would be weighed at every visit, as this is such an important check on your progress. If there are any particular concerns or signs of high risk, your doctor may decide to do more tests, or to inform other people if necessary, to keep you as safe as possible.

This table shows the way risk is assessed from test results:

System	Examination	Moderate Risk	High Risk
Weight and Height	Body mass index	$< 15 \text{ kg/m}^2$	$< 13 \text{ kg/m}^2$
	Weight loss per week	$> 0.5\text{kg}$	$> 1.0\text{kg}$
	Skin Rash		Rash showing signs of bleeding into the skin
Circulation	Systolic blood pressure (BP)	< 90	< 80
	Diastolic BP	< 70	< 60
	Postural drop	> 10	> 20
	Pulse rate	< 50 beats per min.	< 40 beats per min.
	Hands and feet		Dark blue/cold
Musculoskeletal	Limb girdle weakness	Some signs of weakness	Marked signs of weakness

System	Examination	Moderate Risk	High Risk
Temperature		< 35 degrees Celsius	< 34.5 degrees Celsius
Investigations	Full blood count	Concern if outside normal limits	K (potassium) < 2.5
	Urea and electrolytes (including phosphate)		Na (sodium) < 130
	Liver function tests Albumin		PO_4 (phosphate) < 0.5
	Glucose		
Heart	Pulse rate ECG	Rate < 50	Rate < 40 Prolonged QT interval

You can keep a record of your own results and track your progress in improving your nutritional health.

System	Examination	Baseline	10 weeks	End of treatment (20–30 weeks)
Body mass index	Weight			
	BMI			
	Weight loss or gain/wk			
Circulation	Systolic BP			
	Diastolic BP			
	Postural drop			
	Pulse rate			
	Extremities			
Musculoskeletal	Limb girdle weakness			
Temperature				
Investigations	Full blood count			
	Electrolytes and urea			
	Liver function tests Albumin			
	Glucose			
	ECG			
	Bone			
	Other			

TOP TIP: USE INFORMATION ABOUT YOUR NUTRITIONAL HEALTH TO EMPOWER YOU

- Remember it is important not to criticise yourself about the effects your anorexia is having on your health. Instead, use this information to give yourself the wake-up call you need, to spur you on to make different nutritional choices that will enable your body and mind to be on top form.

What do you think about your nutrition and do others agree?

Now you have a lot of information about your nutritional health, you can think about it. Try a simple experiment with the nutrition health ruler. Think about the information you have, then use the ruler to rate the following:

- *How do you rate your nutritional health?*
- *Your therapist or doctor will look carefully at the medical results. Where do they place you on the ruler?*
- *Are there other people who are concerned about your nutritional health, perhaps your parents or other family members? Where do they think you are on the ruler?*

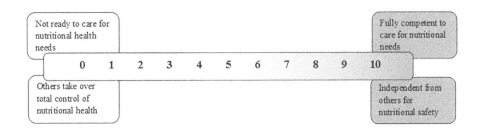

REFLECTION

What have you learned from this experiment?

- Are there any big differences (more than two points) between the different ratings?
- What do you think about the differences?
- If your own score was higher than the score other people would give you, why do you think this is?
- What would have to happen for the ratings to match more closely?

If there is a big difference between the score you gave yourself, and the score that others gave you, it could suggest that the anorexic part of you is strong at playing tricks on you.

Fuel for your body

Your body needs a continual fuel supply to provide energy for all the processes of keeping you alive and functioning, plus physical activity and other processes such as growth, repairing injuries or fighting infection. You also need a store of energy, in the form of carbohydrate and fat, to keep you going between meals, and for times when you aren't able to eat enough, for instance through illness. This energy must come from food, and it is measured in calories. Every individual is different, and everyone uses different amounts of calories every day depending on the changing needs of their body, and the activity they do.

It is possible to estimate the calories we need, from lots of data that have been collected from large numbers of individuals, but it is an estimate, not a precise prediction, and it changes a little from day to day, and over longer time periods.

You may find it helpful to estimate your own energy needs. The answer is in megajoules; you can convert this to calories at the end.

Step 1: First, let's calculate your resting metabolic rate. This is the amount of energy you need every day, just to stay alive, doing no activity at all.

Females	Age	
	18–30	$0.0546 \times$ body weight in kg $+ 2.33$
	30–60	$0.0407 \times$ body weight in kg $+ 2.90$
	Over 60	$0.0424 \times$ body weight in kg $+ 2.38$
Males		
	18–30	$0.0669 \times$ body weight in kg $+ 2.28$
	30–60	$0.0592 \times$ body weight in kg $+ 2.48$
	Over 60	$0.0563 \times$ body weight in kg $+ 2.15$

My resting metabolic rate (RMR)_____ **megajoules**

Step 2: Now, let's consider whether you need to make a metabolic adjustment. If you are very underweight, your body slows down metabolic activity to conserve energy, so if your body mass index is below 16 kg/m^2, multiply your resting metabolic rate by 0.9.

My adjusted resting metabolic rate (RMR)____ **megajoules**

Step 3: Finally, let's think about your activity level. Physical activity uses up energy, so you need to add a factor for that, for your average activity. Multiply your adjusted resting metabolic rate by a physical activity factor to get to your total energy expenditure (TEE).

Physical activity factor

Below average	RMR × 1.49
Average	RMR × 1.63
Above average	RMR × 1.78

My Total Energy Expenditure (TEE) _____ megajoules

Step 4: Converting joules to calories. Most people in the UK use calories to estimate the energy they need, so lastly, convert your answer to calories by multiplying it by 238.8.

My Total Energy Expenditure (TEE) _____ calories

Calories and body weight

If you consistently eat less than your body needs, it is forced to adjust to this. It uses up the stored fuel, and makes changes to reduce the amount that it needs, by stopping or slowing down non-essential processes. You may notice this yourself. Your periods may have stopped. You may feel cold and tired. Your gut can get sluggish, so you feel bloated and constipated. Along with the information in Worksheet 1, these are indicators that you are not providing enough fuel to your body, and you need to eat more to give your body the fuel it needs to restore all its functions, rebuild the body, and recover a healthy weight.

To gain weight

Building healthy tissue uses energy. You need around 7,000 calories to gain 1 kg of new tissue, so to gain 1 kg per week you need to eat your TEE plus 1,000 calories a day. A good aim for weight gain is about 0.5 kg/ week, so you will need your TEE plus 500 calories to achieve that.

Make your own weight gain plan:

- I want to gain _____ kg per week.
- To do this I need to eat _____ (TEE calories) + _____ (extra calories per day).
- Therefore, I need to aim to eat a total of _____ calories per day.

TOP TIP: CALORIES ARE NOT FOR EVERYONE!

- Calories reassure some people (as they provide a boundary of sorts), but they are not helpful for everyone.
- For some people thinking about calories pulls them into something of an obsession with what is OK and not OK to eat, which just promotes rigidity and anxiety. If this sounds like you, then please don't dwell on calories. It's as simple as that. If you have a friend who has maintained a healthy weight for most of their life without much effort and without much variation, ask them whether they count calories; bets are on that they don't!

Nutrients and nutrition risks

Every cell in every part of your body needs not only fuel, but many other nutrients to work well and resist damage.

The following table gives some information about nutrients that are important; remember there are many more.

Nutrient	Blood test	Foods to help	Notes
Iron	Haemoglobin Iron Ferritin	Red meat, especially liver Eggs Breakfast cereals and bread Dried fruit Dark green vegetables Beans and lentils	Tea reduces iron absorption, so don't have tea with meals. Vitamin C increases iron absorption, so vegetables and fruit with meals is helpful.
Potassium	Potassium	Most fruit and vegetables, especially potatoes, bananas, tomatoes Coffee, cocoa, chocolate Meat and fish Milk and cheese	Vomiting and using laxatives can reduce blood potassium to dangerously low levels.
Sodium (salt)	Sodium	Most foods	Vomiting, using laxatives and drinking excessive fluid can reduce blood sodium to dangerously low levels.
Protein	Urea	Milk, yogurt, cheese Eggs Meat, fish Beans, pulses, nuts Bread and wheat cereals	
Phosphate	Phosphate	Milk, yogurt, cheese Meat, fish Peanut butter	

Nutrient	Blood test	Foods to help	Notes
Magnesium	Magnesium	Whole meal bread Whole grain cereals Milk, yogurt Fruit and vegetables, especially bananas	
Calcium	Calcium Bone mineral density (DEXA scan)	Milk, cheese, yogurt Nuts and pulses	You need vitamin D to absorb calcium.
Vitamin D	Vitamin D	Oily fish Eggs and hard cheeses Liver and kidney	You also make vitamin D when sunlight acts on your skin; this is very limited in northern Europe.
Zinc	Zinc	Red meat, especially liver Shellfish Peanut butter, nuts and seeds Cheese	High-strength iron supplements can reduce zinc absorption.

Nutrition supplements

If you have not been eating well for some time, your body could be very depleted in some vitamins, minerals and fatty acids. Discuss your blood results with your team or doctor, and consider if supplements would be helpful for you.

For most people, the best option is a multivitamin and mineral supplement, such as Sanatogen Gold, Centrum Performance or Boots A-Z Complete.

You may need to take extra calcium if you have low bone mineral density. Some calcium supplements contain vitamin D to help you absorb the calcium. Check that you don't take too much vitamin D, as excessive amounts can be harmful. Make sure you are not taking more than 50 mcg altogether daily from any supplements you are taking. A reasonable dose for most people is 10–25 mcg.

You may also want to consider an essential fatty acid (omega-3) supplement, especially if you do not eat oily fish. If low mood is a problem, you may want to take a high EPA (eicosapentaenoic acid) supplement. You will need about 1,000 mg EPA daily to help with low mood.

If you prefer a vegan diet, or a mostly plant-based diet, you will need a multivitamin and mineral supplement. You can get more information about this on the Vegan Society website at www.vegan-society.com.

Common risks

Iron and anaemia

Your blood cells need iron to carry oxygen to all parts of your body. If you don't have enough iron, you can feel drained and exhausted.

Bone health

Osteoporosis, or brittle bones, is a serious long-term risk of poor nutrition. It is caused because your body shuts down some metabolic processes, to save fuel, and this includes the hormones that build bone tissue (the same hormones that make periods happen). Bone-building happens fast during early childhood, and again in the teenage years, and if it is slowed down at these times, bone can remain weaker than it should be. The most important factor in protecting bone health is to recover weight quickly, so that hormones can recover and work to strengthen bone. You also need a good supply of calcium and vitamin D.

Your doctor will consider the risk to your bone health as part of your assessment, and decide whether you need a bone scan to measure bone density.

You can find more information about osteoporosis and eating disorders on the National Osteoporosis Society website, www.nos. org.uk.

Brain nutrition

The brain is a very busy organ, even when you are asleep. It needs 200–300 calories a day for perception, thinking, emotional regulation, learning and memory, and controlling all your body systems.

If your brain does not get the constant flow of energy and nutrients it needs, it quickly begins to slow down any activity that is not absolutely essential. A number of things happen to healthy brain processes:

1 The brain shrinks in size.
2 It triggers the production of the stress hormone cortisol, which has a cascade of effects on your body, as well as on thinking and feeling.
3 The normal process by which new learning takes place is stunted, and it becomes difficult to concentrate, learn and remember new information.
4 Habits become entrenched and difficult to change.
5 Thoughts of food distract attention and concentration.
6 Thinking becomes much more rigid. It is difficult to adjust and be spontaneous.

7 Thinking becomes fragmented and you may be lost in detail and it becomes more difficult to see the big picture.

8 It is harder to be emotionally in tune with others.

9 You become more sensitive to negative and less sensitive to positive emotions.

10 It is harder to regulate emotions: fear, anxiety and anger are accentuated.

11 A large amount of thinking time is taken up by finding ways to cope with anxiety, to avoid facing food fears or by devising ways to compensate or undo the effects of feared behaviours, e.g. exercise, vomiting or fasting (i.e. the so-called safety behaviours).

In turn, this increased and constant anxiety affects appetite. Everyone has experienced loss of appetite when they are nervous or anxious – the 'butterflies in the tummy' effect. This can get you into a vicious cycle of not eating to try to reduce anxiety, starving your brain more, and in the end feeling more anxious and stressed. This seems to create the path that can get people stuck in an eating disorder.

TOP TIP: CAN YOU EVEN REMEMBER HOW YOUR BODY, MIND AND EMOTIONS FUNCTIONED BEFORE ANOREXIA?

Once anorexia has kicked in, people tend to talk as though the anorexic side effects are all they know – that being tired, restless, anxious and cold is just 'them' – now, look back at the preceding list and tick those that apply now and ask yourself the following in relation to each statement you have ticked:

1 Has this always been the case? If not, how were things before anorexia?
2 Do I really want to sign up to these side effects for the rest of my life?

Brain nutritional risk chart

The chart overleaf illustrates the impairment suffered by the average brain at various levels of weight loss. This varies between individuals and it might be helpful to monitor and calibrate your own brain activity. You can do this by jotting down the content of your thoughts, feelings, sensations, images, memories and your behaviours at frequent time intervals during the day. Many people with an eating disorder are surprised at how much time food and anorexic thoughts take up when they take time to track them. Others are surprised that their urge to be on the go and exercise is linked to food and anorexia. Why don't you try the experiment and see what you find out about yourself? Where are you on this chart?

BMI < 12	-Pretty much all (90-100%) of thinking relates to food or "safety" behaviours (exercise, weight etc)
	-Working memory (<25% of normal) with lapses of attention or confusion
	-Inflexible, rule driven and detail-focused thinking at 90% of maximum
BMI = 12 - 13.5	80-90% of thinking relates to food or "safety" behaviours (exercise, weight etc)
BMI = 13.5 - 15	60-80% of thinking relates to food or "safety" behaviours (exercise, weight etc)
BMI = 15 - 17.5	30-60% of thinking relates to food or "safety" behaviours (exercise, weight etc)
BMI = 17.5 - 19.5	15-30 % of thinking relates to food or "safety" behaviours (exercise, weight etc)
	Working memory (>80% normal) with lapses of attention or confusion
	Inflexible, rule driven and detail focused thinking at < 50% of maximum (varies with individual thinking style)
BMI = 19.5-25	Healthy, normal, flexible, thinking, according to your personal thinking style

Why is it difficult to know what to eat?

Our bodies have a complicated and powerful system to regulate food intake, to keep us eating what we need. It has evolved over millions of years to be flexible and to cope with times when food may be in short supply or plentiful. Sadly, it hasn't really adapted to modern environments and lifestyles, and it can go wrong, especially if we veer away from eating in a healthy way.

Natural appetite regulation uses a lot of signals, from our bodies – hunger and fullness, from the outside world, seeing or smelling food, and from learned experience – a regular eating routine. This can get disturbed if we often override the signals of hunger and fullness from our bodies. If the messages don't all agree and work together, we end up with confused signals that are difficult to understand, so it's easy to lose confidence about when and what to eat. This confusion can make it hard to re-establish healthy, normal eating, and can keep an eating disorder stuck.

It can be helpful to understand how these signals work in a healthy way.

First, there are two sets of signals that work together. The first set is the **short-term signals** that help us to know when we need to eat, and when to stop. These work from meal to meal, and combine information about how much is in our stomachs, and nutrients flowing into blood, with our awareness of things like routine mealtimes and what other people are doing. There are also **longer-term signals** that our brains are getting about whether there is enough fuel stored in our bodies. These signals may not match, for instance if your body stores are empty, you can still feel hungry even if your stomach is full straight after a meal, and it is hard to make sense of that. You may begin to feel there is something wrong with your body, as it is making you feel you could go on and on eating even when you are full.

If you have been lucky, and learned and practised from childhood how to eat in a healthy way, you will remember what you have learned and be aware if you go too far astray. With so many other sources of information and misinformation, from advertising, websites about dieting or clean eating and so on, it's easy to pick up ideas that are misleading, and undermine learning how to regulate eating in a healthy way. An eating disorder can make you feel very sensitive to messages from all directions and leave you feeling you don't know where to turn.

Appetite for food is not just about nutrition. Healthy humans also use food for comfort, reward and connecting with family, friends and strangers. When this emotional and social eating is part of the overall mix, it is healthy and helps us to comfort ourselves and maintain relationships with others. If emotional eating becomes too big an influence, we can lose sight of getting the basic nutrition our bodies need.

The way these systems work and interact to help us make decisions about eating looks a bit like this:

Bodily signals	Personal learning, memory and experience	The outside world
• Amounts of stored nutrients in the body (fat and carbohydrate) • Food in the stomach and other parts of the gut • Blood levels of carbohydrate (glucose) and fat	• Liking or disliking a food • Pleasure and reward of eating, or guilt and anxiety about eating • Comfort and soothing from eating • Learned cultural eating habits and expectations • Enjoyment of social eating	• Time of day • Whether other people are eating – or not eating • Seeing or smelling food • Whether food is easily on hand, or difficult to get • Messages from many sources
↓	↓	↓
• Hormone signals • Nerve signals	• Social situation and expectations • Immediate need for comfort, soothing or distraction	• Immediate recognition of meal time • Situational triggers to eat
↓	↓	↓

Our brain processes and interprets these signals

↓

Appetite and Eating Behaviour

Research in animals has shown that if these signals are persistently confused, or interfered with, eating behaviour becomes abnormal and inappropriate.

How animals learn to under-eat and starve

Animals will under-eat if:

- They are exposed to chronic stress
- They are kept short of food but allowed access to exercise as an alternative activity or distraction.

This can explain how compulsive exercise can keep you stuck in anorexia.

How animals learn to over-eat and binge-eat

Animals will overeat or binge-eat if:

- They are undernourished
- Their stomach content is drained after eating
- They are given food at times that are irregular and unpredictable
- They are given food that is highly palatable at irregular intervals.

If animals are exposed to these conditions, they repeatedly overeat (i.e. binge eat), even when they are returned to normal feeding. Binge eating can be provoked many months later by cues that activate memories from the experience that initially caused the overeating. It seems as if this operates via the same mechanisms of neural learning that produce addiction to alcohol, nicotine and other addictive drugs.

You can see from this why binge eating often occurs during the course of anorexia nervosa. It is common for this to be a phase but with some effort on your part you can choose to stop it from becoming a terrible compulsion.

How humans learn to eat abnormally

Overeating in response to the easy availability of very palatable foods is a common place experience in our present environment.

Being kept short of food, for instance by dieting, or persistently ignoring hunger to continue working, can leave people with a tendency to overeat. Vomiting destroys the learned link between food and satiation. It leads to swings in blood sugar that leave you feeling uncertain whether you are hungry or full.

Resetting a disturbed appetite control system

Learning how to get the balance right takes time, but it can be done. Here are some things which will help:

- Eat regularly with no long fasts so that you don't become excessively hungry; your glucose levels are stable and your body learns that food will be reliably available.
- Eat slowly, pay attention to what you are eating, and avoid distractions like the television or your phone.
- Don't eat in secret – that will reinforce anxiety and guilt.
- Eat with others if you can as there is an interplay between social and appetite hormones. Choose foods that travel through the gut slowly. This allows the peripheral and gut sensory systems that signal satiety to work well.
- Choose foods with a low glycaemic index so that your sugar level does not have huge swings and troughs (you can get information on this from books, or the internet).
- It may be helpful to limit your access to foods that have been engineered to be highly palatable.
- You may want to keep chocolate or crisps to eat as a snack when you are out, but not keep a supply at home. Or have a piece of bitter (high cocoa) chocolate after a meal so that it does not cause blood glucose to rise.
- Aim to not spit or vomit or disconnect food from the stomach. The incentive will be to continue eating because the healthy satiation mechanisms are disrupted. Your body will become excessively sensitive to the sight, smell and flavour of food. This sets up food cravings and the drive to binge.
- Aim to get your weight within the healthy range (BMI 19–24). If you are underweight, the biological drive to eat will be strong and switched on all the time. The pleasure and reward mechanisms for eating will be over-sensitised. There may be a rebound of these signals during the recovery process, but they will settle over time.
- Develop a variety of activities that give you pleasure and comfort so that you do not rely so much on food or compulsive exercise.
- Build up a network of people to talk to and spend time with so you can have more enjoyable social interactions.
- Use ways of rewarding all your sensory systems:

  - Touch – body-oriented therapies, massage, aromatherapy, reflexology.
  - Smell – have a warm bath with scented oil, grow plants with scented flowers or keep lavender among your clothes.
  - Sound – making or listening to music, enjoying birdsong in the park.
  - Vision – make your room a pleasant environment with pictures or other items you like to look at; learn meditation techniques so you can hold peaceful, pleasant scenes in your mind's eye.

All these activities activate the left part of the brain that has the soothing system. They act as an antidote to the fight, freeze or flight systems in the right part of the brain, which respond to threat and stress.

REFLECTION

This information aims to help you to think about your nutrition more clearly.

- Do you think you are ready to think about nourishing your body effectively?
- Which area of eating might you make a start with?

1 Eating sufficient amounts
2 Eating a variety of foods
3 Eating as a social event
4 Eating regularly (no long fasts).

A healthy mix of foods and fluid

This picture shows a healthy mix of foods, in five groups.

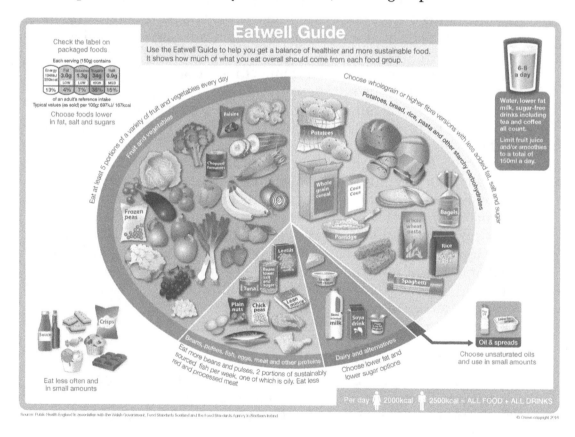

The biggest groups show the foods we need to have most – starchy foods, and fruit and vegetables.

The smallest group shows healthy oils and fats. There are two groups in the middle that are essential in different ways: milk and dairy foods; and meat, fish, eggs, nuts and seeds. Lastly, the picture shows foods we should use just a little: very sweet and very fatty foods.

The right mix of foods will make sure you get all the nutrients you need, and give your body the signals it needs to regulate how much you eat, so that you don't feel deprived and get food cravings, or feel full and bloated.

Think about each group – why it's important and how you can fit it into the way you eat. If you aim to have three meals with small snacks regularly over the day, you will have lots of ways to get all the variety of foods you need.

Fruit and vegetables

Most people know how valuable our '5 a Day' are for good health. We need a variety of fruit and vegetables for the wide range of vitamins and minerals that are essential for protecting many aspects of physical and mental health. They can help prevent conditions such as heart disease, cancer, depression and dementia. Fruit and vegetables also provide potassium, which is necessary for muscles to work, including the heart muscle. Purging by using laxatives or vomiting causes the body to lose potassium, so fruit and vegetables will help to replace it. Fruit and vegetables also have fibre for healthy bowel function and lifelong gut health.

Include fresh fruit or juice at breakfast and as a snack or dessert. Have salad in sandwiches and light meals, and a mix of vegetables with cooked dishes and in sauces and casseroles. Use fruit in desserts such as crumbles and pies, baked apples or stewed fruit. The more variety, the better!

It is possible to *overdo* the fruit and vegetables. More than eight or nine servings a day can make you feel bloated and stop you getting enough of the other foods you need, can give you stomach pain, and even make your skin turn yellow as excess carotene is stored there. It can also confuse appetite regulation; for instance, if you eat a lot of salad, your stomach might feel very full, but there is little flow of nutrients to your blood and brain.

Starchy staples

These foods are powerful signals to the brain to regulate food intake. They give the feeling of fullness after a meal, coupled with a steady rise in blood glucose over the next few hours, giving the brain the message to end the meal, and not start eating again for a while. Having starchy foods regularly helps prevent excessive hunger. If you let yourself get too hungry, your thoughts keep turning to food, and this can increase the risk of food craving and uncontrolled eating.

Use the starchy foods that release glucose *gradually* over several hours (low glycaemic index or low GI), such as granary or seeded bread, porridge and muesli, oatcakes, pasta, sweet potato, brown rice, high fibre cereals like shredded wheat. Whole grain bread, cereals and starchy vegetables also provide protein, fibre, vitamins and minerals, including B vitamins, vitamin E, iron and zinc. Include these foods as cereal, porridge or toast at breakfast; granary bread or rolls, or couscous or pasta salad with a light meal; and pasta, rice, potato or sweet potato with a cooked meal. You can have toast or a scone, or a cereal bar or oatcakes with cheese, or cereal with milk as a healthy snack.

Meat, fish, eggs, nuts, seeds and pulses

This group is quite a mix of foods. They all provide protein, and each offers a different variety of other essential vitamins, minerals, essential fatty acids and fibre. Meat, eggs and pulses provide iron and zinc; oily fish supplies essential fatty acids for brain and heart function; nuts and seeds provide B vitamins and magnesium, fibre and healthy fats for building cell membranes. If you don't get all these essential nutrients, your physical and mental health can be impaired now and in the future. If you don't eat meat, take care to get iron from eggs, dark green vegetables, bread and cereals and dried fruit. If you don't eat oily fish, it is difficult to get enough essential fatty acids and vitamin D; it may be sensible to take a supplement.

Aim for a couple of servings from this group every day. You can use meat or fish or egg or peanut butter or hummus as a sandwich filling or with a salad. You can have a larger serving of one of these foods as part of your main meal. Nuts and seeds make a snack that is easy to carry around with you.

Milk and milk-based foods

Milk, yogurt and cheese are the calcium-rich foods and are also an important source of protein, vitamins and potassium. Calcium is the substance that makes bones and teeth hard. At times of rapid growth, especially the teenage years, your body responds to hormones (oestrogen in girls and testosterone in boys) by rapidly laying down calcium in bones to make them hard and strong. If your body weight is low, production of these hormones may be reduced.

Combined with a lack of calcium, protein and vitamin D, this leaves bones short of calcium and at risk of serious weakness called osteoporosis. If you are under 25 years old, you can make your bones stronger by staying at a healthy weight and getting a high calcium intake – four servings every day from this group.

If you would like more information about calcium and bone health, look at the NHS Choices website (www.nhs.uk/Conditions/

vitamins-minerals/Pages/Calcium.aspx). For information about osteoporosis and eating disorders, see the National Osteoporosis Society information sheet (www.nos.org.uk/document.doc?id=1421).

Cereal or porridge with milk as a regular breakfast gives you a good start. Have yogurt, fromage frais or rice pudding as a dessert or snacks; milky drinks such as cappuccino or hot chocolate or milkshake are good; choose a cheese dish such as macaroni cheese as your main meal sometimes, or cheese as a sandwich filling or with oatcakes as a snack. If you prefer not to have cow's milk, use soya milk with added calcium. Other types of 'milk', such as rice or nut products, are not adequate as they may not provide enough calcium *or* protein. You also need vitamin D to use the calcium – from oily fish, eggs, cheese, and yellow spreads on bread. If you are at risk of osteoporosis (if you have ever been at low weight, even for a few weeks) a vitamin D supplement will probably be helpful. You need 10–25 mcg daily, but don't have more.

Every cell of your body is built from a mix of protein and fats. So you need protein and fat to grow, to repair damaged cells and to replace the ones that are worn out. Many of the active substances that keep all body functions working – hormones, enzymes, substances for fighting infection and getting rid of toxins – are built of protein. We all need a constant supply of protein to keep healthy, and milk provides the high quality protein we need – for most people in the UK, around a quarter of daily protein intake comes from milk and dairy foods.

Healthy oils and fats

All our body cells have membranes made from fats, and many substances such as hormones are also made from fats, so we need the right kind of fats and oils from our foods. These come from oily fish, and also from nut and seed oils and olive oil. Use olive oil, nut oils and rapeseed oil for cooking, dressings and sauces. Fat-soluble vitamins (vitamins A, D, E and K) are present in the fatty elements of foods such as cheese, eggs, milk, butter and spreads, oily fish, nuts and seeds.

Sweet and fatty foods

Healthy eating is not just nutrients. Sweet and fatty foods may not provide much to support physical health, and too much can be harmful, but we really need them for emotional and social health. Enjoying food is essential for us to feel satisfied and comfortable. Pleasure from eating is part of healthy appetite regulation. If we try too hard to avoid these foods, we feel deprived, and this can trigger craving and uncontrolled eating. To take part in social eating, you need to be able to have a full variety of foods. It's not comfortable to feel you have to turn down a gift of expensive chocolate or a cake that a family member has made with love. We all need to learn how to use these foods in a normal way, without having so much that it harms our health. It's best to have these foods when you are not very hungry, so you are less likely to overeat them. One or two servings a day is fine, maybe more some days and less on others. You might like a dessert after a healthy main course sometimes, or crisps or chocolate as part of your light meal. Accept one slice of birthday cake, or a cookie with your milky coffee. You can learn to enjoy your food by including a little, and it will help you to feel comfortable joining with what your friends and family have.

Fluid

Most of us need six to eight drinks a day, each one about 200–300 ml – a large mug.

Every cell in your body needs water for everything it does. Your body is losing water all the time, through your skin, and in your breath, and getting rid of waste products in urine. If you don't replace it, you become dehydrated. If you don't get enough fluid, you may get headaches, or moments of dizziness, for instance when you stand up quickly. Your skin may get dry and papery, and you may be prone to urine infections.

Purging by vomiting or using laxatives makes you lose water, so they can quickly make you dehydrated. Work with your therapist to reduce it, and make sure you get extra fluid to replace what you lose.

You can drink plain water, or tea or coffee, milky drinks or fruit juice. You may need more if you are very physically active, or the weather is hot, or you are unwell, or you have alcohol or a lot of caffeine (from coffee or energy drinks). If you drink alcohol, or strong coffee, have a glass of water for each drink with alcohol or caffeine.

You can overdo fluid intake. If you have too much – more than about 2.5 litres a day – it can dilute the essential salts in your blood, and that may impair your heart function.

Fizzy drinks can cause problems. You may find you use a lot of diet fizzy drinks. This can interfere with recovering natural appetite regulation, and they are very acidic, so they can damage teeth severely, especially if you use them often. If they also contain caffeine (cola and energy drinks), they may interfere with sleep and can make anxiety worse.

You need to take drinks regularly over the day. Aim to have at least one drink with each of your three main meals, between meals and in the evening.

A regular eating routine

To eat in a healthy way you need to have some **structure**, so that you can:

- Meet all your nutrition needs
- Not have too much of the foods that might become harmful in excess
- Be aware of what you are eating without feeling stressed.

You also need to be **flexible** to meet these needs in different ways at different times, so that you can:

- Make adjustments to fit in with the other needs and activities of your life
- Share foods that others prepare for you and eat with you
- Try new foods
- Eat in situations where you cannot choose the food, or choice may be limited
- Make changes so you can join in with celebrations and unexpected events
- Feel normal.

To do this successfully, it helps to have in your mind a **framework for your eating** that you feel confident will meet your needs and preferences, without being too rigid and rule-bound. Most of us develop this framework over the years as we learn to be independent adults, and keep on adjusting it as our lives change. When you have a stable eating routine, you can use it as a benchmark to try new things and experiment, without taking too much risk.

To build your personal framework, think about:

- How often do you eat each day? What's the most often that would be OK for you? What's the least? Except overnight, three to four hours is the longest time you should go without eating.
- What times should you eat? How soon after getting up should you eat? What's the longest you should go between meals and snacks? Should there be times when you do not eat? Should you have a planned snack or drink if you wake in the night?
- When is your main meal of the day? Is that the same every day?

Regular meals provide the **steady supply of fuel** that is important for all the cells in your body, so that they have the energy to work. This is especially important for vital organs that need a lot of fuel, in particular the brain. If you go too long without eating, or eat in an uncontrolled or erratic way, your body systems may be deprived or overloaded, and this stresses them. They respond to deprivation by making changes to stop or slow down non-essential functions. You may notice, for instance, that concentration and learning become more difficult, and mood is more unstable, or you feel cold or tired. They may be unable to respond quickly enough to overload, and eating too much in a short time can stress organs such as your liver, pancreas and stomach, sometimes causing long-term damage.

Regular meals play an essential part in **appetite regulation**. A steady stream of nutrients into your blood is a signal to your brain that you do not need to eat just yet. As it slows down, your brain begins to register hunger. Very rapid shifts in the flow of nutrients, from over-eating or restriction, can confuse the part of your brain that regulates appetite. Regular eating helps you to learn and remember the best ways to feed yourself, to stay comfortable. Hours of deprivation can make you excessively hungry, risking uncontrolled and binge eating, preoccupation with thoughts of food, and stress to your body and brain.

Eating regularly, in more or less the same way as the people around you, helps you to feel comfortable to join others for a meal or snack. Eating is part of most social relationships, and helps keep you **connected to family and friends, and to build new friendships**.

Building a regular eating pattern

For most people, three meals and one to three snacks each day is a pattern that works well. Even if your work means changing shifts, or you travel across time zones, you can use that as a basis for planning. Every day, aim for:

- Breakfast – usually the smallest meal of the day, and the one that is quick to prepare and eat, but it doesn't always have to be in the morning, it may work better for you at a different time, especially if you work shifts.
- A main meal – usually the largest meal of the day, with at least two courses, and including cooked foods.
- A light meal, which may need to be portable, perhaps sandwiches or salad, or a simple dish such as a filled jacket potato, with items such as yogurt, fruit, soup, cereal bar, nuts, crisps, cake.
- A substantial snack, usually in the longest break between meals.
- One or two small snacks, which you might change depending on what you are doing.

Look in the next section, on getting a healthy mix of foods, for ideas of what to eat at each kind of meal and snack.

You can begin by thinking about the times of day that you might eat a meal or snack, perhaps within a one- to two-hour time slot for a meal, for instance you might plan your main meal to be any time between 6 p.m. and 8 p.m. If you need to, you can begin by having something small in your chosen time slot. For example, if you are not used to having breakfast, you could start with fruit or yogurt before 9 a.m.

Try planning your food and drinks for a day using this template. You can make as many copies of the template as you want.

MORNING

AFTERNOON

EVENING

TOP TIP

We often get asked by our patients what is more important in making a plan for improving your nutritional health, consistency or variety. In other words, is it better to challenge yourself to have meals out (e.g. lunch with work colleagues or dinner with friends) once or twice a week or build a regular daily eating routine. Whilst ultimately both consistency and variety matter for happy, healthy eating, early on, consistency trumps variety.

A day in the life of my gut

Now you have worked through a lot of information, you can begin to think about how you relate to your body and its need for food. How is your relationship with your gut, your digestion and what are your feelings for that area?

Have a go at writing a letter from the perspective of a day in the life of your gut. How does your gut feel? What would it like to say to the rest of you? What does it need from you to feel nurtured, cared for and comfortable? How does it relate to the rest of your body and to the world?

A day in my life improving my nutritional health

Getting better nutritional health would keep you out of hospital and stop others stepping in to improve your nutritional safety. Visualise what a day in your life would be like if you improved your nutritional health. Make a detailed storyboard like a film director:

- *What could you do to improve your nutritional health?*
- *What makes you feel confident that you could do that?*

- *What are the things you are currently doing to help your nutrition?*
- *Who else might be able to help you and how, when and where?*
- *What are the further benefits of better nutritional health aside from avoiding hospital?*
- *What is the first step?*

Safeguarding my nutritional health – if . . . then . . .

What would happen if you put such a plan in place? Think about all the blocks that will obstruct your path to good nutritional health and have a back-up plan if . . . then. . . .

- To complete the first column, you need to think about external support. This may mean a person to help, but it also means that the right food is available at the right time and place.
- For the second column, think about your internal blocks.
- Next, run through the behaviours involved in eating several times in your head, like playing a DVD, and add to the third column.
- Lastly, you need to think of the consequences. Think of the negative consequences that will follow eating: fear, guilt, the compulsion to make yourself safe by exercise or purging or restricting more severely. Also, think about the long-term positive consequences of eating, and add these into the final column.

Safeguarding nutritional health

External structure	Internal Blocks If . . . then. . . .	External blocks If . . . then . . .	Long-term Positive Consequences
Who When Where	If my fear escalates rapidly then.	If the timing gets altered then.	e.g. able to care for my nutritional needs independently; enjoy the company of my friends again

Look at the table, can you think of ways to plan for obstacles and not immediately turn away?

- Keep your focus on the positive long-term consequences (e.g. having a bigger life).
- People who successfully recover from anorexia nervosa are resourceful and creative in making these plans and often enrol the help of others. You might want to do the same.

Nutritional change – planning sheet

People who have successfully been able to renourish themselves out of hospital are able to be flexible and able to look at the bigger picture and not get swamped down in detail.

Here is the plan made by Charlotte, who was able to restore her health without intensive hospital care. It might be helpful if you are able make a plan like this and look at it regularly to modify it on a regular basis.

The nutritional changes I want to make are:	To get out of the risk zone for my nutritional health.
The most important reasons I want to make these changes are:	I do not want to go into hospital. I want to have a bigger life and make decisions about my future contribution to the world.
The steps I plan to take are:	I will have a yogurt for a snack and I will not skip lunch.
I can ask others people to help by doing less or more:	Maisie can support me. She will text me at the agreed times for my snacks to cue me in and support me. I will plan snacks with her. I will ask my mother not to quiz me about what I have eaten when I come in.
I will know that my plan is working if:	My nutritional health improves in terms of my place on the BMI chart and my clinical function.
Things that might interfere with my plan and how I will overcome them are:	I will want to exercise more. I will set up an additional plan about my safety behaviours (compulsive exercise, body checking, etc.). When I get the anorexic critical backlash, I will restore my peace and serenity by: • Going for a walk with my brother. • Phoning Maisie, but with non-AN talk. • Asking my Mum to give me a foot massage, brush my hair.

Now it is your turn . . .

**The nutritional changes I want
to make are:**

**The most important reasons I want to
make these changes are:**

The steps I plan to take are:

**I can ask others people to help by doing
less or more:**

I will know that my plan is working if:

**Things that might interfere with my plan
and how I will overcome them are:**

It is usually most helpful to go through these plans with other people. Perhaps you can ask them how to overcome some of the difficulties you will face. Get them to help problem solve some of the if–then passages with you. Good luck!

Maudsley Body Mass Index Chart

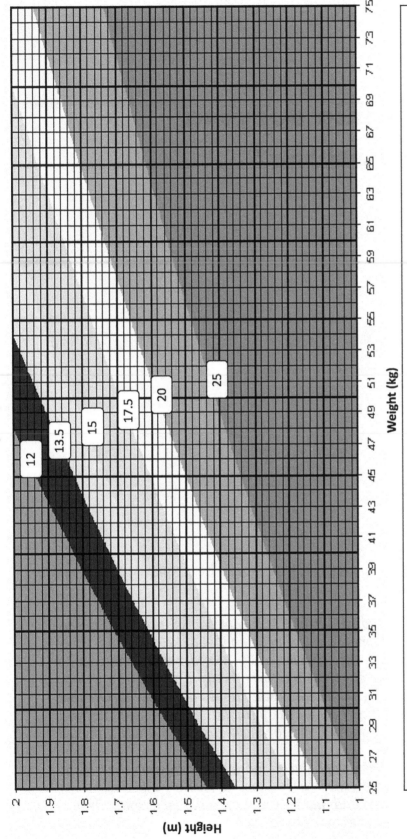

Weight (kg)

Height (m)

Key

<12:	Life threatening anorexia nervosa
12-13.5:	**Critical anorexia nervosa** Inpatient treatment recommended. Organs begin to fail: muscle, bone marrow and heart.
13.5-15:	**Severe anorexia nervosa** All organ systems compromised: muscle, bone, heart and brain. Metabolism reduced by 50%.
15-17.5:	**Anorexia nervosa** Amenorrhoea. Loss of substance from all body organs and structure.
17.5-20:	**Underweight** Irregular or absent menstruation. Ovulation failure.
20-25:	**Normal weight range**

Chapter 5

My anorexia nervosa

Why, what and how?

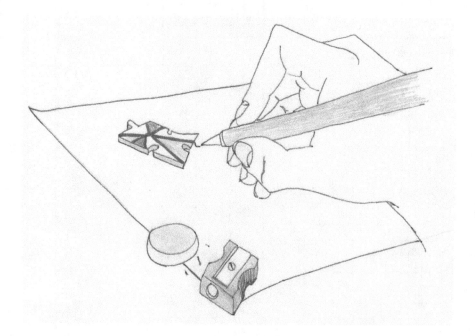

Here's what one of our patients told us about her experience of working through this chapter:

> When I started therapy, I felt like I already had quite a good understanding of how my anorexia developed and what kept it going. However, working through this chapter really helped me to get a clearer picture of this and notice new connections that I wasn't aware of before. Perhaps because I already thought I had an idea of the key factors that kept my anorexia going, I found the formulation itself really difficult at first . . . but, something eventually clicked and the whole thing fell into place.
>
> In the end, I was able to produce a formulation diagram that finally made sense to me, giving me a helpful tool for recovery and a real sense of achievement. Since I had had to work so hard to understand the formulation, it's actually become one of the most memorable sections of the handbook for me. Now that I've left therapy, if I notice any warning

signs or unhealthy behaviour, it's the formulation petals that I find eas-iest to return to for an answer to what might be triggering me and what I can do to combat this.

The aim of this chapter is to help you to understand how and why your anorexia developed and what factors are keeping it going. Kay, who had anorexia for three years, referred to this phase of therapy as 'unearthing her story' or getting to know the early life events and personal charac-teristics that are relevant to how and why her anorexia developed. Kay came to understand that she had always been anxious and sensitive by nature, plus she always liked things to be 'just so' (personal characteris-tics), such that when she moved from a safe, smaller school where she had lots of friends to a much bigger school for her A-levels (life event), she felt wobbly to the degree that she reached out for something (in her case, skipping meals) to help her manage difficult feelings.

Interestingly, the factors that contribute to your anorexia developing – your 'story' – can sometimes be quite different from the factors that keep anorexia going over time (maintaining factors). You see, at first, when Kay began to restrict her eating, her anorexia fuelled itself via all the positive comments she received from people as she lost a bit of weight. However, as her illness intensified, she found that people became cross and fed up with her, and so she withdrew from them and from school, making her bind with anorexia stronger and her life much smaller (maintaining factors).

We will encourage you to reflect upon your 'story', including those personal characteristics and life events that may have contributed to your anorexia developing. However, we won't be able to change these things, they are either enduring characteristics of you (so we wouldn't want to change these!), or they include life events that are now in the past. However, where there is room for movement, where the possibili-ties for change lie, are in those factors currently keeping your anorexia going, those maintaining factors.

Based on many years of listening to people with anorexia and to those who have recovered we have drawn up a model of typical factors that maintain anorexia.[1, 2] The model suggests that once a pattern of coping using anorexia develops, a number of factors can help to keep it going, including: your beliefs about anorexia itself; your general think-ing style; your relationship with your emotions and with other people; and the response of close others to your anorexia.

In this chapter we will ask you to:

- Arm yourself with your wise, reflective 'friend' and with curiosity and compassion; gather the information required to understand your 'story' about why your anorexia developed.
- And then to flesh out those factors that currently maintain your anorexia using our model as a guide.
- Following this, we will guide you to identify the issues that you feel you need to tackle in order to help you move towards recovery.

Before you start

Please mark the scale below to indicate how much you feel you currently understand about how your anorexia developed and why it keeps going? We can review this again later to check that you're getting what you need from this chapter.

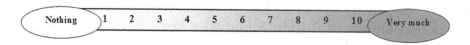

Nothing | 1 | 2 | 3 | 4 | 5 | 6 | 7 | 8 | 9 | 10 | Very much

Your 'story': what you bring to your anorexia

To begin to build your 'story' and to think about how your anorexia developed, we'd like you to consider each part of the following diagram.

What you bring to your anorexia?

Mismatch between challenges and resources

↓

My traits/personality:	My strengths:
Events/challenges/difficulties that have shaped my view of the world:	My supports:

To help you think about what you might write in each section of the diagram, have a read of the following descriptions:

Traits/personality: Your personality traits are enduring qualities of you. When people talk about their traits they usually say things like 'I've always been this way. It's just me'. Jasmine, who had quite severe anorexia for several years, described her core traits as being shy and introverted. Traits often have a genetic component and run in families. For example, both Jasmine's father and brother were very shy and introverted too, whereas her mother and older sister tended to be much more outgoing. Importantly, not every trait that runs in families is totally genetic. Family expectations, culture and learning can also contribute to certain enduring ways of behaving. For example, in some families having a 'stiff upper lip' and not showing difficult emotions is considered the only acceptable way of dealing with intense emotions, and this may to a large extent be a learned behaviour.

Strengths: These are those qualities, characteristics or traits that help you achieve what you want in life and that you are proud of. Jasmine described her top strengths as being hard-working, creative and able to use humour to get through difficult times. Importantly, some traits can be both a strength and a vulnerability and have benefits and a downside. For example, being hard-working, like Jasmine, means she does well in a work environment and gets lots of things done but also can come at a personal cost, i.e. making her vulnerable to exhaustion and others give her more to do.

Events/challenges/difficulties that have shaped your view of the world: Typically when we look back at our earlier life, there are a few key events or challenges that influenced who we are and how we view the world. Jasmine had endured bullying for many years at secondary school which has made it difficult for her to trust people, especially other females. Jasmine's family also moved house and country a lot when she was growing up, and so she had a sense that nothing was stable or predictable.

Supports: This tells us about those resources that keep you buoyant in life, those that help you out during tough times. Funnily enough, they often come in the form of people in our lives that we trust and that are good for us. For Jasmine, her core support person was her aunty Claire, who was a consistent and positive character in her life and who accepted Jasmine just the way she was. Jasmine had other important people in her life, but she came to recognise that they were variable in how helpful they were to her wellbeing and so she learned to lean more heavily on just those people who supported her in positive and helpful ways. Identifying those genuinely supportive people was crucial to Jasmine turning a corner towards recovery.

Mismatch between challenges and resources: What people tell us is that anorexia can develop at times when there is a mismatch between the level of challenge someone is facing and the strengths and resources they have available to cope. We shall return to this later, but for now start to think about your anorexia 'story' and what you might write in each section of the diagram.

TOP TIP: GO WITH YOUR GUT!

- When trying to think about your anorexia 'story' go with your gut impressions of who you are and what has shaped you. Try not to over-think things. You know yourself better than anyone, just dare to reflect.
- If it's frightening to think about yourself and your earlier life, enlist the help of your wise, reflective friend; how would they describe you and the life events that have shaped you?

What keeps your anorexia going?

Once we have explored your anorexia 'story', we will then turn our attention to thinking about those factors in the here and now that keep your anorexia going. Take a look at the following diagram. It looks a bit like a flower. We call this sort of diagram a 'vicious flower' as each of the petals describes a factor that keeps a person locked into their problem, in this case anorexia. We have grouped the petals according to themes that people with anorexia tell us keep their anorexia going. To think about what keeps anorexia going in your life, we will guide you to consider each of the following factors:

- The beliefs you have about anorexia being a positive in your life and perhaps how anorexia has become part of your identity.
- Your commonly used thinking style, such as struggling with flexibility and/or a tendency to focus on detail at the expense of the bigger picture.
- Difficulties 'being with' and/or managing emotions and relationships.
- The influence of key people in your life, in regards to your anorexia.
- Any other factors that keep you stuck with anorexia.

After you've worked through these steps, you will have a personal model that will help you to understand more clearly why anorexia has developed in your life, what keeps it going and how, and this will provide a starting point for thinking about how to change.

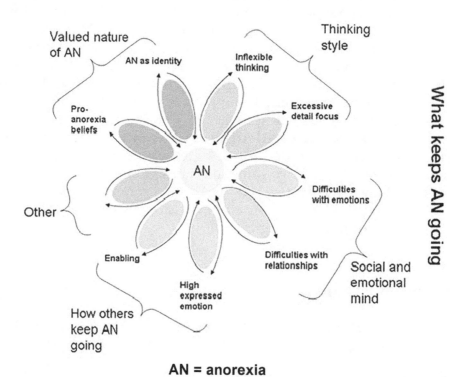

AN = anorexia

REFLECTION

- So far during this chapter we have introduced you to the idea of your anorexia 'story' or the idea that anorexia emerges from somewhere, usually a backdrop of difficult life events that challenge a person's usual way of coping.
- We have also introduced to you the idea that certain themes or tendencies tend to be common for individuals with anorexia that function to keep the anorexia going. We represented these within the vicious flower of anorexia.
- We will now move on to look at your anorexia 'story' and your anorexia vicious flower in a little more detail. But first of all, take a pause.
- Does thinking about your past bring up any difficult feelings for you? It is quite possible that reflecting in this way might feel painful and threatening and there might be a pull to 'cut off', but we urge you to stick with it, people tell us that understanding their anorexia 'story' is the first step toward developing self-compassion, and that understanding what keeps anorexia going marks the beginning of enormous possibilities for change.

1. Your anorexia 'story': what you bring to your anorexia

During this section, we'd like to invite you to think in more detail about your anorexia 'story'. Why you? Why anorexia? Why now? Try to enter this section being as open and honest and compassionate with yourself as you can be. Most people struggle at some point in their lives with something really challenging. In fact most of us will suffer a mental health struggle at some stage during our lives. The key is to embrace this episode as part of your life journey, face it head on and get to know it. Let's begin by thinking about those events/challenges/difficulties that came your way.

Events/challenges/difficulties that have shaped your view of the world

Nobody grows up in a perfect world. Often when people have emotional and psychological difficulties in their lives, they are able to identify experiences from their past that gave them messages which affected how they see themselves, others and the world around them, or life in general. Sometimes, these experiences can be one-off events or they can be more long-standing experiences or challenges, rooted in the person's childhood. Some of these experiences may have been very unpleasant and distressing (e.g. involving some form of trauma or abuse), but others may simply have been unhelpful in quite subtle ways, reinforcing particular messages (e.g. critical comments from a family member about their weight and shape). Sometimes quite regular events that may not bother most people can really bother someone else because it meshes with their personality. For example, in the case of Jasmine, changing school was stressful because she was shy and found it hard to make friends. But for her sister, moving house wasn't an issue (she struggled more with organising herself to meet work deadlines, which was no problem for Jasmine!). So, there are big differences in how responsive and sensitive to stress people are and how likely they are to perceive life's challenges as negative and threatening. Personality, genetic make-up and experiences in utero (i.e. before they were born) all contribute.

CHARLOTTE'S STORY

Charlotte has anorexia nervosa. She has an older brother called James. James has always excelled in his life. He always got top marks at school and at university and now has a job where he earns a lot of money. He has a wonderful girlfriend and they are getting married. Her parents have always been so proud of him and his achievements. Charlotte has also done quite well at school, but has always had to work exceptionally hard to get reasonable grades. She has a small group of friends but has always been rather quiet and less outgoing than James. Charlotte has always felt that James is better than her. She believes that other people think this too, although they are often too nice to say it. Charlotte's family don't talk much about how they feel, they tend to 'just get on with things'. Charlotte's anorexia started after she failed to get the grades for getting into the university course of her choice.

Have you had any experiences in your life that have had a lasting effect on your view of yourself, other people and the world/life in general? Please have a go at jotting some of them down in the following table.

TOP TIP

- Perhaps there is someone from your family or close friendship circle that you can talk to to help you learn about aspects of your earlier life that you may not remember, such as your birth, your toddler years or your early schooling.
- It can be fascinating and very revealing to sit down and look at photos of yourself as a baby or small child and talk to a parent or family friend about how life and relationships were for everyone back then.

Age	Early life experience	Impact on how I see myself, others, or life in general

Age	Early life experience	Impact on how I see myself, others, or life in general

Traits and personality

We've talked about those events and challenges that came your way during your earlier life; now let's think about the you that you came into the world with those traits and personality characteristics that you carry through life. Now, research suggests that there can be certain identifiable 'inbuilt' aspects of temperament or personality that make people vulnerable to difficulties if certain life challenges don't suit those sets of traits. For example, many people with anorexia strive for perfection and give 200 percent in everything they do. These may also be people who are intensely self-critical such that when faced with an outcome in which they don't do as well as they think they should, they suffer enormously as a result of an onslaught of self-criticism.

Many people with anorexia have a tendency to be rather shy, sensitive, introverted and anxious, frightened of anything new or risky. These individuals might suffer in an environment in which there are lots of changes such as house moves, school moves or parents separating. However, the good news is that these traits, such as perfectionism, sensitivity and introversion also have lots of advantages for the person, given the right environment. This phenomenon has been described as the 'dandelion and orchid' phenomenon. Dandelions are resilient and grow under almost any circumstances and anywhere. In contrast, orchids need special conditions to thrive, in terms of soil, temperature and humidity. People with anorexia often are a bit like orchids: put them in the right environment and they flourish beautifully. Read up on how to create the right environment for yourself if you are introverted and shy, in the book *Quiet* by Susan Cain.[3]

- Do any of these traits sound like you?
- Are there any other aspects of your temperament or personality that you think might have an impact on how your difficulties developed or how they keep going?

TOP TIP

- If it feels tricky to identify traits, go back to the life events identified in the previous section and ask yourself what part of me made that life event a challenge/problem? Of course, do remember that some events are just plain awful for anyone (such as abuse), but some more subtle events bother us more because of the way we are wired. These help us identify our traits.

MY TRAITS AND PERSONALITY

TOP TIP: WHO AM I?

- If it's tricky to think about yourself, enlist the help of your wise, reflective friend; how would they describe you?

Strengths

We have thought about the tough times and we have thought about parts of our personality that can make these tough times especially tough. Now let's turn our attention to those people and characteristics that make you strong, those that pick you up following tough times and help you get right back on track. In fighting the anorexia it will be essential to have a good understanding of your strengths.

Think of what you were like before anorexia started. What were the things you enjoyed and did well? Think of the things that have helped you cope with and pull through any periods of difficulty in your life. Some of the things that you have identified as traits that have made you vulnerable towards anorexia may also be strengths, e.g. such as a tendency to have high standards for yourself.

James identified a strength of being a loyal and trusted friend, and as a result he could identify many close confidantes and allies and he thrived on company. However, on the flip side he found that if friendship wasn't reciprocated or if he was let down in some way, he could feel horribly abandoned and fragile. He could see that his ability to form close connections was a wonderful strength of his, but it was also an enormous source of pain when things didn't work out.

TOP TIP

- If you find it hard to think of what your strengths are – what would other people who know and like you say about your strengths?

MY STRENGTHS

Supports

In fighting the anorexia it will be useful to have a good understanding of who is around you to give you support. You may already have completed the support questionnaire in chapter 3.

Karen was very close to her mum – in fact people often referred to them as 'more like friends than mother and daughter'– however, during much self-reflection Karen came to see that although well meaning, her mum wasn't actually allowing Karen the space to grow and to discover herself as a separate person. Karen learned that she needed a degree of autonomy to recapture a life beyond anorexia, and for her this meant a little bit more space from her mother.

TOP TIP: WHO IS GOOD FOR ME?

- We are drawn to people for all sorts of reasons. Sometimes we don't have a choice because they are in our family, or they are friends we have had for decades, but extensive research suggests that anorexia can actually be fuelled by unhelpful relationships, and can be healed within supportive relationships. In Chapter 3 we helped you choose who might be the positive supports in your life. They aren't always the people you spend the most time with. You might be surprised!

MY SUPPORTS

REFLECTION

- We have been thinking about your anorexia 'story'. What have you discovered that you didn't know before? How has this felt to you? Has it brought up any feelings, memories or reflections that you hadn't experienced or thought of for a while? Try to notice any feelings or memories that surface and perhaps jot them down in a little 'emotions diary'.
- Anorexia can lead people to believe that emotions are harmful in some way, but quite on the contrary evidence suggests that learning to welcome and tolerate difficult feelings is actually a first step towards recovery.
- So try not to fall back on anorexia or 'cut off' from your emotions. See if you can turn towards them, let them speak as a guide to your inner world.

---

2. What keeps your anorexia going?

During the following section we will move on to think about those aspects of you and your world that keep your anorexia going. Now let's look at each of the different petals of the flower in turn and how they maintain anorexia.

The valued nature of anorexia

Two of the petals or vicious circles relate to how anorexia becomes valued in the person's life or becomes entwined with their identity. You will already have done some work in Chapter 1 on looking at what anorexia means to you and what its function is in your life. Just as a reminder: research has shown that common pro-anorexia beliefs are:

- Anorexia keeps me safe
- Anorexia numbs my feelings
- Anorexia shows others how I feel.

There are many variations on these themes and many other such beliefs unique to each person.

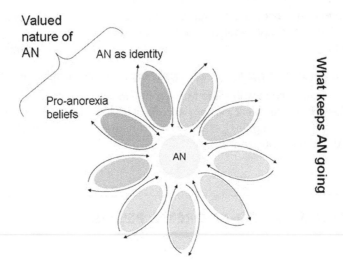

Next, this vicious circle[4] has been fleshed out using the example of Charlotte.

CHARLOTTE

Charlotte felt that anorexia was helpful to her in two ways. First, given that she had always felt overshadowed by her brother, she felt that anorexia made her feel special and that it showed others (mainly her parents) how upset she felt. These thoughts usually became activated when something happened that was a threat to Charlotte's equilibrium. This could be something fairly minor, such as her overhearing her mum talking on the phone to her aunt about her brother's achievements. Listening to the pro-anorexia beliefs had the effect of making Charlotte restrict her food intake even more, and this in turn resulted in her feeling worse and more stuck.

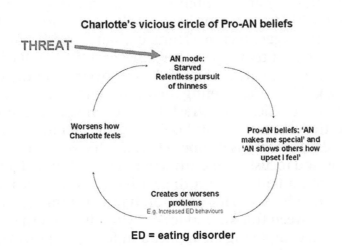

If, like Charlotte, you have beliefs about how anorexia helps you to cope in your life, use the space below to draw your own vicious circle.

TOP TIP: TO DRAW OUT YOUR CIRCLE FOLLOW THESE STEPS:

- Begin with anorexia behaviours at the top of the circle (as in Charlotte's cycle above).
- Then move clockwise and state your relevant pro-anorexia beliefs.
- Then move to the right and list anorexia behaviours that follow and identify how they might have worsened.
- Then identify how you feel (really try to tune in for this), which typically connects back into drawing on anorexia to cope with these feelings (the top of the circle)!
- Remember to keep it simple. Clinicians are experts at making things fit into circles. It's OK if this way isn't for you. If it's a struggle, just list your pro-anorexia beliefs. And think about the role they play in maintaining your anorexia.

MY VICIOUS CIRCLE OF PRO-ANOREXIA BELIEFS

Your dominant thinking styles

Everyone varies in the degree to which they prefer order and predictability versus spontaneity and flexibility and also the degree to which they prefer to work with detail versus have a skill for stepping back and keeping an eye on the bigger picture. Think of managers of large companies; they'd lose the plot if they had to keep in mind the detail of every layer of their organisation! Rather their skill is in overseeing the direction of the company, guiding and steering their colleagues and having vision for the company over time. In contrast, think of the professional who had to proofread the chapters of this book: they needed to check that every word, every sentence was as it should be, and this would have taken considerable time and focus! People attracted to these types of jobs probably have a profile of thinking styles fitting with the tasks of the job; however, ideally one would have capacities for all types of thinking, such that we can meander between thinking styles fairly fluidly such that when detail is called for (e.g. completing an application for a passport) we can apply our detailed, focused 'head', but when overview is needed (e.g. making a five-year plan) we can apply our 'bigger picture' head.

However, research suggests that two thinking styles tend to be associated with anorexia: (1) a tendency to be somewhat rigid and to like predictability and order, while being somewhat threatened by change and spontaneity; (2) a tendency to focus on the detail at the expense of the 'bigger picture'. This section applies to you if your thinking style is:

- Less flexible than other people's
- You like things to be the same and predictable
- Once you have learned something in a particular way, you find it hard to go about the same task in a new way
- You find it harder to multi-task
- You have a tendency to focus a lot on detail rather than the bigger picture in any given situation.

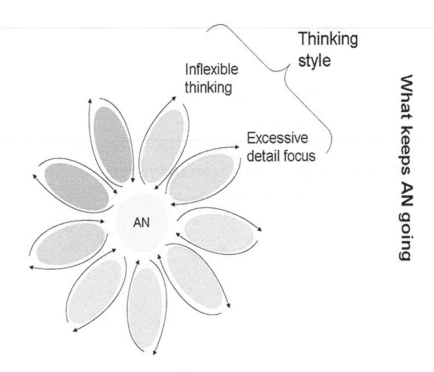

CHARLOTTE

Charlotte's thinking style had always been a little inflexible, with her liking things to be simple and predictable. However, with anorexia in her life this became much more pronounced; she focused a lot more on detail and became unable to see the bigger picture in many contexts.

If Charlotte experienced any stress or threat, her thinking became more extreme. This led to her being even more preoccupied with arbitrary rules about when she would allow herself to eat, what she could have and calorie counting, and would make her focus on the size of particular parts of her body. It would also mean that she worked even harder in her studies and would dwell on small things that were going wrong in her relationships. Taken together, all of this would make Charlotte even more exhausted and fed up than before and would keep her firmly stuck with anorexia.

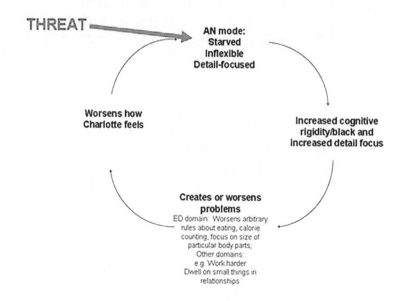

Charlotte's vicious circle of unhelpful thinking style

Having learnt about Charlotte's thinking style, use the box below to draw your own vicious circle.

MY VICIOUS CIRCLE OF UNHELPFUL THINKING STYLE

Your emotional and social mind

This section is relevant to you if you have some difficulties in the area of emotions or relationships. Check out the questions below.

Probes for emotion loop:

- Are you often frightened, confused by or out of touch with your emotions?
- Do you often experience intense and overwhelming emotions?
- Do you tend to avoid or squash emotions at all costs?
- Do you find it hard to tell others what emotions you are feeling or what you need?
- Do you see showing your emotions as a weakness?

- When you have difficult or painful feelings, do you struggle to know how to comfort and soothe yourself?
- Are the emotional lives of others a mystery to you?
- Have you often been told that you should be less hard on yourself and more self-compassionate?

Probes for relationship loop:

- In relationships with others, is there often a pattern, such as you feeling that you are always pleasing the other person?
- Or that you feel:

    - That the other person is always superior to you?
    - That you need to submit to the wishes and ideas of others?
    - That you are desperately in need and clinging to people?
    - That you are terrified that you will be left or abandoned?
    - That you feel smothered by a loved one?
    - That you feel shy and like you want to hide away from everyone?
    - That you feel a burden to others?
    - That you do not feel you belong with your friends and family?

If the answer to one or more of these questions is 'yes' this section probably is relevant to you.

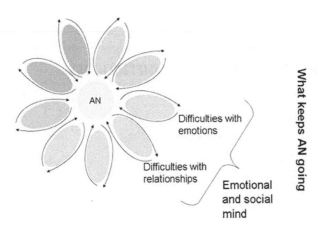

Let's take the example of Charlotte again. As you already know, Charlotte had always felt she compared unfavourably to her brother James. Over the years she had begun to believe that she was 'second best', not just to James but to other people, too. In relationships with other people she therefore always tried to please them to make herself acceptable to them. This left her exhausted, depleted and angry when her efforts were taken for granted or not noticed. People in Charlotte's family tended to have a bit of a stiff upper lip and did not talk much about their feelings. Instead they would just 'get on with things'. Charlotte believed that she must not show her feelings to others, especially not how jealous she felt of her brother, and if she did they would disapprove of her.

The vicious circle of Charlotte's 'bottled up' feelings

THREAT → AN mode: Starved. Belief that must not show emotions or needs

Bottles up how she feels and what she needs

Creates or worsens problems
Makes her feel angry and that others don't understand or care
Alternates between withdrawal and occasional outbursts of emotions
No opportunity to develop more helpful ways for dealing with emotions/relationships

From C. Williams – 5 Area Model of CBT

Worsens how Charlotte feels
e.g. makes her feel lonely, misunderstood iness

In any relationship if someone said or did something that upset her, she tended to bottle up her feelings rather than showing others how she feels. This made her feel angry and that others didn't understand or care about her. As a result she often withdrew from others when she was upset, but very occasionally she had an outburst of emotions, which then left her feeling ashamed and depleted. This robbed her of the opportunity to develop more helpful ways of dealing with emotions in the context of relationships with other people. It increased Charlotte's sense of loneliness and kept her stuck.

MY VICIOUS CIRCLE OF EMOTIONAL DIFFICULTIES

MY VICIOUS CIRCLE OF RELATIONSHIP DIFFICULTIES

How others keep anorexia going

Close others, family, partners and friends usually are concerned about the person with anorexia and want to help. Sometimes this backfires and they may behave in a way that keeps the anorexia going. Research has shown that several things that arise when families talk to each other about anorexia are particularly likely to keep things stuck:

1 **Enabling/accommodating**: This includes the other person going out of their way to be helpful to the person with the anorexia and accepting anorexia's rules, e.g. by going out and buying special foods for the person or giving them lots of reassurance. This usually starts gradually and over time becomes stronger, sometimes ending up with the family member being totally 'bullied' by the anorexia. It is meant to be helpful and reduce conflict. Enabling/accommodating is part of the 'kangaroo response' discussed in chapter 3.

2 **Unhelpful emotional responses**: As we have already discussed in chapter 3 this concerns the other person's emotional responses to the anorexia, which may be overly anxious or avoidant (jellyfish or ostrich) or angry, hostile responses (rhinoceros, terrier) or, as is common, a combination of these. Driven by anxiety and frustration about the anorexia the other person may blow hot and cold. These intense emotional responses have a particularly unhelpful effect if you are living with the person and are spending a lot of time with them.

A vicious circle of how others keep anorexia going is shown below.

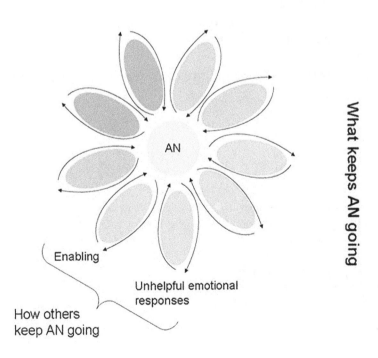

How others keep AN going

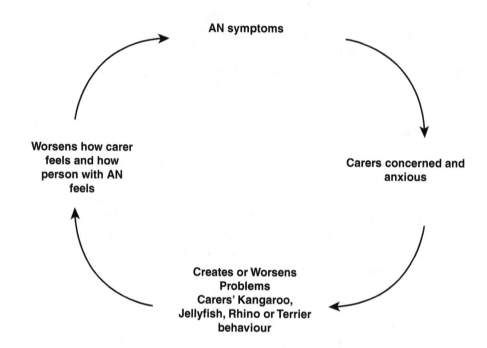

AN symptoms

Carers concerned and anxious

Creates or Worsens Problems Carers' Kangaroo, Jellyfish, Rhino or Terrier behaviour

Worsens how carer feels and how person with AN feels

Does this happen with your family, partner or friends?

- Do you repeatedly ask your close other person for reassurance about what you have eaten, are about to eat or how you look? Have you asked them to strengthen anorexia in any other way?
- Has the other person had to rearrange their life in relation to the anorexia?
- Is the other person making constant efforts to be helpful to the anorexia by buying special foods, staying out of the kitchen, eating at certain times or obeying the rules of anorexia in any other way?
- Has anorexia made the other person scream, cry, shout, nag or withdraw from you?
- Has the other person shown kangaroo, jellyfish, ostrich, rhino or terrier behaviours?

TOP TIP

- People tell us that it can sometimes feel threatening to review key relationships in relation to anorexia, as though you are somehow criticising these important people. Remember, to come to realise that someone's responses aren't helpful in regard anorexia isn't to say that that person doesn't have an important place in your life or that they aren't well meaning, it's just to say that their personality meshes with the ways of anorexia in some ways leading to disharmony! Sometimes people less close to you are more supportive of recovery from anorexia than those who love you dearly and can't bear to see you suffer.

THE ROLE OF CLOSE OTHERS IN KEEPING MY ANOREXIA GOING

Any other maintaining factors

Finally there may be factors not covered in this model that are unique to you in keeping your anorexia going. If you can think of any, here is the place to draw them in.

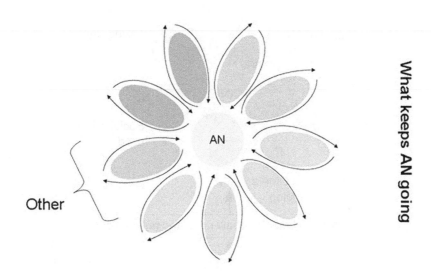

OTHER FACTORS THAT KEEP MY ANOREXIA GOING

Your map: putting it all together

Now consider the diagram on the following page, and use your work from above to fill out each box and petal. When you look at your complete 'map', how much does this help you understand what has been happening to you? In the next chapter we will help you to use this map to guide changes you may consider making.

TOP TIP: TO HELP YOU COMPLETE YOUR ANOREXIA MAP

- Complete the boxes at the head of the map with information from the first part of this chapter.
- If you can, write a couple of personalised examples into the petals of the flower.
- Alternatively, draw out your own formulation on a large (A4) piece of paper so you have plenty of space to personalise this.

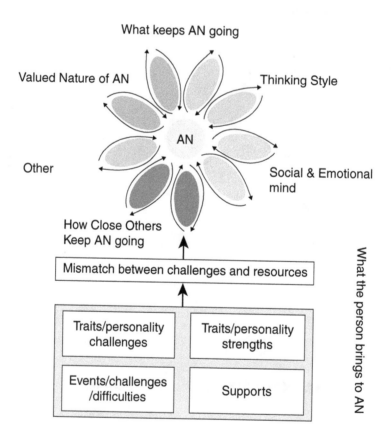

How much do you feel you understand about how your anorexia developed and why it keeps going?

REFLECTION

In this chapter, we have been helping you to consider your anorexia 'story' and those factors that maintain your anorexia in the here and now.

- Has your understanding of your anorexia changed from when you first rated the scale above?
- What have you discovered about your anorexia that you hadn't considered before?
- What has it felt like getting to know your anorexia in this way? What feelings did this discovery process bring up?
- Is there anyone in your life you might like to share your new anorexia discoveries with?
- During the next few chapters we will help you to tackle some of those maintaining factors, if you wish, so that you have options in your coping repertoire beyond anorexia.

Finally, here's a handy tip from one of our patients:

My recommendation for anyone working through this chapter and the rest of the book is to not be put off or give up if you're finding something difficult or confusing. Keep working at it, try to approach the problem from different angles, and ask as many questions as you need to until it makes sense. Like me, you might find that the things you struggle with at first actually have the greatest long-term benefits for your recovery.

Notes

1 Schmidt, U., & Treasure, J. Anorexia nervosa: valued and visible. A cognitive-interpersonal maintenance model and its implications for research and practice. *British Journal of Clinical Psychology*. 2006 Sep; 45(Pt 3):343–66.
2 Treasure, J., & Schmidt, U. The cognitive-interpersonal maintenance model of anorexia nervosa revisited: a summary of the evidence for cognitive, socio-emotional and interpersonal predisposing and perpetuating factors. *Journal of Eating Disorders*. 2013 Apr; 15(1):13.
3 Cain, S. (2012). *Quiet: The Power of Introverts in a Word That Can't Stop Talking*. Crown Publishers. New York.
4 The vicious cycles are all adapted from Greenberger, D., Padesky, C.A., & Beck, A.T. (2015). *Mind Over Mood: Change How You Feel by Changing the Way You Think*. Guilford Publications. New York, NY, USA.

Chapter 6

Developing treatment goals

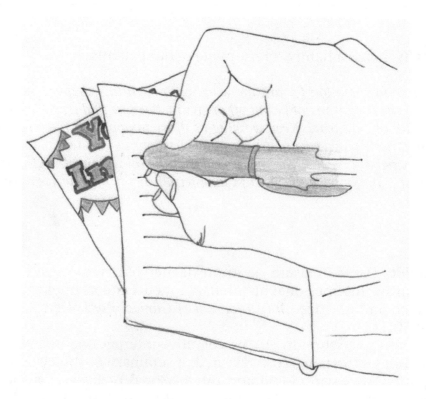

As one of our patients who went on to make a full recovery from anorexia told us:

In the end, you've got find something you want more than your anorexia.

Setting goals

Now that you and your therapist have together drawn up a map of the different aspects of your experience, your difficulties and how they link together, it should be easier to identify areas you might like to work on and decide on some goals for treatment.

It may be worth spending a few minutes thinking about what we mean by this.

Dreams, hopes, wishes or aspirations versus goals

Dreams, hopes, wishes or aspirations may represent a sort of ideal state or solution to concerns. They will be guided by your values and beliefs. Dreams, hopes, wishes or aspirations can be very useful 'bigger picture' kind of ideas that inspire and motivate you, and function a bit like a lighthouse that guides a ship in the right direction. You will have done some thinking about these in the first section of this manual where you imagined your life without an eating disorder.

Goals are different. They are more about the detail of what you want to achieve and how. Whether or not we achieve our dreams, visions, hopes or aspirations may not be totally under our control, but what is clear is that setting yourself a series of goals towards your dream is likely to be the best way of making it come true.

As in other areas of your life, you will need to remain flexible enough to move forward and backward between the bigger picture and the details of how to work towards achieving your dreams or hopes by breaking them down into smaller goals.

SMART goals

Goals should be **SMART**. **SMART** stands for

Specific, **M**easurable, **A**chievable, **R**ealistic and **T**angible.

Specific: Think about what you want to achieve; what the hurdles, costs, constraints and requirements might be; and what are the specific reasons, purpose or benefits of accomplishing the goal. Where appropriate, establish a time frame and a location and name the people that need to be involved.

Example

- **A broad wish** or aspiration may be: have a great social life and a big circle of friends.
- **A specific goal in relation to this** may be: This weekend when I will go out with my trusted friends Jenny and Sarah, I will invite my new colleague Peter along too.
- **Measurable**: Establish concrete criteria for measuring progress toward the attainment of each goal you set. To figure out whether your goal is measurable, ask questions such as: How much? How many? How will I know when I have achieved it?

Achievable: Think here about the steps involved in reaching your goal and the time frame to carry out each step.

Realistic: To be realistic, a goal must represent something that you think is important enough for you to devote your time to and that you are able to do.

Tangible: A goal is tangible when you can experience it with one of the senses; that is taste, touch, smell, sight or hearing. When your goal is tangible, you have a better chance of making it specific and measurable and thus achievable.

Charlotte's aspirations and goals

Charlotte has identified with her therapist some areas aside from her eating and weight that she would like to work on.

'I'D LIKE TO WORK ON . . .'

- My persistent negative view of myself and my self-criticism.
- Always keeping people at arm's length.
- Reducing my perfectionism.
- Always 'numbing out' emotions.
- Expressing my feelings and needs to others.
- Relearning to eat healthily and reducing my exercise.

- She used this list of difficulties to think about what she'd like to achieve in each of these areas and to begin to set goals to work towards.
- This list of wishes or aspirations is helpful, as Charlotte and her therapist can use it to develop SMART goals relating to each one and then make detailed plans about how to reach each of them and how they will measure these.

Area of Concern or Difficulty	Wish or Aspiration
Persistent negative view of myself and self-criticism.	To develop a more realistic and compassionate self-image.
Keeping people at arm's length.	To develop more trust in personal relationships.
Perfectionism.	To learn to accept 'good enough'.
'Numbing out' emotions.	To be able to identify, understand and process emotions.
Hard to express feelings and needs to others.	To be able to assert my feelings and needs to others directly.
Need for rigid control round my eating and exercise patterns.	To learn to have more flexible control over my food intake and exercise.

Your wishes or aspirations

- Based on the work you have done so far, think about what the key areas of concern or difficulty are that you'd like to work on and enter them in the left hand column below.
- Now, think about what you'd like to achieve in each of the areas you have identified and enter your wishes or aspirations in the column on the right.

Area of Concern or Difficulty	Wish or Aspiration

Now you and your therapist can consider in more detail how **you can set yourself some SMART goals** to enable you to work towards these aspirations and measure your progress along the way.

Choosing your goals

Imagine you want to grow a rare flower with beautiful petals and you have been given a bag of seeds to do so.

To produce the plant, you'll need to provide the seeds with regular water, feed, good soil and the right sort of temperature. You may need to seek additional advice on how to produce the best results.

Once the seedlings start to grow, they will need thinning out and replanting, protecting against sharp winds and other extremes of weather, against slugs and pests and so on. Once the plant is beginning to grow big, maybe it'll need staking and weeds growing nearby will need removing, while ensuring that its roots are not damaged. Each and every one of these tasks may not seem to amount to much, taken in isolation they may seem insignificant or trivial, yet taken together they can make your aspirations come true.

Goals can be simple, straightforward, fairly mundane one-off actions such as agreeing to work through a relevant part of this manual or worksheet by a certain time and to reflect on what this means for you.

Other **goals may involve doing something on a regular basis** over a defined period of time. This can be useful where you are trying to learn a new skill (e.g. trying to be more flexible in particular situations or practicing being kinder to yourself) or where you have been avoiding something (e.g. going out with friends) and where it would be helpful to expand your options by doing something extra on a regular basis.

In order to achieve a goal that needs regular practice, you may want to keep a diary or log of how you have practised the new skill. Or you may want to talk to your therapist or another trusted person about how you are doing in relation to this goal on a regular basis.

TOP TIP

- When you set your goals, start small. Especially if you are a perfectionist it is very easy to let high expectations ('I should be able to achieve x, y and z by tomorrow') get in the way and give yourself over-ambitious goals. A variant of this is to work on too many goals at the same time.

Advanced goal setting

WOOP

Even with carefully chosen small goals as stepping stones towards a bigger important goal, it can sometimes be very hard to gain and keep up momentum. It may be hard to keep in mind the reasons why you are doing all of this work and it is easy for obstacles to trip you up. This is where a technique called WOOP is helpful, as it tries to keep these different aspects in mind.

WOOP was developed by Dr Gabriele Oettingen, a psychologist from New York University, and her colleagues.[1] WOOP is short for Wish, Outcome, Obstacle, Plan. The scientific term for WOOP is 'Mental Contrasting with Implementation Intentions' in other words it combines thinking about what you really want and how that would change your life, with thinking about the obstacles that could occur and what to do about them. It is a strategy for helping people find and fulfil their wishes and aspirations, and change unhelpful habits. It is underpinned by lots of studies that show that it helps people achieve goals in diverse areas, such as their health, interpersonal relationships and work/study. It is a simple procedure consisting of four steps.

The four steps of WOOP

If you have never practiced WOOP set aside about 20–25 minutes for this. Switch off your mobile phone and avoid any distractions. Make yourself comfortable. Everything else has to wait. This is YOUR time.

1. **Wish**: Identify a wish. This can be as big or small as you wish, but it has to be something that matters to you or is dear to you. It needs to be something that is challenging, but feasible for you (i.e. possible for you to achieve in a given period of time).

   Write down your wish here (in three to four words).

   ....

2. **(Best) Outcome**: Imagine the *best* thing that you associate with fulfilling your wish or solving your concern, what would it be like and how would you feel? Really take a moment to imagine this properly, close your eyes and let your mind run wild. If you can think of many good aspects, choose the most important one.

   Using three to four words, write down your best imagined outcome here.

   ....

   Close your eyes and focus on experiencing this outcome. Hold it in your mind. Take a moment to really imagine it.

3. **(Key) Obstacle**: Now think, what is it that holds you back from fulfilling your wish? What is it in you? What is your most critical *internal* obstacle? This can be a behaviour, emotion, a thought, an impulse, a bad habit or assumptions you jump to. (You have already taken care of external obstacles by choosing a feasible wish.) Give your imagination free rein. Again if you can think of multiple obstacles, choose the one that is at the heart of it.

   Write down your key obstacle here.

   ....

   Close your eyes and focus on experiencing this obstacle. Hold it in your mind. Take a moment to really imagine it.

(If–then) Plan: What can you do to overcome or prevent your obstacle? Name one thought or action you can take, the most effective one. Then think about when and where the obstacle will next occur. Form an if–then plan. **If** . . . (obstacle [situation, when and where]) . . . **then I will** . . . (effective action [behaviour or thought] to overcome obstacle).

Write down your **if–then** plan here.

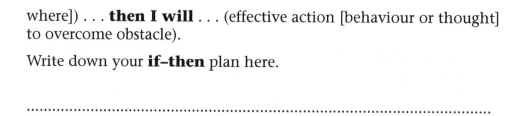

Making WOOP work for you

People often naturally use a part of WOOP by themselves, mainly by dreaming about a positive future and indulging in positive fantasies about how good they will feel when they have finished their exams, work assignment, etc. However, the mental contrasting (i.e. contrasting the wish and desired outcome with the potential obstacles) is something that does not come naturally to most of us, let alone developing an 'if–then' plan. It is all of this together that can powerfully make a difference to your life. To get started, practice WOOP with a wish concerning one particular situation or one day only. Over time and with repeated one-off wishes you can get into a WOOP habit, where you become faster at it and learn to apply it to bigger wishes. Next, we show you a worked example.

Nadia

Nadia had to write an important piece of course work for her studies which she had to hand in within a month. Nadia is a good student, who has very high standards for herself. Because of this, for any piece of work that she tackles, she usually does a vast amount of preparatory work, but only ever gets down to writing the actual assignment at the very end just before she is due to hand it in. This often means that what she writes is overly long and she rarely has any time to check the final product. The stage of writing is usually hugely anxiety provoking and stressful for her, and has on many occasions led to her working through the whole night and feeling utterly depleted and miserable at the end.

Here is Nadia's WOOP.

> **Wish**: I want to finish my course work in good time and find a way of getting the writing done in a more steady unhurried fashion, producing a chunk of text every day and leaving time to review things at the end.
>
> **Three or four words**: *Write steadily without hurry.*
>
> **Outcome**: I would feel a lot less stressed, anxious and overwhelmed, and also less exhausted. I'd sleep better and I would feel calmer and more in control.
>
> **Three or four words**: *Calmer and more in control.*

Obstacle: I do all this preparatory reading to get an in-depth understanding of the subject matter, but then I get drawn into reading about issues that may be very interesting, but are only marginally related to what I am really supposed to write about. I guess I feel unless I go into a lot of depth I will produce a piece of work that is mediocre rather than outstanding. As I am writing this, I realise that at the heart of this is a worry about me not being good enough.

Three or four words: *Worry about not being good enough.*

Plan: If I start to worry about my writing not being good enough, I will take three deep breaths and will tell myself 'what is the worst thing that can happen here? If necessary I can revise it later'.

Throughout the month of writing her course work, Nadia did daily WOOPs specifying the amount of writing she wished to do each day, imagined outcomes and obstacles and reiterated her plan. She comfortably finished her assignment within the month and had enough time to review what she had written at the end. For the first time in her life the course work she produced was within the given word limit. Previously she had always written very lengthy pieces, going considerably over the recommended length and this had sometimes led to her being given a lower mark. Nadia said: 'I was very surprised how well this approach worked for me. Although I was doubtful at first, I did really feel calmer and more in control during the writing, and you know what I also got a better mark than usual'.

TOP TIP

- The most difficult thing about WOOP is to form a good if-then plan. A common mistake in forming 'if–then' plans is keeping the 'if–then' structure but replacing other terms for the ones specified, e.g. **'If I eat more then I will feel better'**. In this example the person has linked their wish to the hoped for outcome. However, the plan that you are creating needs to be linked to the appearance of the obstacle or difficult situation that you have identified: **'If . . . obstacle or difficult situation, then I will . . . effective action to overcome obstacle'**. For example, 'If I don't feel hungry at dinner tonight and am tempted not to finish my meal, I will remind myself that food is fuel for me having a bigger, healthier life'.

A worksheet for using WOOP is given at the end of this chapter.

Behavioural experiments

Sometimes, when we are grappling with a specific difficulty or concern, what makes it is hard to move forward and change our behaviour is that we are held back by certain rules or beliefs. Behavioural experiments are about trying out something new that is relevant and meaningful and gives you the opportunity to reflect on and challenge your usual ways of thinking or experiencing particular situations. Behavioural experiments give you the opportunity to make predictions, observe, experience and reflect on what you have done differently. You will need to discuss with your therapist what would be appropriate behavioural experiments for you to carry out. At the end of this chapter, we have inserted two worksheets: one that helps you think about the thought or belief that may be holding you back and another a sample sheet for conducting behavioural experiments.

Final thoughts

You may be thinking which of these three techniques you should apply in what sort of situations. Actually, all three complement each other and build on each other. Defining and setting SMART goals is a solid first step in breaking down any aspiration or broader wish into manageable action points. WOOP takes this process a step further by helping you keep in mind the bigger picture (best outcome) of why you want to work on a particular area and taking specific action when obstacles occur. If your key obstacle turns out to be a particularly deep-seated belief (e.g. 'I must always give my absolute best in any situation'), then you might want to first do some behavioural experiments that help you revise this, before returning to working on your goal.

WOOP Worksheet

1 My wish:

Three or four words:

_____

2 Best outcome:

Three or four words:

_____

Close your eyes and really imagine this outcome in your mind.

3 Obstacle:

Three or four words:

_____

Close your eyes and really imagine this obstacle in your mind.

4 If–then plan:

If_____ **then** _____

Obstacle (where and when) Action (to overcome obstacle)

Planning behavioural experiments

To help you start developing some experiments you will find it useful to complete the following sentences:[2]

- My old rule (thought/belief) is:

    - --

    - --

- This rule has had the following impact on my life:

    - --

    - --

- I know the rule is in operation because:

    - --

    - --

- It is understandable I have this rule because:

    - --

    - --

- However, this rule is unreasonable because:

    - --

    - --

- The payoffs of obeying the rule are:

    - --

    - --

- The disadvantages of obeying the rule are:

  - --

  - --

- A more realistic and helpful rule would be:

  - --

  - --

- In order to test drive the new rule, the following experiment can help me see if it fits into my life:

  - --

  - --

Recording your behavioural experiments

Planning and Recording Experiments					
Thought to be tested:					
Belief that the thought is true:					
Experiment to test thought	Likely problems	Strategies to deal with problems	Date of experiment	Outcome of experiment	Belief in the thought now (%)

Notes

1 Oettingen, G. (2014). *Rethinking Positive Thinking: Inside the New Science of Motivation*. CURRENT, Penguin Group (USA) LCC. New York, NY. These authors have also produced an app to go with the book.
2 Fennell, M. (1999). *Overcoming Low Self-Esteem*. Robinson Publishers, London, UK.

Chapter 7

The emotional and social mind

Here's how one of our patients talked about her changing relationship with feelings: *The world is such an alien and alienating place when your emotions make absolutely no sense to you. As I gained weight my emotions started to pop up here and there, then they gained in intensity and suddenly they were all over the place, this was initially daunting but with time they calmed down into a rhythm and I have come to see feelings as a barometer that informs me how I'm doing and whether I like the setting I am in and the people I'm with – so, they're kind of handy!*

We and others have shown that difficulties identifying, managing and expressing emotions contribute to the development and maintenance of anorexia. A key implication is that if people with anorexia can be supported to have a better relationship with their emotional world, there is the possibility of their anorexia being less dominant. This chapter is designed to help you develop a sense of curiosity and confidence in relation to your emotional world. Over time, we'd like to support you to develop an easier relationship with your emotions and by so doing to develop or enhance your **emotional and social wellbeing**.

Lara, who had always been successful at everything she set her mind to – she got excellent grades at school, she was good at sports and everyone liked her and admired her – went on to develop anorexia when she was just 16 years old. People had not foreseen this capable girl becoming so devastatingly unwell. However, what people around her had failed to notice was that as Lara approached adolescence and her body started to change and feelings started to bubble up, she felt wobbly and scared and she began to withdraw. People were so used to seeing Lara being capable that they failed to spot when Lara was struggling. Lara described how feelings, which she often experienced as 'messy' and 'confusing', left her feeling out of control and scared. In therapy, Lara learned that for her there was a bit of a divide in how she managed the world: for 'heady' stuff such as doing exams, being head girl at school and performing in a professional orchestra, she felt confident and competent. However, when it came to the messy world of emotions, she felt profoundly unsure and wobbly a lot of the time, and to make it worse, because people were so used to her being so 'capable', she felt unable to ask for support!

This divide between the 'head' and the 'heart' is common among those with anorexia. It's not that emotions are absent – far from it – individuals with anorexia can be some of the most sensitive and in-tune individuals, it's just that when it comes to meandering the uncertainties of emotions and relationships there can be a great sense of unease and even threat, leading to a tendency to want to shut down feelings. One thing we know about long-term food restriction is that it does a pretty good job at shutting down feelings. Lara found that the longer her anorexia went on, the further removed she became from her emotional world and the more entrenched she felt in relation to her anorexia. Thus, for Lara therapy involved rebuilding her relationship with her emotional world, which eventually enabled her to lessen her grip on anorexia and to reach out to others for support and care when she needed it.

So why do we have emotions? Lesley Greenberg, an eminent emotions researcher says:

Emotions are crucial to survival, communication and problem solving. Emotions are not a nuisance to be gotten rid of or ignored; rather emotions are an essential aspect of being human.

Thus, emotions are important signals worth listening to: they organise us to act. They communicate a person's current state, needs, goals and inclinations to others. They also influence other people's behaviours.

Emotional/social wellbeing is being able to:

- Notice, sit with, and listen to your emotions, such that they can guide you towards getting your needs met in life.
- Have an understanding of other people's internal world (e.g. their emotions, intentions or beliefs) from their facial expressions, their tone of voice, their actions and so forth.
- Consider others' points of view and take their perspective, in order to adapt your own behaviour in social interactions and in order to connect to others in nourishing ways.
- Develop a helpful (fair and compassionate) emotional stance to yourself and others.

This chapter has six parts. Only some of these may be relevant for you. Perhaps look through the options with a trusted other to work out which might be useful for you.

Part 1: What are emotions and why do we have them?
This could be useful for you if you dislike your emotions, would prefer life without emotional ups and downs or cannot see what emotions are all about. It might also be useful if you want to find out how anorexia affects emotions.

Part 2: Relationships in context
This part is designed to help you build a picture of the emotional and relationship context in your life. It could be useful for you if you often feel you compare negatively to others, or if there are recurring unhelpful patterns in your relationships.

Part 3: Becoming an expert on your emotions
This part is about listening to your emotions and what they tell you about your needs, identifying your beliefs and rules about emotions and learning to express emotions appropriately and assertively.

Part 4: Learning to manage extreme and overwhelming emotions
This part could be useful for you if you have an anxious temperament or often find yourself in a sea of intense emotions and want to learn skills for soothing yourself.

Part 5: The emotional lives of others
This could be useful if you have difficulties reading other people, or tend to not think much about others' thoughts, feelings or intentions.

Part 6: Learning self-compassion
This could be useful if you are rather self-critical. It teaches about compassion, forgiveness and acceptance.

Part 1: what are emotions and why do we have them?

Here's what one of our patients told us about her experience of learning about her emotions: *Exploring the different aspects of particular emotions helped me to be able to identify and differentiate between them as well as provide evidence to challenge my immediate negative perceptions of others' body language and therefore emotions/thinking.*

Emotions are responses to events in our environment, or to internal triggers such as thoughts we have about things that may happen or will happen in the future, or which have occurred in the past.

Particular emotional states such as happiness, anger or anxiety consist of several aspects, including bodily sensations, thoughts and action tendencies. Have a go at the examples below.

TOP TIP: TUNE INTO YOUR HEART, NOT YOUR HEAD!

- When trying to get in touch with emotions consider choosing a quiet moment, closing your eyes and tuning into your body. Wonder about where your feelings are located, what images go along with your feelings and what memories you have that link with these feelings.
- If it feels daunting or overwhelming to be in touch with feelings, just try tuning into them for a couple of minutes to begin with and build up from there.

EXAMPLES

ANGER

The emotion of anger can go along with:

Bodily sensations of tensing your muscles and your hair standing on edge.
Thoughts of perhaps hating the person who has made you angry and what you would like to do to them.
Images of you looking hot in the face or of shouting at the person who has made you angry.
Action tendencies of making an angry face (frowning, staring), raising your voice, leaning forward and making yourself bigger (i.e. puffing yourself up), making threatening gestures (e.g. shaking your fist).

FEAR

Now think of the emotion of fear. Try to remember a situation where you felt very frightened, try to gather an image of this situation in your mind. Once you have the image in mind, reflect on your bodily sensations, thoughts and action tendencies going along with this? Write in the boxes below.

Bodily sensations

Thoughts/images

Action tendencies

DID YOU KNOW THAT. . . ?

Research has shown that in the brain there is a fast and a slow road for producing emotions.

- The **fast route** produces an emergency emotional and action response (e.g. when a ferocious dog is running towards you). This can clearly be very helpful as it allows you to act quickly without wasting valuable time by thinking through your response. In our modern world, it is usually not wild animals that trigger this response but social encounters with other people.

In people with anorexia, the fast route into emotions can be overly sensitive and the person responds to any minor change or challenge as if it was a major threat, a matter of life or death, rapidly going into emotional overdrive and activating the 'fight or flight' system. Even neutral or slightly ambiguous/uncertain situations (such as someone looking at you in a way that you can't quite fathom out) can be perceived as threatening by a person with anorexia and activate their fast emotion response system. This may be part of an anxious temperament that predates the onset of anorexia, but once anorexia is in a person's life this often gets worse and the person becomes more sensitive to perceived threat (as being severely malnourished is a major stressor on the body). People often tell us that restricting their food intake helps to numb their emotions and makes them less anxious in the short term so that their immediate response to any stress is often to want to eat less. This dual impact of starvation on the body may sound confusing but is a bit like the effect of alcohol on the brain in someone who is depressed. In the short term a person may cheer up when they have drunk, but drinking too much over a period of time often makes them more depressed.

If this is relevant to you, part 4 of this chapter may be of use.

- In the **slow route**, emotionally significant information from the environment is processed in parts of your brain. It is then integrated with other information, allowing you to think about your responses in a more leisurely way. This is important for processing more ambiguous or complex information and for correcting first emotional impressions.

Take, for example, someone who while sitting on a bus, hears a woman passenger sitting somewhere behind them give off a high-pitched scream. The immediate emotional response of the person hearing this may be fear. Their heart may start beating loudly and they may want to run away. However, the scream is followed by laughter and when the person turns around they see a young woman messing about with her friends. Having reappraised the situation in light of the additional information, their emotional response shifts to either being amused or slightly irritated by the noise.

Types of emotions

There are six **basic emotions** that can be found in any culture. These are:

JOY
SURPRISE
DISGUST
FEAR
SADNESS
ANGER

- Whatever part of the world someone comes from, the facial expressions associated with these basic emotions are always the same.
- In addition to these **basic emotions**, we have many other more **complex emotions**. These are shown on the diagram below.
- Millions of years ago, our basic emotions were enough to guide us and help us figure out how particular events affect our wellbeing. However, in our complicated modern world,

we have more complex relationships with other people, and these complex emotions can give us a lot of important information.

Complex emotions:

GUILT
JEALOUSY
DISAPPOINTMENT
SHAME
ENVY

When and how do emotions cause problems?

There are a number of different ways in which emotions can give people trouble.

Evidence from research shows that people with anorexia can have difficulties in any of these areas. See if you can relate to any of these.

Too much or too little emotion: Emotions can give us problems if they are very long-lasting, intense and distressing, or if they arise and persist in response to minor triggers and/or out of proportion to the threat posed by the trigger. Jackie, for example, would switch between feeling fairly numb and then literally flying of the handle. For her, monitoring triggers for her surges of emotion was really helpful in helping her capture and contain the outbursts. As mentioned above, in the starved state negative emotions can become magnified. At the other end of the spectrum is an inability to experience any emotions, pleasurable or otherwise. In the starved state people with anorexia often find it hard to experience pleasure or positive emotions. Jane used to refer to her emotional cut-off-ness as 'The Wall' or the barrier by which she hid from the demands of the world and relationships.

Reading emotions: Some people find it hard to read emotions in themselves or others. This difficulty with accurately picking up emotional signals can make it harder to know what they need themselves or what others want from them. In the starved state the ability to read one's own emotions becomes impaired. In part this is because people with anorexia often find it hard to listen to and interpret their bodily sensations that tell them what they feel. Reading others' emotions and states of minds also is impaired. This makes social interactions more stressful. Jackie, who would tend to fly off the handle, noticed that triggers for her anger were often thinking that people were ignoring her or rejecting her. Over time she came to see that this was in part caused by her tendency to interpret her friends' facial expressions as meaning something negative.

Expressing emotions: Other problems arise if a person does not know how or finds it too frightening to express their emotions. Cultures differ in terms of how acceptable and desirable it is to express emotions in particular social situations. For example, the English have a reputation for having a stiff upper lip, whereas the Italians are much more emotionally expressive. Within families, too, there can be different emotional styles, with some families being expressive and others emotionally restrained. Families can also teach people rules about expressing emotions, such as 'crying is for sissies'. In anorexia, starvation and stress tends to make emotional responses muted. In addition, many people with anorexia often actively hide their emotions and are less expressive than others, because they are fearful that showing their emotions might have negative consequences. If someone *always* bottles up, squashes or tries to ignore certain emotions, this is unhelpful. It isolates them from what they need and cuts them off from other people and often makes the squashed emotion bubble up when the person least expects it (see pink elephant effect overleaf). For example, when Jackie first started to try to get a handle on her explosive emotions, she made the mistake of thinking that managing emotions was the same as squashing them. Like a bubbling cauldron, she tried to bite her lip, only to feel low and drained sometime later because she had been ignoring her feelings. Things got better when she learned to spot the early signs of anger and to express this before they dominated her.

When someone doesn't show emotions in social situations this is hugely disquieting for others around them. The majority of our communications are made through non-verbal signals, in particular our facial expressions. When these are muted or lost in anorexia, the individual can be perceived as robotic, cold or unfeeling. In computer-generated imagery (CGI) this is known as the 'uncanny valley' effect. In reaction to an emotionless person, others become aroused with raised blood pressure and they have an urge to distance themselves from this aloof and unreal person. We suggest you look on YouTube to see what happens to a baby when their mother briefly pretends to be distant and does not show any expected emotions in her face (search YouTube for the still face paradigm). To a large extent this lack of emotion expression in AN is not chosen, it is a secondary consequence of starvation which may serve to isolate and stress the individual even more, creating a vicious circle.

This does not mean that venting emotions per se is necessarily always good thing for a person or for those around them. The philosopher Aristotle knew this a long time ago. He noted that anyone can become angry, but to be angry with the right person to the right degree at the right time and in the right way is a skill.

THE PINK ELEPHANT EFFECT

Paradoxically, if a person avoids a particular emotion or emotional memory because they are scared of the effect this might have on them, the avoided material may bubble up to the surface even more intensely than before. This reinforces the person's belief about the effect of the emotion and they feel they must redouble their efforts to avoid it. To show how this works, please take a moment to do the following experiment.

EXPERIMENT

- For one minute, try to think of a pink elephant.
- Imagine what it would look like, what shade of pink it is, whether shocking pink, piglet pink or any other kind of pink; really conjure it up in your mind's eye.
- Now, for another minute, try very hard NOT to think of a pink elephant. What do you notice?

LEARNING POINT

A lot of mental effort is involved in suppressing thoughts and feelings!

REFLECTION

Being able to recognise our own emotions and those of others, and using them as a guide for action, is important for helping us identify our needs both as individuals and in relationships, as well as the needs of others. Can you think of an example of this that feels meaningful to you?

In anorexia people often have a highly sensitive fast route into emotion, leading them to experience emotional responses of life-or-death intensity, disproportionate to the threat/perceived threat of a situation. To what degree is this true of you?

The short-term effect of food restriction can be to numb emotions, but the long-term effect of starvation is to increase stress sensitivity. Has your appreciation of the role of starvation in your emotional world changed at all? If so, have a think about how.

Anorexia often makes it harder for people to read their own and others' emotions and mind states, which makes social interactions bewildering and frightening. To what degree can you relate to this?

Taken together, these things can set up an unhelpful vicious cycle.

Part 2: relationships in context

It takes a village to raise a child

As humans we are social animals. At the level of our most basic needs (food, shelter, protection from predators) we cannot survive without support from others. Growing up and learning to function in the wider world takes about 20 years of being nurtured and cared for, protected and taught by the immediate family and the wider social group (i.e. 'it takes a village to raise a child'). Over the millennia of human development, we have evolved to form strong attachments to close others (care givers, partners, children), and to love them, even if they don't treat us well. We are also programmed to want to belong, be accepted and be part of a wider group. This is a particularly strong feature in adolescence when the peers suddenly become extremely important. Overall, we derive enormous pleasure from close bonds with others and from the social signals inviting close and trusting relationships such as smiles, warmth, playfulness, kindness or compassion.

The imagined or real threat of being ousted from our immediate or wider social group is very threatening and being alone and experiencing loneliness is very unpleasant for most of us. Anorexia has the tendency to isolate people and make them feel alone.

Social rank and 'keeping up with the Joneses'

Groups usually have a leader and organise themselves in terms of a clear 'pecking order' or social hierarchy or rank. Such hierarchies have probably developed to deal with competition for resources (such as access to food and mates) and to regulate people's behaviour and maintain group cohesion. Traditionally, it would be the physically strongest male who would lead a group. In the animal kingdom, animals of low social rank tend to behave submissively towards dominant others in order to avoid attack. As long as the animal of lower rank has the opportunity to escape, this is not problematic. However, when the submissive animal has no opportunity for escape (i.e. it is trapped), it will experience severe distress or may even die. Professor Paul Gilbert proposed that in human beings depression is the psychological manifestation of such submissive behaviour when there is no opportunity to escape some dominant other or dominating (entrapping) situation. Other consequences of perceived low rank in humans include low self-esteem, shame and humiliation.

A related idea is that of social comparison, which is to do with how you feel you compare against others in terms of *rank* (inferior-superior, incompetent-competent, untalented–more talented, weaker-stronger, etc.) or *how well you fit into a group* (left out–accepted, different-same, outsider-insider) or in terms of *attractiveness* (unlikeable-likeable, unattractive–more attractive). People with eating disorders often feel they compare negatively to others. They may have had this tendency even before their eating disorder started, but usually it becomes stronger once the eating disorder is in the person's life.

The power of negative social comparison to make us feel resentful, envious and hard done by is shown in the poem below which we found on the internet.

'The Other Fellow' by Edgar Albert Guest

www.poemhunter.com/poem/the-other-fellow/

If you are female you may want to replace 'the other fellow' with 'the other woman' or 'the other girl'.

Individual needs and wishes versus group demands

Within any group there is always some tension between the needs and rules of the group and the needs and wishes of an individual. In some groups/societies there are very strong pressures to conform to the needs and rules of the group (e.g. some religious groups), whereas in modern Western society there is sometimes the sense that the individual's needs and wishes should always override the needs of the group. Balancing your own needs and those of others around you requires significant social intelligence and skills.

Relationship patterns

Whilst there are many different ways in which human beings relate to each other, there are some very basic interaction patterns and accompanying roles that underlie these. As adults we want to be able to adopt all of these roles flexibly where needed and switch between them as appropriate. Things go wrong when people get stuck in one particular pattern and use this inappropriately or when they oscillate between two extreme roles (e.g. submission and rebellion).

Caring–being cared for

This pattern characterises the relationship between a parent and their child. The parent's role is to nurture and protect and the child's role is to be cared for, and to depend on and defer to the parent.

Jackie was brought up in a house in which her older brother had a disability which meant that he needed lots of care. Jackie's parents were extremely stressed a lot of the time and expected Jackie to look out for her brother. As she grew up the expectations of this role seemed to expand to her being the main carer of her brother. When she was older and left home, Jackie noticed that she was drawn to repeating this relationship pattern such that with her boyfriend she suppressed many of her own needs to keep him happy. Her therapist helped her to realise it was no wonder she often had anger outbursts given her needs were getting squashed all the time!

Karen, on the other hand, always felt that just as she felt settled in life, things changed. She felt continually anxious about what the world appeared to demand of her and flooded by thoughts that unless she could deliver perfectly there was no point in bothering. When she had a cold at school, her mum let her stay home. When she felt anxious about going to university her mother suggested she take her time and stay home for another year. Karen liked being cared about and protected from things, but with her therapist she realised that she was feeling smothered and prevented from finding her own feet in the world. To truly care about herself was to get out into the world and make some mistakes!

Positive and negative characteristics that can go with these roles

Caring: Prioritising other person's needs, nurturing, providing resources, being selfless/altruistic; rescuing, being a martyr, smothering the other, abandoning.

Cared for/eliciting care: accepting help, care and resources, depending, being dependant, focused on own needs, being rescued, helpless, signalling need for care of protection, clinging like a limpet, abandoned.

Compete–cooperate

This pattern characterises the relationship between partners, or peers (i.e. people who are equal). In order to obtain resources people need to be able to work together (team work), but also need to be able to compete. Jo tended to compare himself and compete with others all the time, this took up a lot of his energy. Over time he learned that working with people and alongside people could also bring good things into his life.

Positive and negative characteristics that can go with these roles

Cooperation: being a team player, pooling resources, sharing, not dissenting from majority view, blending in, prioritising others' needs over own needs.

Competition: bettering yourself, going the extra mile, striving, seeking advantage over others, one-upmanship.

Dominate–submit

This pattern characterises the relationship between people of different social rank (i.e. where there is a real or perceived power differential). Trishna, for example, always 'gave' others the power. She had a tendency to look up to people and always see herself as inferior by comparison, she tended to submit to the demands of other, but over time learned to 'take back' some of that power and stand proud in relation to her own ideas and beliefs.

Positive and negative characteristics that can go with these roles

Dominating: senior, expert, leader, boss, pushing through own agenda, controlling, criticising, coercing, abusing, bullying.
Submitting: junior, beginner, follower, deferring, pleasing, placating, controlled, crushed, criticised, coerced, abused, bullied.

In what follows, let's try to figure out how some of the above might relate to you.

My relationship map

Now have a think about who the key relationships are in your life. Place yourself at the centre of the following diagram and then add the other people in your life. Include family and friends, people who are alive or dead, people who live near or far.

- Place people according to how close you feel to them, so those who are close and supportive would be nearer to you than casual friends.
- If there are people in your life who are important, but where your relationship is more mixed, difficult or painful also include them on the map, but place them further away from yourself.
- Now, choose a different colour and do the same task again, but this time think about where your relationships were before anorexia started.
- Finally, ask yourself the question: where would you put your anorexia on this map, and has that changed over time?

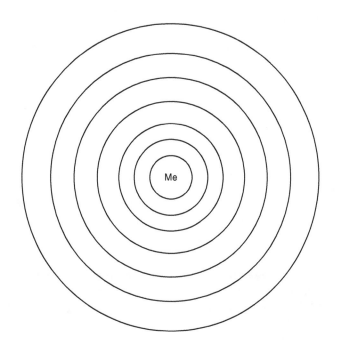

REFLECTION

- What you have learned from this?
- Any surprises?
- How have your relationships changed since your anorexia started?

Mapping relationship patterns

Now think about the different relationships that are part of your life and which figure on the relationship map that you completed. Are there any relationship patterns or roles that you frequently adopt? Think about the role you take on in that relationship and the needs this fulfils in you. What are the positive and negatives linked to this?

TOP TIP: RELATIONSHIP PATTERNS

- If you're finding identifying your relationship patterns quite tricky, ask yourself 'what is common across my main relationships?' Michelle could see that she tended to hang around with competent and 'perfect'-seeming friends that she tended to envy. She unpicked that her relationship pattern was to submit to people she perceived as superior. This gave her a sense of comfort in that they made all the decisions but it cheated her of the fun and companionship that can come from more equal and 'real' relationships, where there is more give and take.
- Have a go at completing the box below; if you are struggling, call on the help of your inner wise and reflective friend to help you 'look on' at your relationship patterns.

Relationship role/ pattern	What need does that signal in me	What do I gain?	What do I miss out on? How does this leave me feeling?	What is my challenge? What other ways can I get this need met?

Note: Often, if a person feels that they compare negatively against others they will either behave more submissively (please others, avoid conflict, etc.) or very competitively and strive to better themselves and do better than others. Either pattern is often found in eating disorders.

REFLECTION

- What you have learned from this?
- Are your close relationships balanced or imbalanced?
- Are there similarities or patterns in how you relate to different people?
- What does that tell you about yourself?
- What are the emotions that go with particular relationship patterns in your life? What emotions and needs get expressed and which ones are hidden? How has this changed since the onset of your anorexia?

The hidden parts of me

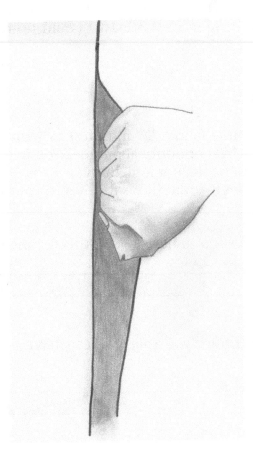

Only we can truly know ourselves, and sometimes important parts of us are actually hidden from other people, even our nearest and dearest. These can be parts of us (e.g. thoughts, feelings, personality traits, things we did or were involved in) that we actively hide, or they may be aspects of ourselves that we would love others to notice, but are not sure how to communicate them. Anorexia has the tendency to assume a dictator like position in relation to one's personality and so you may find you have quite a lot of hidden aspects! The experiment below helps you look at these hidden parts.

TOP TIP: THE HIDDEN PARTS OF ME

- Getting in touch with the hidden parts of yourself will require looking beyond your anorexia. By this we mean, putting to one side your anorexia for a few minutes and daring to look on at the 'you' that is left, the parts of you that are struggling to be seen and heard.

Here's what one of our patients told her therapist after writing her very moving version of the letter above: Well I bet you never realised all that was going on inside of me. . . ! I just feel I can't risk telling people about what's going on for me underneath this damn anorexia. . . . It's embarrassing . . . people have this false idea about me . . . I don't know why . . . I just can't . . . I felt safer writing about it . . . I felt sad writing it, but at least I could do it and at least you know now.

Writing experiment[1]

- Set aside some time (about 20 minutes) to write about 'the things others don't see, hear or notice about me'. You may wish to write this as a letter to a friend, real or imaginary.
- Think about the points/questions to cover in your writing before you start:

  - How ready are you to have a go at this writing experiment?

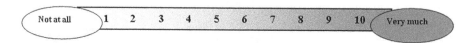

  - How confident are you that you can have a go at this writing experiment?

    - I predict the outcome of doing the experiment to be. . . .
    - Obstacles that might get in the way of me completing the experiment are. . . .
    - Ways I might overcome the obstacles are. . . .
    - I will make time on. . . (insert date and time) to do the experiment.
    - I will conduct the experiment in. . . (where).

---

1 If you want to know more about how writing can help, see Appendix 2 at the end of this workbook for information. Many of the writing experiments in this chapter are based on those found in Dr. James' Pennebaker's excellent self-help book 'Writing to Heal' (see further reading section at the end of this chapter for details).

REFLECTION

Immediately after completing your writing experiment rate the following on a scale of 0 to 10.

- To what degree did you express your deepest thoughts and feelings?

1	2	3	4	5	6	7	8	9	10

- To what degree do you currently feel sad or upset?

1	2	3	4	5	6	7	8	9	10

- To what degree do you currently feel happy?

1	2	3	4	5	6	7	8	9	10

- To what degree was today's writing valuable and meaningful for you?

1	2	3	4	5	6	7	8	9	10

Now spend a few minutes (no more than 3 or 4) noting down how your writing went.

- What did you learn?
- What do these hidden aspects say about you and your relationships with others?
- How does anorexia come into this?
- In what ways do you long for things to be different?
- If you feel brave, speak with a trusted friend or family member about some of the hidden parts of you.

Part 3: becoming an expert on your emotions

During this section we want to help you see how wonderful it can be to listen to your emotions, believe it or not, they can be really helpful! We want to support you in getting to know your emotional rule book and learning to express emotions and needs appropriately.

Exploring emotions and making them work for you!

How we feel isn't always easy to put into words. Edward, a young man who had anorexia for a little over two years, told us that whenever he expressed his feelings or needs he came away feeling guilty, and that long periods of time bottling them up had left him existing in a numb and desolate state. Edward, really struggled to name his feelings, but he knew that things needed to change. For Edward, feelings were like distant relations he once met but had never really bothered with. They were just so unfamiliar to him, he did not know where to begin. Edward's first step in reconnecting with his feelings was to pick up a pen and express himself via drawings. Edward told us that this felt 'safer' to him than struggling to find words. This was a real turning point for Edward and the beginning of his emotional world having more colour to it and less grey!

- Why don't you have a go? Use magazines, newspapers, the internet or your own art work to make a picture, a collage or image that represents a couple from the list of feelings below.

  Fear
  Sadness
  Anger
  Disgust
  Shame
  Happiness
  Envy
  Guilt
  Numbness

- You might even want to put down a poem, a part of a book or the words of a song – there's no right or wrong here, it just matters that you choose something that has meaning for you.
- Be as creative as you like and produce something just for you. *Remember*, creative work is about putting aside any ideas about being perfect or producing the 'right' type of work.
- It's important that you let your creative side take charge in this exercise because we know that the part of your mind that deals with feelings is much more at home with pictures, songs, poems and so forth than with logical thinking and debate.

TOP TIP: EXPLORING EMOTIONS AND MAKING THEM WORK FOR YOU

- You may notice the critical side of you butting in during this activity saying 'this is silly' or 'what I'm doing isn't right or good enough'. Just notice the critical dialogue and pop it to one side, pop it on the chair next to you. Try not to engage with it, just notice it and carry on trying to engage with your feelings. Remember that feelings are what make us human. You have a basic right to be in contact with them.

Making emotions work for you!

Emotions help us out

We are equipped with emotions to help us in life. This can sometimes be hard to believe, especially if an emotion is strong, feels unpleasant or if we are worried or ashamed of others seeing how we really feel. However, Edward (who we met above) found that once he started to notice his emotions, he realised they were actually informative and helpful. He turned up to one therapy session saying he had noticed an agitated feeling all week, he found a poem and a postcard that depicted how this felt for him, he then managed to notice that the feeling came whenever his partner was critical towards him. No wonder Edward was feeling agitated! His feelings were trying hard to tell him something, they were trying to tell him that he no longer appreciated being in a relationship in which he was put down. You can imagine that as Edward started to hear what his feelings were telling him, he made some life changes!

Look at the images you've produced and, for each one ask yourself:

What does this emotion do for me/others?
How does it help me/others?

Write down the *positive* things each emotion can signal to you or achieve for you.

For example, think about. . .

- Emotion = **Anger**

  What positive things does anger do for you or others?

  Edward's example: anger can tell me that someone is not treating me right and realising this helps me make life changes that lead to me feeling brighter.

- Emotion = **Shame**

  What positive things does shame do for you or others?

  Karen's example: shame made me sit up and realise that my anorexia was actually hurting those around me. Shame was difficult to endure but it was the springboard to me turning things around.

- Emotion = **Sadness**

  What positive things does sadness do for you or others?

  Leanne's example: sadness may not sound like a great feeling to be aware of, but for me, it made me realise that sitting at home all day thinking about calories and exercise regimes was not the most fulfilling way to spend my days!

Add your own.

Emotion = _____

How does this emotion help you or others?

_____

_____

Emotion = _____

How does this emotion help you or others?

_____

_____

Emotion = _____

How does this emotion help you or others?

_____

_____

Making emotions work for you!

Emotions tell us what we need

Whether we like it or not we are all have certain basic needs. Such as the need for warmth, nourishment, human contact and also the need to stretch ourselves and to go some way towards reaching our potential. Emotions can be a signal, a kind of signpost, indicating that we need something either from ourselves or from other people.

Again, look at your picture and pull out the different emotions you have included. Ask yourself, what sorts of things people experiencing this emotion need?

Edward took his agitation and sadness with his partner as signs that his basic needs for care and respect were not being met, he needed to reach out to people who treated him nicely and to be loved for who he was and cared for and comforted.

For each image write down some examples like this:

- People experiencing **sadness** need ....

  ....

- People experiencing **anger** need ....

....

- People experiencing **shame** need ....

....

- People experiencing **fear** need ....

....

- People experiencing **disgust** need ....

....

- People experiencing **envy** need ....

....

- People experiencing **guilt** need ....

....

TOP TIP: EMOTIONS TELL US WHAT WE NEED

- If you are struggling to get in touch with the need behind the feeling, it may be because you are using your adult 'head' rather than recognising that needs are more primitive and basic than this. They stem from when we were babies/children. So if you're struggling to identify needs, tune in to children that may be in your life or that you have read about or seen in films. What do children need (such as love, warmth, guidance, nourishment, safety/protection, challenge)? In what ways are these needs being met in you?

Making emotions work for you!

What are emotions in my life trying to tell me?

OK now, look at each image in your picture and the emotion it represents. Find an example of times when you've felt this emotion strongly.

- Where were you? Who were you with? What was happening in your life?
- Consider how this emotion was trying to help you out.
- Finally think about what this emotion tells you that you needed.

It's important that you allow yourself to connect with the feelings so that this exercise uses more than your logical mind alone. We suggest that you close your eyes and gather an image that goes along with the feeling, really embellish that image, it doesn't need to be accurate in any way or a memory, just any picture that goes along with those feelings.

Situation	What emotion(s) did I feel?	What positive things did this emotion intend to do for me in that situation?	What do I need when I feel this emotion?
Charlotte's example: My sister passed her GCSE's and got lots of praise. I remembered everyone ignored me even though I was stressing out in school because of all the course work.	Angry Jealous	It was a signal that I had important needs and feelings and didn't think they were being recognised.	I needed help and praise too! I need support and reassurance (a kind word or a hug) that lets me know that my needs and feelings matter too.

Practising recognising *what you feel* and *what you need*

Try this quick quiz to see how you go about getting your important needs and feelings met from people close to you. For each statement indicate how often you act in each way by ticking rarely, sometimes or mostly.

How do I signal my needs	Rarely	Sometimes	Mostly
I ask assertively by explaining my feelings and asking for what I need.			

How do I signal my needs	Rarely	Sometimes	Mostly
I wait for others to see into my mind and know what I feel and need.			
I give up on any hope that others can meet my needs and sink into sadness.			
I bottle up my feelings, but secretly show how unhappy or angry I am with little signals like refusing to speak or not eating and leaving others to guess what I need.			
I rebel against the injustice of being ignored by letting rip with my anger and demanding that my needs are met.			
I don't really know what I feel or need, but I know what I don't want and hope that others will guess for me.			
I don't feel anything and don't know how I signal my needs.			

REFLECTION

- Which of these approaches do you use mostly?
- What are the advantages of this style of getting your needs met?
- Are there any downsides?
- What might work better for you?

Examining your beliefs about emotions

People have all kinds of different beliefs about emotions and feelings. Some examples we have come across in people with anorexia include:

- I can't bear having strong feelings.
- It's not safe to show your feelings.
- Feelings are dangerous.
- Others will punish me or hurt me if I show my feelings.
- I am weak, bad or out of control if I have strong feelings.
- People should only have good feelings.
- I am a bad person if I experience 'bad' feelings (e.g. anger or jealousy).

Do any of the above beliefs apply to you?

With the help of your trusted friend work out what your beliefs about emotions and feelings are.

It might help to **think about:**

* What would be the worst thing about having strong feelings?
* What would be the worst thing about sharing your feelings with others.

Experimenting with your beliefs about emotion

Once you have identified your beliefs about feelings you might dare to have a go at the behavioural experiment worksheet with your therapist to come up with a way of testing your belief.

SAM

Sam believed that she couldn't trust others not to hurt her and that if she showed her feelings they would see her as weak and reject her or hurt her. This made her shut away her feelings inside and put on a tough face to the world.

To test out this belief, Sam asked people close to her to write letters to her about what she meant to them and what upset them most about her anorexia. Sam read the letters aloud with people close to her and took the risk of showing her feelings to test out what happened.

She was surprised to find that others showed warmth and care for her rather than treated her as weak.

ELLEN

Ellen had intense feelings of disgust and shame when she ate in public. She believed that she could not bear these feelings.

In an experiment with her therapist she had lunch in a café. The therapist encouraged and supported Ellen and helped her track how strong and how bearable her feelings were. Ellen found the experiment very hard, but learned that, as time passed, the intensity of the feelings decreased – Ellen learned that some feelings are strong and difficult to tolerate but that they she could bear them.

In future, Ellen was able to remember that 'I might not like it but I can choose to bear this' when she had a strong feeling.

TOP TIP

* Designing your own feelings 'experiment' might sound scary, but in essence it's just a way of discovering whether your ways of coping still work for you and whether there might be alternatives ways of being in the world that offer you greater satisfaction. So try to be brave and have a go. The examples below might help you to think of experiments of your own.

- If you want to test out your beliefs about feelings, it's important to involve your heart as well as your head. Getting active helps engage the heart.
- Have a think with a trusted friend about what experiment would make sense for you.

My feelings experiment

Belief to be tested: _____

How strongly do I believe this? _____ / **100**

Date	Situation	Prediction	Experiment	Outcome	What I learned?
		• What exactly did you think would happen? • How specifically would you know?	• What did you/ could you do to test the prediction?	• What actually happened? • Was the prediction accurate?	

How strongly do I believe this now? _____ / **100**

Now have a go at summarising your new learning in one simple sentence – a new belief. For example, Candy's new belief is that 'it's OK to express my feelings; others might not always like it, but it won't destroy them'.

Josh learned, 'I had more fun out with my friends when I shared something about myself with them'.

What is your new belief? What have you learned about yourself from carrying out an experiment?

My new belief:

_____

Expressing your needs and feelings: being assertive!

Now that you have begun to identify your own needs and feelings, you may want to take the next step and think about how you would use these pieces of information to help you make things different when faced with a situation. To help you learn how to do this, we use a technique called the scripting approach. Many people find this approach helpful – give it a go.

Scripting[1] involves planning out in advance in your mind or on paper exactly what you want to say in a structured way.

This is a four-stage approach that covers:

- The **event**: the situation, relationship or practical problem that is important to you.
- Your **feelings**: how you feel about situation or problem.
- Your **needs**: what you want to happen to make things different.
- The **consequences**: how making these positive changes will improve the situation for you and/or for others.

In scripting, you plan out what to say in each of these areas.

- **Event**: Say what it is you are talking about.
  Let the other person know precisely what situation you are referring to.
- **Feelings**: Express how the **event** mentioned **affects** your own **feelings**. Opinions can be argued with, **feelings cannot**. Expressing your feelings clearly can prevent a lot of confusion.
- **Needs**: People aren't mind readers. You need to tell them what you need. Otherwise people cannot fulfil your needs and this can lead to resentment and misunderstanding.
- **Consequences**: Tell the person that if they fulfil your needs, there will be a positive consequence for both of you. Be specific about the consequences.

A good way to begin to practice scripting is to **write down** what you want to say before you go into a situation.

The 'event' and 'feelings' aspect of this can be used as a part of a broken record. Once you have engaged the person in discussion you can bring in the needs and consequences.

EXAMPLE

Brother and sister, John and Annie, share a flat. When they moved in with each other, they decided that they would have a rota for cleaning, shopping and cooking. Last week was John's week to do these jobs and Annie was away. When she returned from her trip on Sunday night the bins were overflowing, the fridge was empty and the kitchen was a mess. John later texted her saying he was staying with his friend Lee until the following day. When he returned they had the following conversation:

ANNIE: *'Hello, how are you?'*
JOHN: *'Fine. Did you have a good time?'*

ANNIE: 'I did, thank you. But I did not expect to come back to an overflowing smelly bin, an empty fridge and lots of dirty dishes in the sink. It was your turn to do all that stuff last week.' **(Event)**

JOHN: 'I was really busy all week, so I thought I'd do the cleaning and shopping at the weekend, but then suddenly Lee called and invited me to come over to his and go to this very special gig with him, so events overtook me. I had meant to text you before you got back to let you know, but then forgot once I was with Lee.'

ANNIE: 'I was really tired after the long journey back and looking forward to being home. When I saw all the mess I felt very angry and upset and not having anything to eat made it worse.' **(Feeling)**

JOHN: 'I'm sorry. I really did screw up big time.'

ANNIE: 'I really like sharing the flat with you and sharing the jobs normally seems to work well for both us usually. I'd like us to continue living here together in a friendly way, but I need to feel I can trust you.' **(Need)**

JOHN: 'Yes, I feel the same. I know what I did is not acceptable. Please forgive me. I won't make this mistake again. I want us to get on.'

ANNIE: 'Thanks John. Let's both try our best to keep to our side of the bargain. And if there is something that gets in the way of doing our bit of the rota in time, let's try to give the other person a bit of an advanced warning, so that the situation can be dealt with in a way that is not causing major disruption or upset.' **(Consequence)**

Plan out your scripting conversation here by writing into the four boxes:

TOP TIP

- For your first go at this, don't choose the most challenging conversation you can think of; have a go at something that feels manageable and doable. You can work up from there!

EVENT

FEELINGS

NEEDS

CONSEQUENCES

REFLECTION

- What was it like experimenting in these ways?
- What have you learned about you and your emotional world?
- What two things will you do differently as a result of your new self-discoveries?

Part 4: learning to manage extreme and overwhelming emotions

People with anorexia often describe a polarised relationship with their emotions. That is either they strive for feelings to be bottled up, or they fear they will explode or overwhelm them in some way. Can you relate to this? During this section our aim is to help you to think about these more extreme emotions and to help things become more manageable and balanced. Our aim is to help you to realise that your feelings, even the tough ones, are there to help you learn something about yourself and how you are living your life. Jessica had a sudden realisation halfway through her therapy that, as she put it, 'turning toward' difficult feelings took the fear out of them and actually helped guide her towards organising her life in a way that was more nourishing and rewarding for her. She realised that her feelings had had to become explosive because anything less and they got ignored! It's like if you ignore a crying baby, they start screaming in a desperate bid to try to be heard, and then if their screams are ignored they eventually give up and shut down in a numb and exhausted state. Over time they would probably oscillate between being shut down and screaming. Only through care and compassion towards one's feelings can these desperate lurches between extreme states begin to calm down.

Have a think about your relationship with tough feelings and complete the following boxes.

What do I do to manage difficult or upsetting emotions?

What do I gain from managing difficult feelings or emotions like this?

What are the unintended downsides of managing difficult feelings or emotions like this?

Thinking about what you gain and what you lose; **where does this leave you?**

Taking a break from painful emotions

On the whole, it's better to work through upsetting emotions than bottle them up or squash them down; it is generally not a good idea to manage feelings with behaviours that ultimately chip away at your self-esteem or cause harm to you physically or psychologically.

Sometimes, though, we all need to find ways to help us calm down and give us a break from stressful or overwhelming feelings. Planned breaks from our feelings and the stresses of life are essential for all of us.

Following are some harmless ways that people can take breaks from or manage difficult feelings. The suggestions below are based on ideas by Dr Marsha Linehan, who has developed many ideas for how people can self-soothe to tone down overwhelming and intense emotions.[2]

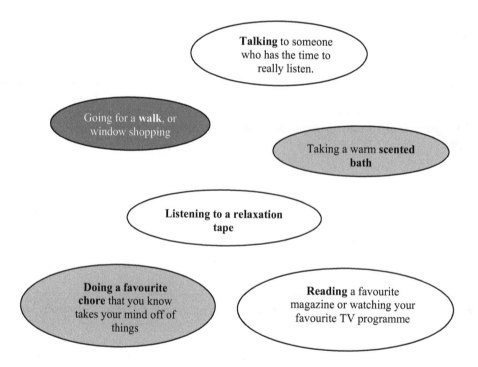

The key things are:

✓ It should be **something you really like**
✓ Something you usually feel **very motivated to do**
✓ Something you can **lose yourself in**.

✗ Make sure it is not something that is harmful to you
✗ Make sure it is not going to provide fuel for your eating disorder (compulsive exercising or calorie counting in the supermarket probably aren't going to be helpful).

If you are interested, there are also mindfulness and relaxation classes available in most cities advertised that can be booked onto at a reasonable cost.

FURTHER PRACTICE

1   *Make your own self-soothing list.* Fill in the bubbles below with all the self-soothing things that you could try that might work for you.

2   *Keep a diary of your emotions:* Note down the situations that aroused the emotion and how you soothed yourself.

A sample diary sheet is given in Appendix 3 at the end of this book.

Part 5: the emotional lives of others

The social brain

A big portion of our brain specialises in understanding social relationships. Our social brain is closely linked to the parts of the brain that deal with emotions. We know about this from brain imaging studies. Our social brain helps us to interact with other people. It allows us to predict what is going to happen next in an interaction with another person. Obviously, the better we can predict what someone is going to do next, the more successful our interaction with them will be. The most important attribute of the social brain is the ability to make predictions about others' behaviour on the basis of their states of mind or thoughts and feelings. This ability to read other people's minds is called '**Mentalizing**' or '**Theory of Mind**'. A lot of this is to do with accurately being able to pick up emotions and thoughts from others' facial expressions, their tone of voice or bodily posture, and also from a given social context.

Importantly, the part of the social brain which handles others' communicative intentions is also the part which handles thinking about our own mental state. This makes a lot of sense, as any communication between people involves thinking about our own thoughts, feelings and intentions and those of the other person/people in relation to each other.

Anorexia and the ability to read other people's minds

Research has shown that people with anorexia often struggle with thinking accurately about their own and others' states of mind. Different factors contribute to this. In general, when people are stressed it is much harder for them to think about others' states of mind, and they can become very preoccupied just with one point of view or perspective or perceive things as much more threatening than they are. Likewise, starvation impairs the ability to read other people and therefore dealing with social situations becomes much harder. We did an experiment with healthy volunteers who were starved for 24 hours only and we then tested their ability to read the mind of others. This was significantly impaired compared to other volunteers who had been eating normally.

Furthermore, research has shown that people with anorexia, when shown pictures of other people's faces, do not spend as much time scanning them as fully (they avoid looking at the eyes) as a comparison group without anorexia and may therefore find it harder to pick up clues as to what the other person feels or thinks. Finally, in the context of close relationships, people can often find it much harder to reflect on their own mental state and that of others.

How skilled are you at understanding the emotional lives of others?

Becoming better at understanding the minds of others can help us understand their behaviours and responses to us. This is called developing **empathy**.

Having **empathy means** that you can really understand how things are for others and why they react the way they do.

- Pick some situations where you've had conflict or tension with people close to you and work with your therapist to build a mental picture of their perspective. The following table might help.
- Afterwards, you might want to go through the table with the person involved or get them to fill in a separate version and compare notes.

Example situation	What emotion(s) did X (e.g. my mum) feel?	What thoughts did X have?	How did this thought make them behave?
At breakfast I spilled my orange juice.	Anger	She did that on purpose because of the anorexia – I'm so worried about the anorexia.	Scream and shout about the mess and say that the spill was deliberate.

Example situation	What emotion(s) did X (e.g. my mum) feel?	What thoughts did X have?	How did this thought make them behave?

REFLECTION

- What are you learning about the emotions of others?

WRITING EXPERIMENT 1

Understanding the perspective of others.
Use the writing experiment sheet at the end of this book (Appendix 2) to prepare for this task and to reflect on it afterwards. Spend about five minutes on each part of the task.

Remember the last time you argued over your eating with one of the people most closely involved in your life (this could be one of your parents or a partner).

1   Write a letter to that person expressing all the strong emotions *you* felt.

How did you feel? Use lots of vivid emotional words (don't censor yourself – the person concerned never has to see this).

TAKE A BREAK

2   Pick up your pen again. Now see the situation from the eyes of the *other person*.

What did they feel? What emotions did they have? Why were they angry or upset? What was it like for them?
Write a letter as if you were the other person writing to you. Express all the emotions the other person felt.

3   After reading through the two letters, write a third letter, this time from the perspective of a *wise and fair person*. If you do not know someone like this, make them up.

What is their opinion? What do they see? What emotions do they recognise in both of you?

More exercises to help understand the emotional lives of others

Below are some other exercises and experiments that people with eating disorders have found helpful in learning more about the emotions of others. Choose one or two that appeal to you and have a go.

Gather information:

1   Collect letters: You may already have asked people close to you to write you a letter explaining what you mean to them; if not, do so now (these can be read through with your therapist or with the people who care for you).
2   Survey: Conduct a survey to find out what people you know think and feel about different situations (your therapist can help you design this).

Experiment with writing:

If you enjoy writing, you might find the following experiments useful.
(Use the writing experiment sheet (Appendix 2) at the end of this workbook to prepare for and reflect on these tasks).

1 **Write the story of a day in the life of someone close to you**.

Make sure you write about their feelings, their beliefs and their behaviours. Who do they meet during the day? What do they do? What things occupy their mind?

2 **Use writing to switch perspectives on emotional upheavals or trauma**.

Almost all upsetting events in our lives involve several people, and the more you can look at things from everyone's perspective, the more you will be able to process and understand what has happened. It is also helpful to be able to move between the 'bigger picture' perspective and the detailed perspective that each individual person involved in the situation brings to it.

In the following experiment, we would like you to write about an upsetting event four times, shifting perspectives each time. You will need to write continuously and honestly, and do the whole task in one go.

I. The Big Picture: Write about the emotional upheaval or trauma that you have been thinking about. Describe what happened and who was involved. How did you and others react to this event and how is it affecting all of you now? (five minutes)

II. I, Me and My: Write about the same event, but focus exclusively on your own perspective: What do you think, feel and do? How have your behaviours affected others? What would you like others to know about your situation? (five minutes)

III. The Other People: Again writing about the same emotional upheaval, focus on the role of another person or group of people: What was and is going on in their minds? What did they do and feel? What do you think they would like others to know about their perspective?

Try to look into their hearts and assume that they are at least as complicated as you are. (five minutes)

IV. Another Big Picture: Before you begin writing, look at what you have written so far. Have you been honest with yourself and about the other people?

For this last five minutes, again tell the story of the upsetting event, but this time take a broad perspective in terms of what happened. What value and meaning can you and others draw from this experience? (five minutes)

Practice:

1 **Practise your empathy skills** – Ask a trusted friend to help you with this and take turns in practicing silently listening to each other.

  • Pay the other person your full attention.
  • When they have finished speaking summarise what they have said.
  • Say what you think they feel.

2 **Empty chair work** – There are many variations on working with an empty chair to explore your own emotional life and that of others.

- One approach people find very powerful is to talk to an empty chair as though they were someone you have a challenging relationship with, expressing how you feel about them.
- Once you've done this, you can swap chairs and have a go at being the other person talking back to you about your feelings.
- You will need the help of your therapist to get the most out of this exercise.

REFLECTION

- What does this teach you about your emotions in this situation?
- Are there emotions you avoid?
- Are there things you might need to express?
- Are there things you might need to understand about the other person?
- Are there losses you might need to accept?

WRITING EXPERIMENT II

Understanding the emotional lives of others in order to make changes.
Is there someone in your life that you want to be different or want something more from? The following experiment is designed to help you approach this.

Use the writing experiment sheet at the end of the book (Appendix 2) to help you plan for and reflect on the task afterwards. Spend about five minutes on each part of the task.

1 Write a letter to them telling them about the hurt or pain you feel.

Explain how you feel let down or ignored or that you need something more from them.

TAKE A BREAK

2 Pick up your pen again. Now think about your relationship through the other person's eyes.

What do they feel? What pressures or problems affect them? What leads them to behave as they do? Write a letter as if you were the other person writing to you.

3   After reading through the two letters, write a third letter, this time from the perspective of a *wise and fair person*. If you do not know someone like this, make them up.

What is their opinion? What do they see? What emotions do they recognise in both of you? What advice would this person give to you? Should you ask for what you need? Should you give up and accept the sadness of never getting what you want?

Wanting someone to be different

Sometimes knowing what you feel and what you need and assertively asking for it won't help. Sometimes we desperately want someone to treat us differently and to help meet our needs, but they are unable to.

LISA'S STORY

Lisa's father used to be very close to her when she was small; she has lots of memories of going everywhere with him and having fun together. Things changed when Lisa was 10. Her mum and dad began to argue a lot. Dad began to spend lots of time in the pub and was drunk each night and during the day at weekends. Lisa wanted her old closeness with Dad back, but he just seemed angry and drunk whenever she approached him. Lisa kept trying everything she could to get his attention and love back, but even when she started restricting her food and making herself sick she couldn't get him to stop drinking and care for her.

Part of Lisa's recovery involved looking at all the things she had tried to get her Dad to see her needs and feelings (including being assertive, threatening, pleading and being ill). She learned that there wasn't anything she could do to make her Dad change. Lisa had lost the Dad she knew. He is still in her life and she still loves him, but now he is often unreliable and lets her down due to his alcoholism. He is emotionally insensitive and has unpredictable mood shifts.

What kind of emotions might Lisa feel when she realises she will never get her old dad back?

Are there relationships in your life where you might want to consider if it's really possible to get the kind of emotional care and support that you really want?

You might be trying really hard to get the kind or care and support you want – are you being realistic?

What will tell you that it's time to accept that perhaps you'll never get what you hope for even if the person is in your life every day?

Lisa found it helpful to write a letter (just for her to read) in which she wrote:

'A goodbye to the dad I hoped for'.

In this letter she wrote about all the things she hoped to get from a dad but didn't in the past, the hopes she would have to give up on in the present and the things she would probably never have in the future.

She wrote another letter from herself to herself titled:

'The dad I really have'.

This letter aimed to give an honest and balanced account of her dad, including his good points, bad points, strengths and limits. In it she was honest in writing about what he could give her and what he can't.

You might want to have a go at writing some letters like this.

Recognising kind intentions in others

Especially if communication with another person is somewhat difficult or leaves you upset it is easy to focus on the content and outcome of the interaction, rather than on the other person's motives and intentions. Over the next week, try and see whether you can spot the kind intentions of others towards you. This could be something small, like the first example below – it doesn't have to involve grand gestures, or be something big. Use the table below to record these – have a go at seeing if you can understand the thoughts and feelings that prompted the other person/s kind intentions.

What happened?	What did X do?	What did I think? How did I feel? What did I do?	What were X's kind intentions?
I overslept my alarm and was going to be late for work.	My mum was awake and noticed I hadn't got up, so came into my room and woke me up.	I thought it was nice of her to realise that I was going to be late, and that I was lucky she did! I felt relieved to have enough time to just make it to work on time, and thanked her.	Mum wanted to save me the anxiety and embarrassment of turning up late for work.

What happened?	What did X do?	What did I think? How did I feel? What did I do?	What were X's kind intentions?
My auntie visited – she had last seen me when my anorexia was really bad.	She said that I looked so much better now.	At first I thought – this is terrible, she thinks I am fat! Then I calmed down a little and remembered what a nice person she is and that she would not want to hurt me.	She wanted to give me honest feedback and show her relief and pleasure at seeing me get better.

Here's how one of our patients found this exercise: *I was able to look at another perspective on a situation and not only find myself getting less frustrated or upset at what they did or said (if I automatically saw it negatively), but I was also able to realise that I am surrounded by people who support me and try to do good for me, making me appreciate them more, feel closer to them and generally see them as allies against anorexia rather than 'enforcers'.*

REFLECTION

- What are the pros and cons of being more aware of the intentions of others?
- If you notice kind intentions in others, how does this affect your view of that person and yourself?

Part 6: learning self-compassion

Many people with anorexia tell us that they have a strong self-critical or demanding voice in their head. Often this voice is very demanding, attacking and harsh. Sometimes people can locate this internal voice to a past figure in their lives. Amy's father had been a very academic man and a rather demanding character. On reflection she thinks he probably only wanted the best for her, but at the time, while she was growing up, she internalised this voice that demanded perfection and high standards from her at all times. As a result she was always striving in relation to her demanding internal voice but never feeling good enough or OK about herself. Frances, on the other hand, had been abused by a family friend when she was a little girl. The nature of her internal voice as a child and then as an adult was ruthlessly critical and condemning. This was the only voice Frances ever knew, and so to her this level of day-to-day bullying was 'normal'. Internally the voice of the abuser is a dreadfully sad and unfair legacy of abuse, and if you recognise this type of abuse we would recommend you seek therapeutic support so that you have a companion to help you sift through the tough times imposed on your when you were little. You deserve to lay these events to rest so that you can become the adult you want to become!

So if you struggle with a critical and or demanding internal voice, have a think about the exercise below.

TOP TIP

- People tell us that their internal voice can be so automatic and quick firing that they get to a point where they almost cease to notice it. It's as if they have become so used to this constant negative chatter that it feels like all they know. If this is you, try to use your wise reflective friend to step back and then 'look on' at that voice inside of you. What tone does it speak to you in? What types of things does it say to you? Does anyone from your past come to mind? Or if it's no one specific, what image goes along with that internal voice?

- Use all you discover above to help you with the following exercise.

What kind of critical voice do you have?

Think of a time when you ate more than you planned or ate something you would normally avoid. Write down the kinds of things your critical voice would say.

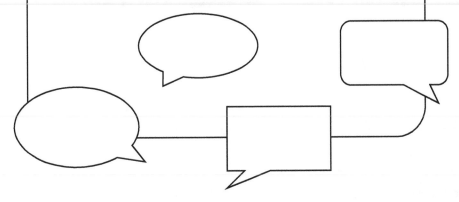

How does your critical voice talk to you?
For example: What's the tone of the voice? What kind of language does it use? Does it call you names or tell you that you are bad or that you will make something bad happen?

What does this make you feel?

What behaviours does this make you want to do?

Pros and cons of my critical voice

Write down all the good and useful things about your critical voice.

- *What is its positive intention for you?*
- *What do you worry might happen if it wasn't there?*

Write down all the downsides of having this voice in your head.

- *What effect does it have on how you feel about yourself, on what you can and cannot do?*
- *What would be the best thing that might happen if the voice changed and became kinder and more encouraging and supportive?*

REFLECTION

- What type of internal voice do you have?
- What are the pros and cons of your internal voice?
- What is your take-home message from exploring your internal voice?

When the voice gets out of hand

Some researchers and therapists think that people have a self-critical voice for very good reasons, but that at times it can get out of hand and operate in ways that are damaging to your sense of worth and your ability to get what you really want in life.

Professor Paul Gilbert, a researcher specialising in shame and self-criticism, says that we sometimes talk to ourselves in a self-attacking way because we worry that we are in danger of doing things that might stop us achieving important goals (like being accepted by others or being good enough to be loved).

The problem is that, sometimes the self-attacking voice is so harsh it makes us feel overwhelmingly bad about ourselves. This can then lead us into unhelpful behaviours (like trying really hard to be good enough by controlling everything we eat). These eventually lead to even more self-criticism.

Ellen's example

1 Ellen grew up being told that she had to do her best and be in control of her feelings. She learned this message so strongly that she worried that she would be rejected if she didn't achieve everything perfectly or if she showed that she was upset.

2 To make sure that she wasn't rejected for not being good enough Ellen adopted all kinds of coping strategies including striving to be perfect in everything she did and hiding upsetting feelings from others. Ellen also tried to achieve perfect control over her eating. The positive side of this was that Ellen felt she could be safe from rejection and in control.

3 Unfortunately these coping strategies had **unintended side effects**. Her anorexia made her parents concerned for her but also angry and rejecting at times. Hiding her emotions isolated her and meant others couldn't get close.

4 When Ellen saw the **unintended effects** she saw herself as a threat to herself and criticised herself for causing problems, for not being good enough, for upsetting her parents, for being weak and being a failure.

5 The harsh criticism of Ellen's self-attacking voice led her to redouble her efforts and try even harder to be perfect, hide her feelings and make sure she was safe from being rejected.

What do you think might be the problem with this way of dealing with your demanding and self-critical voice?

One of our patients told us: Exploring my critical voice, its tone, how it talks to me, enabled me to differentiate it from my own internal voice and therefore view it as a nasty intruder when it gets out of hand.

Developing qualities of inner compassion

We can see that being self-critical can be very stressful and makes us feel worse. One way of coping with our critical voice or 'inner bully' is to learn to be compassionate to yourself. This requires a number of things:

Valuing compassion: Some people are worried that if they are compassionate with themselves they may somehow be weak, self-indulgent or lack the drive to succeed. Thus they don't really value compassion. However, people who are renowned for their compassion, such as Buddha, Jesus, Gandhi, Florence Nightingale and Nelson Mandela, can hardly be regarded as 'weak' or 'unsuccessful'. Learning to be compassionate can actually make us stronger and feel more confident.

Empathy: Empathy means that we can understand how people feel and think; see things from their point of view. You will have practiced this in part 5 of this chapter. Similarly, when we have empathy for ourselves we can develop a better understanding for some of our painful feelings of disappointment, anxiety, anger or sadness. This means we may need to learn to be sensitive to our feelings and distress – rather than try not to notice them or avoid them. Sometimes we tell ourselves that we shouldn't think or feel as we do, and try to deny our feelings rather than working with them. The problem with this is that we don't explore them to understand them and then they can be frightening to us. We can learn to understand how and why we became self-critical, often because we feel threatened in some way. Becoming empathic to yourself means coming to see the threats that lie behind self-criticism. Emma went through a phase in her therapy of feeling very sad and mournful about all the years she had lost spent listening to her internal 'bully'. She had come to recognise her internal bully as the voice of her father and it took a long while to appreciate that he was not worth listening to! However, once she realised this, she was left for a time with deep feelings of sadness for the parts of her that had endured his criticism in person throughout her childhood and then in her own head. Unlike when she was a child with little control, she was relieved to learn that as an adult she could choose whether to listen or not to that voice in her head.

Sympathy: Sympathy is less about our understanding and more about feeling and wanting to care, help and heal. When we feel sympathy for someone, we can feel sad or distressed with them. Learning to have sympathy for ourselves means that we can learn to be sad without being depressed (without telling ourselves that there is something wrong or bad about feeling sad). We can also focus on feelings of kindness in our sympathy. Emma (above) also came to feel some sympathy for her father who had been mercilessly bullied by his father. This did not excuse his behaviour towards her when she was a child, but it helped her understand things a little.

Forgiveness: Our self-critical part is often very unforgiving and will usually see any opportunity to attack or condemn as an opportunity not to be missed. Learning the art of forgiveness however can be important. Forgiveness allows us to learn how to change; we are open to our mistakes and learn from them. Emma forgave her father, and then she forgave herself and allowed herself to be kinder towards herself.

Acceptance/Tolerance: There are many things about ourselves that we might like to change, and sometimes it is helpful to do that. However it is also important to develop acceptance of ourselves as human beings 'as we are'. Acceptance isn't passive resignation, such as feelings of being defeated or not bothering with oneself. It is an open-heartedness to all our fallibilities and efforts. It is like having the flu and accepting that you have to go to bed perhaps but also doing all you can to help your recovery. Greg came to accept his sexuality and to tolerate knowing that his parents could not. He learned to live his life in a way that made him happy and fulfilled and let go of needing to please the unpleasable!

Developing feelings of warmth: This requires us to begin to experience and practice generating feelings of warmth for the self. To do this we can use images and practice feeling warmth coming into us. When we are depressed this feeling may be very toned down and hard to generate – so we will have to practice. This can seem strange or even frightening, so we need to go one step at a time. Greg was not used to feeling warmly towards himself because he grew up being told that how he lived his life was unacceptable. He had to rechannel lots of negative energy away from himself and learn how to generate warmth and love towards himself.

Growth: Compassion is focussed on helping people grow, change and develop. It is life-enhancing in a way that self-criticism is not. When we learn to be compassionate with ourselves, we are learning to deal with our fallible selves such that we can grow and change. Compassion can also help us face some of the painful feelings we wish to avoid. Greg once said to his therapist 'when I denied who I was and how I wanted to live my life I was stunted and sad all the time and now I am open and respectful about all parts of me, I feel alive for the first time ever'. This is growth.

Taking responsibility: One element of learning self-compassion is taking responsibility for one's own self-critical thinking. To do this we can learn to recognise when it's happening and then use our compassionate mind to provide alternative views and feelings. This can be so empowering because taking responsibility means we have choices to make. This is your internal world we are talking about. Have a say in what it says to you!

Training: When we attack ourselves, we stimulate certain pathways in our brain but when we learn to be compassionate and supportive to our efforts we stimulate different pathways. Sometimes we are so well practised at stimulating inner attacks/criticisms that our ability to stimulate inner warmth and compassion is rather under-developed. It will need lots of practice to develop this. The training part can be like going to a physiotherapist, where you learn to do exercises and build up certain strengths. The compassion systems in your brain are the ones we are trying to strengthen with our exercises. You may well have had decades of training in how to be mean and rotten to yourself, so don't expect self-compassion to grow overnight; it will take dedication, practice and commitment!

The consequences of being compassionate to yourself

Learning to relate to ourselves in a more accepting, kind and forgiving way could impact on your life in a wide variety of ways. Consider the following questions and think about how learning to be more compassionate to yourself could help you change and become more like you want to be.

For each question, consider:

- In what ways will this be different to now?
- How will you notice this happening?
- How can you build on this?

1 How would being more compassionate to yourself affect how you feel and relate to yourself?

2 How would being more compassionate to yourself affect how you deal with challenges, difficulties and problems in life?

3 How would being more compassionate to yourself affect how you interact with people?

4 How would being more compassionate to yourself affect how you choose and work towards life goals (both in the short term – in the next few days, weeks and months – and over a lifetime)?

5 How would being more compassionate to yourself affect how you deal with errors and mistakes, setbacks and life crises?

6 How would being more compassionate to yourself affect any other life issues that are important to you?

REFLECTION

- Do you think that being able to relate to yourself more compassionately would be a good thing?
- How can you build self-compassion into your everyday life?
- What might make this difficult?

Compassionate letter-writing

Here's what one patient told us: *This type of writing I did whenever I judged myself badly, or felt guilty about a situation. I carried a notepad and pen around to complete it anywhere, anytime and have managed to practise it enough to be able to verbally say it to myself without needing to write it and it has become a much quicker response, hopefully it will develop into an immediate response whenever I have critical feelings.*

If you are frequently self-critical, it will not come naturally to be compassionate to yourself and you may need to practice your self-compassion skills. To help you make a start, you may want to do the following writing experiment. You will need to set aside about half an hour for this.

Think about an event that emotionally matters to you. Choose something over which you have criticised yourself, where you have felt ashamed or guilty.

The task is to write about this to two different audiences and then, in a second step, to write back to yourself from *their* perspective.

STEP 1

1 **A Fair Authority Figure:** Imagine you are telling a fair authority figure about this particular event.

   - This should not be someone who was involved in what happened. It could be a teacher, judge, priest, parent or someone like that. It should be someone who you know will be fair and who you respect. If you do not know someone like that, then make them up.
   - Tell this person about the event and what happened and about your thoughts and feelings then and now, and the impact this has had on you and continues to have.

2 **A Close and Compassionate Friend:** This time you are asked to write about the same experience, but with a very close friend in mind, someone you deeply trust and who will accept you no matter what you say.

   - This friend should not be linked to the experience in any way. Again, if you can't think of anyone, invent one.
   - In your writing, tell your friend about what happened, about your thoughts and feelings, your self-criticism and how this has affected your life since.

   Write continuously for 10 minutes.

STEP 2

In a second step, write back to yourself:

- First from the perspective of the **fair authority figure**, and
- Second from the perspective of the **close and compassionate friend**.

Again, write continuously for 10 minutes.
Then stop and reflect.
(Use the writing worksheet at the end of this module to help you do this.)

TOP TIP: COMPASSIONATE LETTER-WRITING

- We don't underestimate how challenging it can be to generate self-compassion when you have spent so long being critical of yourself. It can feel alien and even 'not allowed' for a time. But our belief is that **everyone** deserves to be cared about and we'd love to help you feel better about yourself. Have you ever known anyone who showed some compassion towards you? Even just a little bit? Maybe a teacher, aunt or family friend? Or a figure you remember from a film? If so, try to gather a mental image of that person and enlist them as a guide when doing these exercises. Think about the qualities they exude, and use their guidance to mentor you in developing self-compassion.
- If a person doesn't come to mind, is there a scent or a piece of music that you associate with kindness and calm? If so, carry this around with you for a while and try to let the kindness in. Have this with you whenever you need to be compassionate towards yourself.

Developing your sense of self-compassion – more ideas

Here are some other ideas for developing your sense of self-compassion.

1 **Getting curious about your anorexic voice** – Write a description of your self-attacking or anorexic voice, describing it as vividly as possible.

   How does it talk to you?
   Whose voice is it?
   Where did it come from? Does it sound like anyone you know?
   What are its qualities? What are its credentials for advising you?
   What's good and bad about it?
   Does it deliver what it promises?
   Does it make you feel happy, sad, guilty, ashamed or frightened of making a mistake?
   What are its catchphrases?
   What are its prejudices?

To learn more about the voice, you can talk to your therapist about other techniques.

- Some people find it helpful to **keep a record** for a week or so of how the voice talks to them and how this makes them feel.
- Some people find it useful to use an **empty chair technique**, where you can take on the role of the critical voice and explain what your **positive intention** is and then respond explaining how it makes you feel to be spoken to like this.
- You can also try **letters** from your critical voice to you and a warm letter back from you explaining how you feel when spoken to so harshly.

2 **Building a caring part** – It can be very helpful to practice developing a really caring and compassionate voice to help nurture and guide yourself instead of being harsh and critical to yourself.

Try writing about how your mind is when you've cared for someone (e.g. a pet, a child, someone you recognise as innocent and deserving of care).

What kind of thoughts do you have?
What are the qualities of this kind of thinking?
How do you speak?
What do you do?
What's your positive intention?

- Why not **choose a picture** or item that for you captures a sense of compassion and caring? Use this to remind you of the caring voice you described in your letter. Make this your **personal reminder** of your ability to be compassionate when you are tempted to be harsh on yourself.
- You may ask your therapist to help you with other exercises on building compassion such as **visualisation exercises**.

3 **Applying the new perspective to yourself** – Develop a new compassionate relationship with yourself.
Ask your therapist to video a therapy session or watch a home video of yourself. As you watch, imagine this is someone else, someone you don't know but feel great sympathy for.

Look and listen with care and warmth and hear any sadness or hurt. Be compassionate for that person's hurt, guilt, fear or sadness.

- Write the person in the video a letter of support – show them care, understanding and as much warmth as you would give to someone you love if they were suffering.
- Try eating something you would normally avoid while reading your letter of support and warmth or using your picture of compassion to bring warm thoughts to mind. Notice what happens to the feelings of guilt.

4 **Applying the new perspective to others** – Apply curiosity to the minds and behaviours or your peers and key attachment figures.

What matters most to them?
What fears, hopes and loves do they have? Why do they do what they do?

5 **Recognising and accepting your needs and feelings** – Make a plan of how to express your feelings in appropriate way that makes your life bigger and takes you forward.

Final thoughts

This is the end of this chapter. There is lots in here to be thought about, and perhaps you remain somewhat overwhelmed and daunted by the idea of radically altering your stance to emotions and relationships and the tasks ahead.

Try to conjure up the image of a four-leaved clover. This is to wish you luck but also to remind you that in any difficult interpersonal situation it will be helpful to you to think about four things: being **fair** and **compassionate** to **yourself** and the **other** person. If you keep this in mind as the essence of this chapter you can't go far wrong.

Notes

1 Williams, C. Overcoming depression: a five areas approach. 1992. www.leeds.ac.uk/studentcounselling/sections/2/Beingassertive.pdf.
2 Linehan, M. M. *DBT Skills Training: Handouts and Worksheets*. 2nd edition. Guilford Press New York, NY, USA, 2014.

Further reading

James W Pennebaker (2004) *Writing to Heal: A Guided Journal for Recovery from Trauma and Upheaval*. Oakland CA, USA: Hew Harbinger Publications.

The Compassionate Mind Foundation was founded by Professor Paul Gilbert, an eminent researcher in the field of compassion. The site contains many useful resources. https://compassionatemind.co.uk/.

This website by Dr Kristin Neff has many helpful resources and exercises on self-compassion. You can also complete a self-compassion rating scale assessing how well you treat yourself. http://self-compassion. org/ 878-034-0-90586-9.

Chapter 8

Exploring thinking styles

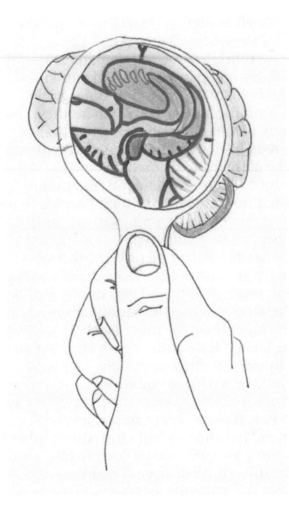

One of our patients described her experience of learning about thinking styles as follows:

> I often find myself laughing and saying 'there I go again . . . getting
> obsessed with the detail' . . . or 'there I go again . . . following the same
> old routines in the same old ways'. I try to pull myself out of behaving in
> these kind of scripted ways. Its liberating! But I also realise, these ways of

being aren't bad and they may not change any time soon, they are just one way of tackling the world and now I know how to play to my strengths.

When we approach a life task, such as planning a holiday, there are two core mental ingredients that make this happen. Most obviously there is the *content* of our thoughts/images. These might include thoughts about the time period in which to take a holiday and images regarding the part of the world we'd like to visit; reflections on what the weather will be like at that time of year; and the activities that will be available to us (skiing, sunbathing, walking, etc.). Of course, all of this mental content has the potential to generate a host of feelings ranging from excitement and happiness to worry about everything that needs to be achieved at work before the holiday season arrives! What we may be less consciously aware of is that as well as mental *content* there are also mental *processes* involved in the management of life tasks. These tend to involve *how* rather than *what* we think, and we call them *thinking styles*. For example, in planning a holiday one person might like to know all the details in advance, book the holiday well ahead of time, go with the same opera-tor as always, to a similar sort of place, where they know exactly what to expect, in terms of what is available, what the costs are and where they will be staying. This means that when arranging their next holiday their search will be narrow and focused. In contrast, someone else might be looking at many different holiday options and just have a few broad criteria for choosing from these. They might decide to just book a flight and a couple of nights of an accommodation, and then go wherever they spontaneously desire. Crudely put, this process is about whether you are more of a flexible 'bigger picture' thinker who is good at impro-vising, or whether you tend to be a more detail focused 'planner' who values routine and predictability and gets drawn into detail. As you can imagine, both thinking styles are important and some tasks lend them-selves to one style more than the other (such as applying a detail focus when completing an application for a passport), but what is fascinating is that there are individual differences here – we tend to be more prone to one type of thinking style than another.

Another important thinking style involves how you respond when there is a need to switch plans. For example, if you plan to go on a skiing holiday with a friend but she suddenly introduces other ideas about the 'perfect' holiday, how able are you to flexibly take on board these new ideas and involve them in your overall thinking about the holiday, or does this new input feel derailing and overwhelming? Crudely put, this thinking style is about how 'flexible' you are in your ability to accom-modate new information.

We call these two core processes *thinking styles*, and research suggests that people naturally vary in their proneness towards these ways of being. Research within our team has shown that many people with anorexia tend to show a particular profile of *thinking styles*. Can you guess how this profile looks? Well, they tend, if anything, to have an acute atten-tion to detail at the expense of the bigger picture, and to be less flexible and thus find change or uncertain situations harder than most people.

This typical anorexia thinking style often goes hand in hand with a fear of making mistakes and a tendency to set very high standards for yourself. Can you relate to this profile of thinking styles? Research has also shown us that these traits become more extreme as individuals with anorexia lose weight, but on the positive side their thinking can 'free up' as they reach more normal weights. The important thing to keep in mind is that no profile is good or bad. It's more about whether your dominant thinking style suits the task at hand and whether you have the ability to move between thinking styles based on the needs of the task at hand. Research within our team has shown that under certain conditions rigidly following a limited set of thinking styles can contribute to the maintenance of anorexia. So the key here is for you to become curious and aware of your profile of *thinking styles* and to know when to turn it on and when to reign it in!

In this chapter, we will '*think more about thinking*'.

- We will talk about **how** rather than **what** you think, and what this means for you in different areas of your life: the challenges and the opportunities. We will look at the action tendencies associated with particular thinking styles.
- We will help you to broaden your repertoire of thinking styles so that you can choose the optimal thinking style appropriate for different contexts and situations.
- We will look at what circumstances make particular thinking styles more prominent and how to manage thinking styles that are unhelpful in certain contexts. Together, we will think about how to manage your environment to suit your personal traits.

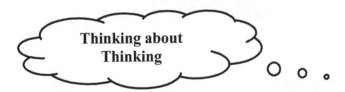

An introduction to thinking styles

Different people have different ways of thinking that we call 'thinking styles'. A person's thinking style tends to go with their personality traits and affect the way they behave or respond to situations (action tendencies).

For example, some people find it very easy to accommodate new information and switch between different ideas and concepts. These people are often keen to seek out new stimuli and are attracted to environments that provide these. They may also be the sort of people who can juggle many different tasks (multi-task). They may see changing circumstances and uncertain situations as exciting opportunities.

Others like to concentrate on one thing at a time, are slower to integrate new information and find it disruptive or overwhelming if they are interrupted or if they have to switch between tasks. These sorts of people may be very good at finishing things or 'seeing something through, no matter what'. These people may find new or changing situations hard.

Some people are good at seeing the bigger picture, whereas others are focused on detail.

Some people spend a long time doing things meticulously, whereas others are satisfied if things are 'good enough'.

We focus mainly on two aspects of thinking styles:

1 How easy you find it to switch between different thoughts, rules and tasks.
2 How detail focused you are.

As mentioned earlier, these thinking styles often go with a fear of making mistakes and having excessively high standards for yourself, and we will think about these things too.

These things are not related to your intelligence but have to do with how the 'wiring' in your brain organises incoming information.

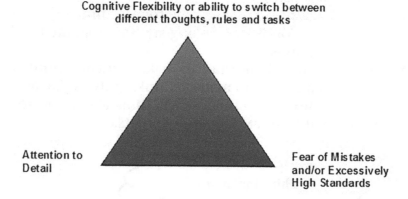

Cognitive Flexibility or ability to switch between different thoughts, rules and tasks

Attention to Detail

Fear of Mistakes and/or Excessively High Standards

One of our patients beautifully described something she learnt from this as **_zooming out_** _and watching myself doing things . . . and_ **_nipping myself in the bud_** _when I get carried away with all that detail._

TOP TIP: ZOOM OUT AND LOOK ON AT YOURSELF!

- 'Zooming out' and watching oneself doing things is a lovely way of describing the perspective we urge you to take during this chapter. Keep 'zooming out' and looking on at yourself in order to maintain a curious and reflective stance.
- Another helpful strategy can be to look on at other people you know who go about things differently to you. For example, perhaps you have a friend, partner or family member who isn't too bothered with details (maybe this niggles you sometimes!) but who has a wonderful capacity to capture the essence of something or to cut to the chase. Watch them for a week. See what differences you spot in their approach and yours. See if you can learn to 'nip yourself in the bud' when you get carried away!

Am I overly focused on detail at the expense of the bigger picture?

We are now going to invite you to take part in a fun set of activities to get you thinking about your thinking and to encourage you to learn about your dominant ways of being. Let's begin by having a think about your proneness to focusing on the detail at the expense of the bigger picture. Here is a rough and ready task to test this out.

Read a newspaper or magazine article that interests you and pull out two or three key points from the article that really matter to you (e.g. key events, key themes or key lessons learned):

1 _____

2 _____

3 _____

If you can do this easily, you are probably good at seeing the bigger picture, deciding on priorities, and letting the 'small print' be just that. If you have real difficulties with this task, you may be too focused on detail. Sometimes this can stop you from 'seeing the wood for the trees'.

Please have a look at the two pictures below.

- Did you see more than one image almost immediately?
- Were you able to switch between the images easily?

If you didn't find it easy to interchange between the images, do you think this also says something about your abilities to switch between different thoughts and tasks in your life, or how easy you find it to take different perspectives when thinking about a situation? (You can find more such pictures online, e.g. www.coolopticalillusions.com.)

The balance between speed and accuracy

With any task, there is usually a trade-off between speed and accuracy. Bear this in mind while completing the following task.

Look at the sets of lines and shapes shown overleaf and use a pen or pencil to mark the midpoint of each line or shape (exercise adapted from

Tchanturia, K. et al., Cognitive Remediation for Anorexia Nervosa. www.
national.slam.nhs.uk/wp-content/uploads/2014/04/Cognitive-remedia-
tion-therapy-for-Anorexia-Nervosa-Kate-Tchantura.pdf).

You must not use any tool to measure the shape or line; just give a
rough estimate of the midpoint. **Try not to miss any lines, but do
the task quickly!**

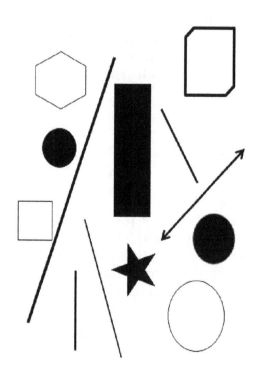

REFLECTION

1 Did doing it quickly go against your usual way of doing things?
2 Would you normally spend a lot of time over this kind of task and check repeatedly that you
   had done it right?
3 What have you learned from this task?

If you are someone who would normally spend a lot of time over this
kind of task and check repeatedly that you have it right, this may be due
to having a **fear of making mistakes** or having **very high standards for yourself** or both. In the following task, we will look some
more at what your personal thinking styles may be and think about the
implications of these for you in your life.

A thorough way of assessing your thinking styles is to take part in a
detailed neuropsychological assessment, and this is how thinking styles are
assessed for research studies. However, this isn't the only way. The following checklists may help you identify how these thinking styles might trip
you up in everyday life. Have a go and see what you discover about yourself.

Checklist 1: the impact of attention to detail on everyday life

(Remember there is a tendency to have more of a detail focus under times of stress and high emotion, so also think about those times.)

Life situation/problem	Tick here if you have noticed this	Rate how strongly you endorse this: 0 = not at all; 10 = very strongly
I depend on others to help me get things into perspective as I tend to have rather a blinkered view on things in my life		
I often feel vulnerable and unsafe as I am unable to see threats (or opportunities) that are out of my field of vision		
I have high levels of anxiety/discomfort as I can see/feel/hear/taste things that might not be quite right		
I can get very focused and persist on one particular aspect of a task or situation		
I tend to analyse potential problems in depth and focus on all the things that could go wrong		
If something goes wrong, I can't help dwelling on all the details of what happened		
I find it difficult to remember the story line in films, plays or books, but can remember specific scenes in detail		
Sometimes other people get frustrated as they think I am being pedantic		
If other people look upset, I usually assume it is because of something I have done		
I feel hurt if others do not remember to finish a message with a kiss or use a pet word		
I can get angry if people do not do things my way		
I have problems with time management (I take longer than expected with most tasks)		
I am often exhausted as I put in more time and effort with tasks than others do		
I spend the same amount of time on a task regardless of whether it is very important or not		

Life situation/problem	Tick here if you have noticed this	Rate how strongly you endorse this: 0 = not at all; 10 = very strongly
I have difficulty prioritising		
I may get hung up on details when reading rather than understanding the gist		
I need clarity and rules when facing a new situation; without rules, I easily feel lost		
I find it hard to write concisely; I often overrun word limits and then can't decide which details to leave out		
I have an eye for detail that others can miss		

REFLECTION

Having completed these questions, reflect on your answers using the following three questions:

1   Does my attention to detail create problems for me in certain situations?

  Yes ☐   **No** ☐   **Sometimes** ☐

2   Has this reduced my confidence in things and led to an increasingly restricted life?

  Yes ☐   **No** ☐   **Sometimes** ☐

3   Overall, has this worsened how I feel?

  Yes ☐   **No** ☐   **Sometimes** ☐

If you have answered **Yes** or **Sometimes** to all three questions, you may want to do some work on this area. The strength of your endorsement of particular items may help you figure out where to start.

Checklist 2: the impact of a difficulty in flexibility on everyday life

Life situation/problem	Tick here if you have noticed this	Rate how strongly you endorse this: 0 = not at all; 10 = very strongly
I get very distressed if plans get changed at the last minute		
I get upset if other people disturb my plans for the day by being late		

Life situation/problem	Tick here if you have noticed this	Rate how strongly you endorse this: 0 = not at all; 10 = very strongly
I find it difficult to go back to a job that requires concentration if I have been disturbed by a phone call		
I have difficulty starting when going back to a task that has been left unfinished for a time, but eventually get into it		
I find it difficult to do several things at once (multi-tasking)		
I like doing things in a particular order or routine		
I dislike change		
When others suggest a new way of doing things, I can get a bit anxious or unsettled		
I like to make plans about arrangements such as journeys or work projects, and get annoyed if they get disrupted		
I can be called single-minded or stubborn as it is difficult to shift from one point of view to another		
I find it difficult to see a different perspective in a specific situation		

REFLECTION

Having completed these questions, reflect on your answers using the following three questions:

1   Do my difficulties in being flexible or changing focus cause problems in my relationship with the world and other people?

   Yes ☐   **No** ☐   **Sometimes** ☐

2   Has this reduced my confidence in things and led to an increasingly restricted life?

   Yes ☐   **No** ☐   **Sometimes** ☐

3   Overall, has this worsened how I feel?

   Yes ☐   **No** ☐   **Sometimes** ☐

If you have answered **Yes** or **Sometimes** to all three questions, you may want to do some work on this area. The strength of your endorsement of particular items may help you figure out where to start.

Checklist 3: the impact of anxiety about making mistakes on your life

Life situation/problem:	Tick here if you have noticed	Rate how strongly you endorse this: 0 = not at all; 10 = very strongly
I take a longer time checking things than other people		
I am reluctant to raise my hand and ask questions in public in case I say the wrong thing		
I rarely take the lead in conversations		
I put off doing complex tasks because once I've started, I have to do it thoroughly and completing the task takes forever		
I try to avoid responding to problems or difficult situations until I have had the opportunity to think about it from all angles		
I dislike, and so avoid, speaking in public or performing complex tasks (e.g. dance routine, role play) when others can see		
I spend a long time remembering repeatedly a specific situation in which I think I could have done a mistake		
In a new situation I rather observe others' behaviours before doing anything		
I always like to get reassurance from other people that the things I have done or am planning to do are alright before delivering a final product or committing myself to a course of action		
I find it hard to be creative and tend to use other people's opinions and ideas for fear that my own may be wrong or incorrect		
I find it hard to be criticised		

REFLECTION

Having completed these questions, reflect on your answers using the following three questions:

1   Does my anxiety about making mistakes have an impact on my relationship with the world and other people?

    Yes ☐   **No** ☐   **Sometimes** ☐

2   Has this reduced my confidence in things and led to an increasingly restricted life?

    Yes ☐   **No** ☐   **Sometimes** ☐

3   Overall, has this worsened how I feel?

    Yes ☐   **No** ☐   **Sometimes** ☐

If you have answered **Yes** or **Sometimes** to all three questions, you may want to do some work on this area. The strength of your endorsement of particular items may help you figure out where to start.

Checklist 4: identifying excessively high standards impact on my life

Life situation/problem	Tick here if you have noticed this	Rate how strongly you endorse this 0 = not at all; 10 = very strongly
Always have to give my best, no matter what the task		
Am often exhausted because of giving it my all		
Others will come to me to sort things out because they know I will do the best job		
Even when I have given my best I do not feel satisfied and think I should have tried harder		
If I don't feel totally exhausted at the end of the day I feel I have been lazy		
Sometimes I get into trouble with others because I find it hard to hide my disapproval at their shoddy standards		

Life situation/problem	Tick here if you have noticed this	Rate how strongly you endorse this 0 = not at all; 10 = very strongly
Others rely on me to sort things out and sometimes take advantage of me		
I always keep my environment (home, work) neat and tidy		
I check things over and over again to make sure that I deliver the perfect product		
Before I go out I spend a long time checking my appearance and clothes to make sure I look immaculate		
If a dress has a tiny stain I will not wear it again, because it is spoilt		
I expect a great deal from myself		
People should always do their best		

REFLECTION

Having completed these questions, reflect on your answers using the following three questions:

1   Do my high standards create problems for me in certain situations?

    Yes ☐   **No** ☐   **Sometimes** ☐

2   Has this reduced my confidence in things and led to an increasingly restricted life?

    Yes ☐   **No** ☐   **Sometimes** ☐

3   Overall, has this worsened how I feel?

    Yes ☐   **No** ☐   **Sometimes** ☐

If you have answered **Yes** or **Sometimes** to all three questions, you may want to do some work on this area. The strength of your endorsement of particular items may help you figure out where to start.

What does your thinking style mean for you?

In the following figure, we display the traits of flexibility/focus (set shifting) and detail/bigger picture thinking as two dimensions. Perhaps you can plot where you are on this map based on your sense of yourself.

TOP TIP: SEEING THE WOOD FOR THE TREES!

- Sometimes we are so used to our way of being that we can't see the wood for the trees. If it's tricky to place yourself within the following figure, why don't you summarise to a trusted friend what you have learned about thinking styles so far. Try to make four key points (watch that attention to detail doesn't run away with itself if this is an issue for you!).
- Then, ask your friend to plot where they think you might be within the dimensions below. They could also plot themselves and then you could both have a discussion about how your profiles pan out in your daily lives.

Cognitive style summary

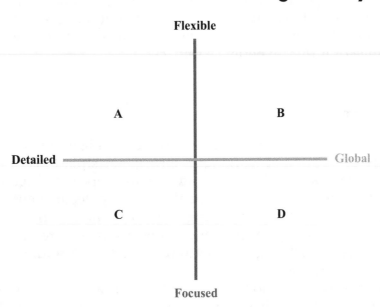

How do thinking styles play out in the world?

In the following examples, we describe some of the strengths and weaknesses associated with each of these quadrants. We look at their value for vocational function and their impact on social function. Have a read and see if you can relate.

Flexible and detailed

A person with this pattern of styles is good at using detail when needed. This is their default preference. However, such an individual is able to shift and take in other viewpoints or use other strategies. A shift to a bigger picture approach might take more effort and energy, but it is possible.

Vocation: People with this temperament can be good at jobs that require adjusting to uncertainty and change and yet require the ability to be analytical. For example, a person with such traits might work as a journalist: at times, it would be helpful for them to concentrate on detail, use analytical traits to follow a lead and track down clues. However, when it is time to write a report, they need to be able to paint a bigger picture and the headline must summarise the gist. Similarly, a surgeon could do well with these traits. Much of the job might involve an ability to zoom into the detail. However, if something goes wrong with the patient's physiology, the surgeon needs to be able to zoom out and step back and attend to the crisis in the overall condition of the patient.

Social: If the tendency to go for detail is taken to extremes it can be exhausting for the individual and for those around him. Pleasant conversational banter can be difficult, as the detail-oriented individual may persist in one focus. At times, they may seem pedantic as they cannot take up the gist of what another person may be signalling. However, such an individual can adjust well when plans change or if they experience setbacks.

Flexible and global

Vocation: If you can multi-task and see the bigger picture, you are likely to be good at working in emergency situations or any area where you have to think on your toes and cope with high pressure, e.g. busy reception areas or in the casualty department. You will find it easy in a complex, changing environment to triage risks and emergencies and prioritise tasks. However, if you are in a situation where you need to get something done very carefully and accurately, it may feel onerous and boring.

Social: A flexible and global individual may always want to be on the go doing new things. They may find many 'cultural' things such as theatre and cinema uninteresting. They may appear to others to be unreliable, disloyal and somewhat shallow if judged in a negative light, but in a positive context they can be seen as carefree and fun-loving.

Detailed and focused

Vocation: It might be useful and helpful to be very focused and analytical. Not changing your mindset or shifting your cognitive style or approach to tackling situations and problems can sometimes be beneficial, for example if you are someone who needs to examine data by searching for errors, or work with complex computer programs. If you are a fighter pilot or air traffic controller, it is important to spot anomalies and make detailed adjustments if necessary. You need to follow a set of rules and procedures and not stray from them whatsoever.

Social: Individuals with these traits may feel lost in the plot of stories or find it hard to follow some social conversations. Others may find some of the extreme expectations of detailed and focused individuals exhausting and their attention to detail and compulsive interests can appear pedantic and boring. On the other hand, individuals with these traits are usually loyal and reliable and get things done.

Global and focused

Vocation: This type of style might fit very well with artistic endeavours or teaching a class of students. For example, when directing a film or play or when making an installation it may be important to be able to conceptualise the whole and not get overly preoccupied with one element, but it is also important to be able to keep the eye and momentum fixed on where the direction of the project is going. These traits are also useful when teamwork is essential, such as in the Armed Forces. It can be easy to feel overwhelmed and anxious with this sort of style because good leadership skills are required to keep all elements moving towards the goal. Individuals with these traits can be good entrepreneurs.

Social: Others may get rebellious and see the fixed rigid position with an emphasis on following rules or a plan difficult. At times individuals with these traits can be seen as a bullying; on the other hand, individuals with these traits can be effective and get things done.

Here's how one of our male patients, Jake, found this chapter: *This chapter helped me understand that there can be a mixture of different ways of thinking and the pros/cons of these. There are also techniques to help . . . such as increasing my flexibility or decreasing my drive for perfection.*

REFLECTION

- In what ways is your profile of thinking styles working for you?
- In what ways is it making life hard sometimes?
- How does your profile of thinking styles affect your emotional world?

We continue to think about what your cognitive style means for you over the next few pages by looking at social situations.

Can you think how it might influence your social situations?

Your relationship with other people

Strong detail focus

If you really think about it, meandering our social world is heavily influenced by our thinking styles. The social worlds we choose to enter are influenced by our cognitive ways of being, as is what we take away from social interactions and how they make us feel. For one thing, your relationship with people can be difficult if you see the world in a different way from others.

Most people score highly on global function. People with high global functioning can get very frustrated with tasks where it is essential to focus on small details, such as proofreading a lengthy piece of written work. They just cannot see what people with a high detail focus see. As a result, they may get irritated and cross with your detail focus when in fact you are just doing things as you see them.

It is as if you are going round with the camera on zoom rather than widescreen. You are seeing the world as if it is a technical drawing, whereas the rest of the world sees it as an impressionist painting. It may not be just your visual perception that acts in this way, but all of your senses: touch, taste, smell and sound.

Sometimes your detail focus may get you into conflict with others. Things that devastate and really upset you can be unimportant to others. Your tendency to think over and over again on a detail may make others impatient or frustrated. In turn, you may be angry if a loved one misses an 'X' from the end of their text to you. You expect others to be able to see and do things the right (i.e. your) way.

You may find perceptions that are too intense (loud noise, strong smells and flavours, high emotions) overwhelming and unpleasant. This may make you say 'no' or avoid many things in life rather than going with the flow. You may be so exhausted attending to each detail that you withdraw from other people. This can alienate you and make you lonely, creating a sense of emptiness.

People with high-functioning autism or Asperger's syndrome also see the world in this fragmented, intense way. You may find books written by and about people with Asperger's interesting to see how they can learn to cope and optimise relationships. We provide a selection of books at the end of the chapter that you might find helpful, but there are many others you may come across which give you pause to reflect.

Limited flexibility

If you have a focused approach to life, this can make you somewhat rigid compared with others. You may be unhappy to break your routines and rules and change plans. Others will depend on your planning ability, reliability and loyalty.

However, if you get upset, it is difficult to stand back and 'look at' rather than 'be in' the emotion. This can lead you to do and say things you regret later. This can make others rather wary of you and keep their distance at times.

How do high standards and a fear of making mistakes fit in with these thinking styles?

Excessively high standards

You may always put your work before your friends and family, and this can create tensions. You may try to have 'perfect relationships', endlessly trying to please/give to others and not allowing yourself to have any needs or demands. You may try so hard to always do the right thing and aspire for moral virtue that others see you as rather 'preachy' or 'sitting on a high horse'. You may strive so hard to be better, cleverer or more hard-working than others that it is hard for them to relax in your presence.

Fear of mistakes

An intense fear of making mistakes can lead to the person developing a restricted life and becoming dependent on others to feel safe and help them make decisions. They may procrastinate and not get on with projects, tasks or meetings because they are frightened of what could go wrong. A person's detail focus often gets recruited to reduce the likelihood of making any mistakes. For example, the person may feel they have to check every piece of work multiple times or make endless plans trying to anticipate any potential problem or mistake, and exhaust themselves in the process. They may dwell on any mistake or social gaffe and see this as a catastrophe.

How do these thinking styles impact on your life, work and friendships?

By now, you will have some idea of what your personal thinking style might be and have identified that each different style has its own strengths and weaknesses in various environments. It might be useful to think now about how your style fits in with your individual life and relationships with others.

- How do your thinking styles affect your various life roles as partner, parent or peer?
- How do they affect your thoughts, behaviour, feelings and physical state?

Use the grid below to jot down how you think your style impacts in your life.

Before you start, you might find it helpful to think about the example of Jane given below:

JANE'S STORY

Jane is in her early thirties. She has had an eating disorder since age 18. Jane worked in IT. She was strongly supported by her boss who was her mentor, and through his support, she was promoted to be on the board of management. She found this much more difficult, and she became particularly anxious when her boss was asked to leave after a takeover. Her eating symptoms deteriorated and her relationship with her partner broke up.

Jane had a detailed neuropsychological assessment before her therapy for anorexia began. Her neuropsychological assessment showed that Jane had a high degree of detail focus and, on discussion, it emerged that she set extremely high standards for herself. After the feedback session and completing the checklists above, Jane was able to draw up a list of pros and cons of her detail focus and high standards in her life.

Relationships with others	Education, career and role
Thoughts	**Behaviour**
Feelings	**Physical state**

TOP TIP: REMEMBER TO KEEP ZOOMING OUT!

- Remember that you need to shift perspective in order to explore thinking styles, you will need to 'look on' at your usual ways of doing and approaching things. This is not easy. One way to help with this can be to gather the help of a supportive other to help you gain this new perspective.

Jane's list of pros and cons for her thinking style

Pros ➡	Cons
Doing everything to **perfection**	Problems with **time management**
Precision	**Exhausted**
Focus	**Depend on others** as blinkered life view
Persistent	**Vulnerable,** unsafe, unable to see threats (or opportunities) that are out of field of vision
Single minded	**Anxious**
Heightened perceptions, emotion, etc.	**Black/white thinking**
Systematic	**Catastrophic thinking**
Good at remembering names, numbers, **detailed information**	**Obsessive,** compulsive focus
Able to **analyse a situation** in its individual parts, and so come quickly to the heart of any problem	**Difficulty in remembering the story line** especially in films and books
Good at seeing similarities and detecting differences	**Limited creativity**
Consistent, reliable, and dependable	**Difficulty making connections** between related issues or information
Being thorough, accurate and precise	Difficulty getting a balanced view of the whole, often focusing on one aspect of a situation so it becomes out of proper proportion and other aspects are ignored

Jane began to pick out the pros and cons of her thinking style in her life

- Jane recognised that her detail focus had made her very good in her job in IT systems. However, she began to realise that colleagues who had made mistakes were able to let it wash over them and carry on as if nothing much had happened. She put in a great deal of effort to make sure she never made mistakes and would have been mortified to deliver a less than perfect product at work.

- She did not find it easy to generate new ideas or think strategically. However, she was able to work up an idea when she was given one, although she found it anxiety provoking without support.
- She acknowledged that the opportunity of having a boss who was very supportive of her had allowed her to flourish. She understood why she had to compensate in her present situation with a new boss who was less directly involved with her. She also realised that when she was promoted to be on the board, it meant that she was outside her comfort zone in terms of skills and abilities.

Jane started to work with her therapist to develop the ability to stand back and see the bigger picture. Here is how Jane filled out the grid:

Relationships with others	Education, career and role
Let down when others do not do what I expect/ have planned for them to do. E.g. plan date Thursday rather Saturday; insist that plans are made in detail; stick to itinerary for every day's activities on holiday.	Focus is great and useful when following plan for IT systems. Difficult to generate new ideas. Find change very difficult.
Thoughts	Behaviour
Life planned in detail 3–7 days in advance, what to wear, when to wash hair, etc.	It's as if my body rebels to get a pleasure fix, e.g. binge food.
Feelings	Physical state
Feel ignored as cannot fit easily with other's plans. No time for joy in the moment or ability to go with a flow of wellbeing, creativity, etc.	Not thought about – ignored.

REFLECTION

- How do your thinking styles play out in your social world?
- In what domains do they work well for you?
- In what domains are they tricky or non-optimal?

How to make the most of your hand

The metaphor of a game of cards such as bridge can be helpful. People who are able to approach the game of life playing suits in which they have strengths and accepting that for some games they have weakness and may need to work strategically with a partner, do better than those who want to be perfect and win each round in isolation as they go 'solo'.

Sticking to your usual game plan – help or Hindrance?

We are all creatures of habit to some extent. Habits, routines, rules, doing things always in a particular way or order, at a particular time, and keeping things in a particular place in your home or at work can be tremendously helpful. Habits and routines allow us mentally to go on autopilot. This makes life manageable and predictable, reduces time and mental energy spent searching for things or deciding about options, and can reduce anxiety and uncertainty or chaos.

However, people with a less flexible thinking and detail-focused thinking styles are usually more dependent on habits than others and there can be downsides. Rigid rules or habits can get in the way of new opportunities and experiences; they may isolate people and lock them into eternal boredom and shrinking horizons; they may make relationships go stale; and when habits or routine are disrupted (illness, injury, loss, etc.) the individual may end up very upset. Take for example a child trained to a very particular rigid bedtime routine, which culminates in him hugging a very particular teddy bear. If that teddy bear suddenly is lost, all hell breaks loose.

It may be that you need to adapt and take on different skills or work in conjunction with those with other skills in order to fit more comfortably with your environment and the other people in your life.

Before we begin thinking about developing your skills, look at the following tables and reflect on the pros and cons of your thinking styles. Think about which skills you might want to strengthen.

Detailed, analytical vs. global, big-picture thinking

1   How does your eye for detail (or whichever bias you have) manifest itself? Can you give specific examples at work, in learning, in relationships, at home, at play, with the family? What about your other perceptions such as taste, smell, sound, touch?

2   How does your eye for detail manifest itself with eating or with body shape?

3   What are the pros and cons of having an eye for detail (in general and over the life story)?

4   What are the roots of this trait (do other family members show this trait, were you encouraged in this trait in your early environment, etc.)?

5   What are the pros and cons of the other side of the coin – the tendency to see the bigger picture? Can you do this too? Do you have close others who can do this?

Multi-tasking vs. focused attention

1   How do your strengths in focused attention or weakness in multi-tasking manifest themselves – at work, in learning, in relationships, at home, at play, with the family?

2   How does your single-minded focus manifest itself with eating or with body shape?

3   What are the pros and cons of having a single-minded focus (in general and over the life story)?

4   What are the roots of this trait (do other family members show this trait, were you encouraged in this trait in your early environment, etc.)?

5   What are the pros and cons of the other side of the coin – the tendency to be flexible and adaptable, and see the bigger picture? Can you do this too? Do you have close others who can do this?

High standards and anxiety about making mistakes

1   How do your high standards and/or your anxiety about making mistakes manifest – at work, in learning, in relationships, at home, at play, with the family?

2   How do your high standards and/or your anxiety about making mistakes manifest themselves with eating or with body shape?

3   What are the pros and cons of having high standards and/or being more anxious about making mistakes (in general and over the life story)?

4   What are the roots of these traits (do other family members show this trait, were you encouraged in this trait in your early environment, etc.)?

5   What are the pros and cons of the other side of the coin – the tendency to allow yourself to be good enough rather than perfect, be carefree and more confident? Can you do this too? Do you have close others who can do this?

REFLECTION

1   What is the balance between your ability to focus and not make mistakes with your ability to be flexible, adaptable and quick, and to make do with good enough rather than perfect?
2   What is the balance between your ability to go for detail and to analyse events, perceptions and thoughts, and your ability to see the bigger picture and synthesise these elements?

Strengthening your skills

The facts about toning up your brain

One step toward making the most of your thinking styles is to get used to 'zooming out' and giving awareness to your thinking style profile. You can start to shape your environments to better suit your ways of being. Or you can simply note when your ways of tackling things might be making more work or stress for you, and notice this and understand it rather than beat yourself up for it. But can thinking styles change? Can we cultivate our less dominant thinking styles? In a nutshell, you will probably always lean towards your dominant ways of being, but that's not to say with some conscious retraining and practice you can't sharpen your less dominant thinking styles. This could be fun!

First, let's give a little care and consideration to that organ that manages us day in and day out: the brain. Did you know that our brain is a hungry organ needing several hundred calories in running costs?

The brain is constantly working and developing. It is never too late to learn. Exercising the brain can improve mental fitness, just as exercising the body can improve physical fitness.

The brain is a highly 'plastic' organ and is shaped by how we use it; the more you use it in diverse ways, the more new neurons and networks flourish. Stress and poor nutrition put a strain on this process. As the saying goes, 'use it or lose it'.

You need to optimise your health and wellbeing before brain growth can occur. Once you have started attending to your body's basic nutritional needs, think of ways in which you can tone up your mind. You may need to work hard at first and put in lots of practice. As with all things, it does get easier.

As we have discussed, for people with anorexia, toning up your mind usually means practice to become:

- Flexible
- Able to see the whole picture rather than being hooked on a detail
- Learning to allocate an appropriate amount of time and energy for the task in hand
- Learning to be good enough rather than strive for perfection at all costs.

If you reflect on your thinking style self-assessment, you may realise what exercises will encourage your thinking to be toned up and fit for any purpose.

Here are some basic ideas:

If you:	Then you might want to:
Strongly endorsed many of the items on the attention to detail checklist	Ensure that you can zoom out to the bigger picture
Strongly endorsed many of the items on the difficulties with flexibility checklist	Practice flexibility and breaking rules, routines and habits
Are slower on tasks than most other people	Practice balancing your resources of time and energy with the demands of the task
Strongly endorsed having excessively high standards and/or being frightened of making mistakes	Practice being good enough rather than perfect and taking mistakes in your strides

The following exercises are designed to help you tone up the thinking areas which are less easy for you, strengthening your skills in these areas.

Strengthening bigger picture thinking

Read the following ideas and tick any that you are willing to have a go at:

- Practice by using images, diagrams, flow charts, mind maps, bullet points, or newspaper-style headlines to synthesise your thoughts, memories, feelings and perceptions and reflect the bigger picture.
- Read a newspaper and summarise an article from it in one or two sentences.
- Start by telling a friend about something that has happened to you today using only 15–20 words. Try to get to the point where you can easily limit your text messages to less than 10 words and limit emails to one to five sentences.
- Listen to what others are saying and try to summarise the gist of what they are saying.
- Watch/listen to a TV/radio programme or read a book and describe in three sentences what the programme/book was about.
- Visualise how you want your life map to appear. Think in terms of physical and psychological health, connections with partner, friends, family, citizenship and the world, etc.
- In five short bullet points, describe what you imagined your life would be when you were a child, or what your current life looks like, looking back from an older, wiser self.
- Think back to goals and ideals that you had in the past. How would you like these to evolve in the future?
- Try to step back from the detail and see the bigger picture every day in each domain of your life at work: when learning, in relationships, at home, at play, with the family, when eating. Try to make a note at the end of each day of the bigger picture of the day's events.
- Keep on the lookout for and note down as many examples as you can spot of other people taking a bigger picture rather than a detailed approach.
- Rank all the things that have consumed your physical and psychological energy last week. Next to each one, write the percentage of your total energy pool it used. Then ask yourself, 'In the grand scheme of my life, how important is each of these things to me?' and write their percentage importance. Look at the two percentages you've given each thing: how similar are your rankings of importance and energy allocation?

TOP TIP

- Be prepared to be out of your comfort zone: start small and work up.
- Particularly if you are very much at an extreme on one or more of the thinking styles, trying to challenge this well-practiced way of being might feel rather like writing with your left hand if you're right-hand dominant! You might feel anxious, exposed and awkward – like you want to run right back towards your usual way of doing things! We urge you to trust the process and to begin small, perhaps by noting the behaviours of people with different thinking styles to you and then gradually working up to trying out new ways of being.
- Watch the tendency to become self-critical. Make a note if that inner voice kicks in to say 'you can't do this' or 'this is silly'. Just notice that voice, pop it on the chair next to you and carry on regardless!

Once you have tried some of these, you could start to think about the bigger picture in relation to your food and nutrition and also how you think about your body and weight. This will be particularly important if you are the sort of person who weighs themselves multiple times a day or spends a lot of time checking different parts of their body. This unhelpful focus on detail helps keep the person locked into their illness. Research has shown that people with eating disorders spend more time looking at the parts of their body that they like least compared to their most liked body parts. However, when they look at other people, they spend more time looking at the other person's best features. People without an eating disorder do the opposite. This means people with an eating disorder judge themselves harshly and unfairly. So, next time you are drawn to checking the size of your thighs, zoom out and think of what is the bigger picture here.

TOP TIP

- Ask yourself – what is the bigger picture here? Will anyone else notice? Will it matter to them? What are the aspects of your body that you do like? Is anorexia simply playing tricks on you? Is there a kinder and more compassionate way of thinking about yourself? You could also make a plan as to how to gradually reduce unhelpful weighing and body checking.

Life lesson

It is impossible to have an encyclopaedic knowledge of the world and people in it. You need to be able to be able to extract the gist so that you are not overwhelmed by an information overload. A work assignment or academic course is not only valuable for its final mark, but also in the transferable skills – what you have learned along the way that will be useful for you in your life's journey.

Strengthening flexibility

Read the following ideas and tick any that you are willing to have a go at:

- Try to implement some 'planned flexibility' into your life. Go through the script of your day and think about what you can do differently. For example, change your morning or night-time routine, or try out a different route to college or work.
- Become a rule breaker. Each day, try to make a small change in your behaviour in each domain of your life: at work, when learning, in relationships, at home, at play, with the family, with eating. Some people start by challenging themselves to cope with chance (e.g. set up tasks related to the throw of a die or opening sealed envelopes).
- Note situations that could be described or perceived differently depending on your perspective (news, opinions, etc.).
- Try to understand the viewpoints of other people. Maybe you can fill in the six areas of the life grid to describe what was going on in the minds and bodies of a friend or family member during some recent interaction with you. (If you are also trying to strengthen bigger picture thinking, try to use one sentence for each domain.)

Relationships with others	Education, career and role
Thoughts	Behaviour
Feelings	Physical state

- Keep on the lookout for and note down as many example as you can spot of other people being flexible.
- Multi-task on gardening or cleaning the house.
- When you tidy or clean, leave one area for next time.
- Try out a new leisure activity, e.g. go to an exhibition you normally would not normally go to or see a film in a genre that you would not normally choose.
- Read something that you would not normally consider. It doesn't matter whether it's an obscure book or a trashy magazine.
- Select a TV programme you have never watched, switch channels on the spur of the moment or start listening to the radio.
- Shop for a novel item not related to food (stationery, flowers, bubble bath, candles, a new CD).
- Sit in a different place from where you usually sit. This could be at mealtimes or in the lounge, just anywhere other than your habitual place to sit.
- Change around a small item of furniture or lamp in your room.
- Explore a new street, public park or other recreational facility in your local area.
- Choose a different ringtone on your phone.
- If working with text on the computer a lot, select a different font for the day.

Once you have tried some of these, you might think about how to introduce more flexibility into your relationship with food, eating and your body and appearance.

TOP TIP

- If you have lots of different rules and routines about when to eat, where to eat, the dishes you use, what to eat, what foods to combine and so forth, make a list of them and see how many there are. People are often surprised to see how long their list is, how much it has grown since anorexia came into their life and how these rules keep them locked into anorexia. Some of these rules may be helpful rules (e.g. 'always start your day with a breakfast'), but many will be directly related to anorexia and be rigid, arbitrary and unhelpful. Rank these rules in terms of how difficult they will be to break. In tackling these rules, it will again be important to start small and to try not to be self-critical or impatient. Breaking engrained rules and routines takes courage, time and consistency.
- As you are gathering momentum with breaking unhelpful eating and food-related rules, you may also want to think about establishing one or two overarching and more flexible rules governing your food intake. For example, 'until I am back to a healthy weight I will have at least two snacks a day in addition to my meals' or 'I will only weigh myself once a week to gauge my progress'.

Life lesson

There are many routes from A to B. Remember, life is a journey and it consists of many small steps. Listening to others, getting them to help or working as a team can produce more creative and successful outcomes. We live in a world where there are few certainties, and so being able to absorb and react to change is a useful skill.

Strengthening being 'good enough'

Read the following ideas and tick any that you are willing to have a go at:

- Think about your standards. Do you always give at least 200%? What about your fear of making mistakes. Is it realistic? What would friends and family say about these aspects of you? Is this all rather out of proportion, making you procrastinate, or slowing you down because it has to be perfect without any mistake?
- Start something that you have been avoiding for fear of not doing it well enough. See how you are getting on.
- Halve the amount of time you take to do your hair or put your make-up on.
- Halve the amount of time you take to tidy your room.
- Only check something you've written once, e.g. text, letter, email, report.
- Do something spontaneous, such as inviting friends over on the spur of the moment rather than for a perfectly planned evening.
- Find out more information and reflect on this by reading one of the books on perfectionism that are listed at the end of this chapter.

Once you have tried some of these, you might think about trying to be good enough with your eating, your appearance and your exercise routine.

TOP TIP

- If you are someone who exercises a lot as part of your eating disorder and you subject yourself to punishing routines where you drive yourself on relentlessly, try to give yourself some days off from this, or on a daily basis do slightly less than you would like to do.

Life lesson

Error-free learning or working is pretty impossible, unless you are learning much less than your full potential or working much more slowly than you should. In order to be creative and stretch yourself, you need to step beyond your comfort zone and take safe risks. Remember the motto: 'Every mistake is a treasure'.

Strengthening general skills

Problem solving

As we have seen, your thinking style can influence your life and behaviour in a variety of ways. A final thing to think about might be how your thinking style affects your ability to solve problems.

For example

- It can be hard to solve problems if you are so focused on the detail that you cannot see the overall context.
- It is also hard to solve problems if you have a set of rules about how to do things and do not find it easy to change to new rules.
- It is hard to solve problems if you avoid taking any risk.

Therefore, you need to make a special effort to work on problems and difficulties. This takes several steps.

1 Step back – look at the bigger picture; **what is the problem** you should prioritise in your life?
2 **Break the problem down and make a list of all the different parts**.

   Have you looked at the wider context of the problem and from multiple perspectives so that you know what the problem really is?
   What does it actually consist of?
   Are there separate components you can tackle one at a time?
   Make sure that you are not overly focused on a small detail that you can see, but is irrelevant to others.

3 **Think about how others would see the problem**.

a How would someone who could see all perspectives set about solving the problem? What solutions would they come up with? In order to implement these solutions, what sort of things would have to happen first?
b How would a wise person (or committee) who could oscillate between being flexible and focused and attending to detail and seeing the bigger picture solve the problem? What would their plan be?

4 Plan to **practice these wise solutions** in small steps.
5 **Reflect on the bigger picture** from time to time: to what extent do you think you are getting closer to solving the problem?
6 If what you tried did not work as well as you would have liked, what would be the new ways of working it through? **Be flexible, change the rules**!

REFLECTION

- Reflect on two ways in which your thinking styles directly fuel your anorexia.
- Allow yourself to be a rule breaker.
- Remember the bigger picture, and if in doubt, zoom out.
- Consider sharing these new ways of being and self-reflections with a trusted friend or family member.

Further reading

Perfectionism and obsessive compulsive behaviours

Anthony, M.M. & Swinson, R.P. (1998). *When Perfect Isn't Good Enough: Strategies for Coping with Perfectionism*. Oakland: New Harbinger Publications.

This book is clearly written and contains many ideas. It has a specific chapter on dieting and body image.

Shafran, R., Egan, S. & Wade, T. (2010). *Overcoming perfectionism: A self-help guide using scientifically supported behavioural techniques*. Robinson, London.

Hyman, B.M. & Pedrick, C. (2005). *The OCD Workbook* (2nd edition). Oakland, CA: New Harbinger Publications.

Veale, D. & Wilson, R. (2005). *Overcoming Obsessive Compulsive Disorder*. London: Robinson.

Asperger's syndrome

People with Asperger's also tend to be great at picking up detail. This can lead to problems in social relationships because they may expect too much of others. They can be too honest and literal and not recognise the role of white lies and negotiating a solution. Also, too high anxiety can cause friction in interpersonal relationships. These books illustrate some of these problems.

Haddon, M. (2004). *The Curious Incident of the Dog in the Night-Time: Adult Edition*. Vintage Books, London, UK.

We have had several people with anorexia nervosa tell us that this story resonates with how they see the world.

Tammet, D. (2007). *Born on a Blue Day: A Memoir of Asperger's and an Extraordinary Mind*. Hodder and Stoughton, London, UK.

This is an autobiography of someone with Asperger's who has immense skills in learning languages and remembering numbers. He writes about how he has been able to negotiate his pathway through life to attain a state of equilibrium.

Boyd, B. (2003). *Parenting a Child with Asperger Syndrome*. London: Jessica Kingsley.
This is written to help children with Asperger's as children, but it is wonderfully clear and well written and might give you some ideas.

Chapter 9

Identity

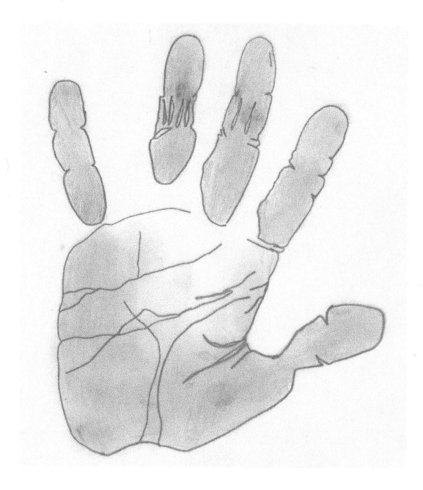

Here's how Amber, one of our patients, found this chapter: *The identity chapter was the most helpful for me. This is because it helped me to finally make-up my mind that recovery was what I truly wanted and life became 'good' again. I started by reflecting on who I wanted to be by listing features . . . For instance, I wished I was strong and confident in myself. Instead of harshly berating and punishing myself for my flaws and mistakes, I wished I could just be OK with it and just learn from the experience. I also wished I could be like one of those kind of people who manage to be happy even in the*

darkest times and support others with their brightness and optimism. I then thought about some inspirational individuals and explored why one in particular inspired me.

Anorexia and my identity

As you begin to turn a corner in regard your anorexia and recognise longings to get more from life, you might find yourself wondering: 'But who will I be without anorexia?' 'What will be left?' 'How will I cope if anorexia is not there?' A sense of fragility around one's identity can maintain anorexia – better to stick with the devil you know than to risk not knowing. This can be especially the case if anorexia was rife at a time when identity naturally evolves (i.e. during adolescence) or if you have had anorexia for a long time such that life has reduced to a point where anorexia is the biggest constant in life. It can also feel terrifying if one of the functions of your anorexia is to squash feelings, and this is because change necessarily involves some degree of uncertainty and upheaval. It can feel a big leap of faith to loosen one's grip on old coping methods and to begin to trust in new ways of being.

One of the things we have heard over and over from people who go on to recover from anorexia is that a tipping point arrives when they realise they want something else more than they want anorexia. Lucy desperately wanted to make it to university to study design. She knew she had a real talent and she knew she had a make-or-break summer ahead of her to get herself well enough to go, otherwise she would change the course of her life in a way she knew she would one day regret. Rhia had a wake-up call when a friend of hers died young. She had a glimpse of the fragility of life and of time passing quickly followed by a surge in her sense of wanting more from life. She looked on at herself and her situation; she decided that enough was enough and that she no longer wanted to be ruled by anorexia. Rhia for the first time boldly asked for help; she embarked on psychological therapy with a genuine commitment and motivation; and with the support of her therapist she went on to recover. Alan, a man in his twenties, had battled with body image worries and urges to restrict for a very long time, until along came his baby daughter. Alan longed to be a positive role model for this little girl; he wanted her to look up to him and to be proud of him. Someone had come along for Alan who was more important than anorexia, and this reshuffled his priorities and made getting well top of that list.

Please don't think that any of these people found recovery plain sailing – far from it. There were ups and downs and setbacks along the way, but all of them went on to recover and all of them told us that they preferred their life free from anorexia. They all set their sights on something bigger and better than anorexia, something that would not or could not be the same while anorexia was around. These types of goals can mark turning points in your journey.

REFLECTION

- Step out from your anorexia for a moment and have a think about what for you is more important than anorexia. This could be an ambition, a life goal or a relationship; it could be to align yourself more with a core value or principle you hold.
- If this is tough to think about, fast-forward to picturing yourself in retirement. What will you be talking to your grandchildren about? What do you want to have been the defining moments, achievements and relationships in your life? Or if your retirement seems too far away, think about your next big birthday. What would you like people to say about you on that day, about the kind of person you are, how they see you, what they like about you and how you have affected them?

During this chapter, we will encourage you to begin to be curious and creative about the 'you' beyond anorexia, those sides of you keen for a chance to be heard and to get some of the goodies from life. If anorexia is still a big feature of your identity, we will encourage you to put your anorexia aside for now and to be curious about your needs, wants and wishes beyond this side of you. If you are on the road to recovery, perhaps you have started to become aware of some longings, or interests, but perhaps engaging with this feels precarious and scary. We will encourage you to be **bold**, to be **curious** and to **have a go**!

TOP TIP

- Go back to Chapter 2, 'Getting Started'. Did you write a letter from the future without anorexia? If so, are there any hints in there as to what your flourishing self beyond anorexia might look like? If you haven't written this letter, do so now.
- Likewise, go back to Chapter 7, 'The Emotional and Social Mind'. Have you previously written a letter to the hidden parts of yourself? If so, are there any pointers in there as to parts of you that you would like to develop more? Try to hear the longings; try to feel the pull for new beginnings. If you haven't done this letter, do so now.

The way we think about it is that many people who have had anorexia for a long time find that their true identity has been submerged as anorexia becomes their defining characteristic. It is almost as though their authentic self is squashed by the values of anorexia. We use the adjectives 'submerged' and 'squashed' because for many people we have met, that is what it feels like. For others there is truly a sense of not knowing who they are without anorexia. This can be the case if your anorexia started very early in life. We have never met anyone who went on to get well from anorexia who didn't eventually flourish in regard to their identity. In fact, many people recovered from anorexia evolved into quite amazing people! Coping with, surviving and beating an illness in itself creates resilience, growth and new strengths. The person may have feared that there would be nothing there, but it was more a case of trusting the process of rediscovery, of getting back in touch with their core self and/or of daring to step beyond their comfort zone to let their healthy flourishing self begin to grow. If you let yourself go a little, this could be exciting!

OK, now let's think about what anorexia does to your identity:

- The following figure is one way of representing anorexia's domination of identity.

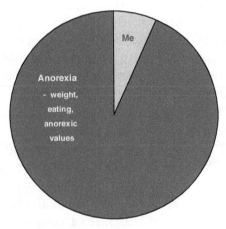

- Once a person's identity has re-emerged and had a chance to develop beyond anorexia, with time it may be represented more like below, with the different components of your life having blossomed.

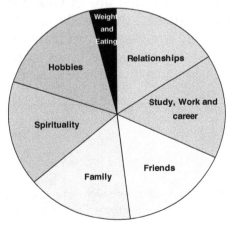

- Grab a piece of paper and sketch out your own identity pie chart, perhaps of when your anorexia was at its worst and another for how things look now.

- Consider asking a good friend or family member to either talk to you about or even better to write you a letter about *all the sides of you they love and miss and would like to have more time with*. If you dare, ask them to read this aloud to you.

REFLECTION

- How has anorexia affected your identity? Which parts of you have been squashed by anorexia?
- What have others missed about you? Which parts of you would they love to spend more time with?
- How does it feel thinking about your non-anorexic identity? What feelings does it bring up for you?

Getting to know the 'me' beyond anorexia

It might not be easy to imagine the 'you' beyond anorexia. Anorexia can be a very dominating beast! We just ask you to commit to learning one or two new things about your non-anorexic side which might then act as a springboard to you going on to find out lots more, when you feel ready.

In Chapter 2, 'Getting Started', we encouraged you to get an image of your anorexic side and your non-anorexic side. We will be using and elaborating these images during this chapter. Don't worry if these images have gone from your mind or indeed have changed since you worked through that chapter. As your relationship with anorexia changes, we would expect your images to ebb and flow and to evolve.

So we'd like you to begin by closing your eyes and getting an image of your anorexia side. Use the following prompts to guide you:

- What do you see? What are the physical characteristics of your anorexia, how big or small is this side of you; what is its colour, shape and texture?
- Try to put some language to the qualities of this side of you. What sort of character is your anorexia? What are the motives of this side of you?
- When you are in touch with this side of you, how do you feel? What are the feeling qualities (if any) that go along with your anorexic side?
- Are there any associated images or even real memories that you link with this side of you? Are there any times from the past or present that have the same tone and qualities as this side of you?

REFLECTION

- Has your image of anorexia changed from the image you had at the beginning (Chapter 2)? In what ways?
- Are there any ways in which your relationship with your anorexia image has changed? How do you feel towards your anorexia? Has it softened or evolved at all?

So now we'd like you to close your eyes and get an image of your non-anorexia side; we are going to call this side your healthy flourishing self. This includes two components: first, elements of the you that was there before anorexia and that houses personal qualities, likes and dislikes, and strengths and talents that were submerged by anorexia; and second, parts of you that you would like to build and develop to become the best possible version of yourself. Use the following prompts to guide you:

- What do you see? What are the physical characteristics of your healthy flourishing self? How big or small is this side of you? What is its colour, shape and texture? Does this side of you smile or frown? Is this side of you faint or bold? Does this side of you like the seaside or snowy mountains?
- Try to put some language to the qualities of your healthy flourishing self. What are your core values? What is your favourite film? What last made you smile? What annoys you? What do you long for? Try not to dismiss anything as too small or trivial.
- When you are in touch with this side of you, how do you feel? Do you notice any seeds of excitement? Do you notice fear or longing? Try to welcome all feelings.
- Are there any associated images or even real memories that you link with this side of you? When was your healthy flourishing self last in the driving seat? What were you doing and how were you feeling? Any times from the past or present that have the same tone and qualities as this side of you?

REFLECTION

- Has your image of your healthy flourishing self changed from the image you had at the beginning (Chapter 2)? In what ways?
- Are there any ways in which this side of you has changed or developed? How do you feel towards your healthy flourishing self? Has it grown or changed in tone or quality?

Especially if you have had anorexia for a long time, it can be difficult at first to gather a clear sense of a healthy flourishing self. It might be helpful to stand back a little, consider people you like and value and who get what they want from life. This might include well-known figures, characters from a book or film, but also ordinary people who have values and ways of being and relating that you look up to and long for. Who comes to mind? Perhaps you have or had a role model at some stage in life who guided you or nurtured you – a fairy godmother of sorts. Does anyone come to mind?

Close your eyes and let your mind wander a little.

- Who comes to mind when you think of someone who has really made a go of life, someone who lives life in a **meaningful** and **nourishing** way?
- Someone who can be **happy** and **content**, but someone who can also **accept** and tolerate negative emotions.

- Someone who has good relationships and who holds principles you admire. Someone who is their own person.
- Jot down the names of two or three such people in the space below (you could even paste in a photo or magazine clipping).
  Remember they may be people you know personally, well-known people, figures from fiction, or examples of both. The people you choose may be quite similar to each other or they may be very different. They are likely to have good and not so good attributes.

- ....

- ....

- ....

- ....

It is important to remember that people are different and no one is perfect (that would be dull). Instead we are all a mix of qualities and human failings that ebb and flow and evolve with time. Even these people who you like and respect have both strengths and weaknesses and their personalities are not static.

If you think about the people you admire, what different strengths do they have? What are the qualities they have that make them special to you?

Qualities of those I admire

-
-
-

Again, thinking of these people, what struggles do they have? What aspects of their personalities sometimes trip them up? What strategies do they have to cope with these?

Struggles of those I admire and coping strategies

-
-
-
-
-

Values

By virtue of the fact that you chose these people, they are special and meaningful to you in some way. They hold qualities that intrigue you.

- What values do you imagine are important to these individuals?
- What are the principles that guide their lives?

Have a look at the list of values in Chapter 2 and jot down the top five values you think might be important to **the people you admire**. What do you guess would be their least important five values?

Least important to people I admire	Most important to people I admire
1 _____	1 _____
2 _____	2 _____
3 _____	3 _____
4 _____	4 _____
5 _____	5 _____

Try to imagine that your anorexia has been put to one side such that your healthy self has flourished for a few years. Imagine yourself five years from now, when you are well. What values do you think this future self would hold?

Some values you already hold you may wish to make part of your future life.

Least important to my future self	**Most important to my future self**
1 _____	1 _____
2 _____	2 _____
3 _____	3 _____
4 _____	4 _____
5 _____	5 _____

TOP TIP

- Keep in mind that there are forces at work that move us away from our true selves and towards a false self (a constructed, inauthentic self). Social media, for example encourages people to communicate only parts of themselves to the world (usually their highlights), which can give others the impression that their lives are 'perfect' and to be envied. Be wary of this; no one's life is perfect, and trying to pretend that it is only leads to misery and a sense of sadness and alienation from the world. Be true to yourself and if you find you get lured in by social media and this affects your mood, delete it or limit its use! There is now research to suggest that prolonged social media use, especially passive browsing of pictures and comparing yourself against others, is associated with worsening mental health in young people. The Eating Disorders Unit from the South London and Maudsley NHS Foundation Trust have produced a guide on social media use (Social Media – Friend or Foe), which you might helpful. Check out the Resource Section on the website www.FREEDfromED.co.uk to download it.

Life domains

Think about the people you admire and their values. **What** do these individuals **do** that **you admire**?
Think about:

- The sorts of relationships are they in.
- How they fill their time.
- How they manage their health.
- Within each domain, remember to consider how they cope when things don't go to plan. What helps them bounce back?

Think about the following life domains and jot down some thoughts:

- **Relationships**:

- **Career**:

- **Hobbies**:

- **Health**:

REFLECTION

- What would you like to be doing differently in life?
- What are your goals and dreams?
- What would your healthy self be doing across the life domains if you allowed yourself to flourish and fulfil your potential?
- What are useful coping strategies when life is a challenge?

Considering these life domains, what would you be doing differently if your healthy self could flourish?

Write below a goal statement about how you would like things to be within each life domain.

Underneath each goal, write out the steps you would need to take to achieve this.

- **Interpersonal relationships**:

  My goals are: _____

The steps I would need to take to achieve these are:

  -

  -

  -

  -

- **Career**:

  My goals are: _____

The steps I would need to take to achieve these are:

  -

  -

  -

  -

- **Hobbies**:

  My goals are: _____

The steps I would need to take to achieve these are:

  -

  -

  -

  -

- **Health**:

  My goals are: _____

The steps I would need to take to achieve these are:

  -

  -

  -

  -

New self-beliefs

What do we have to believe about ourselves to make our dreams possible? Think about the people you admire, the values they hold and the things they have achieved.

- How do you think they would complete the following **guiding beliefs**?
- Have a go at completing the phrases below in the role of **your flourishing sense of self**.

I am. . .

Others are. . .

The world is. . .

REFLECTION

- How do these beliefs compare with the beliefs you currently hold?
- Think about your flourishing sense of self:
    - How would you see yourself?
    - To make your dreams come true, what would you have to believe about yourself, the world and others?

Rules for living

In line with your new beliefs and values, what rules would you live by?

You may want to look back at the formulation that you and your therapist drew up a while ago, and if appropriate also your work on your thinking style and your emotional rule book. In all of these you will have identified unhelpful rules that keep the anorexia strong. Can you think of some alternative rules that would help you get what you want from life?

Try and jot down as many as you can. Remember, these tend to take an 'if–then' format.

My rules

- **If** _____

  Then _____

- **If** _____

  Then _____

- **If** _____

  Then _____

- **If** _____

  Then _____

REFLECTION

- How do these differ from your old set of rules?
- Are they more flexible?
- Are they less punishing?

Feelings

Now close your eyes and really try to think about your flourishing sense of self.

Try and draw up an image of your flourishing self:

- Think about your **posture**. How would you hold yourself?
- Think of the **values** you hold, the new **things you would be doing**, the **beliefs** you hold about yourself, the world and others?
- How would you be **feeling**?

Welcome and try to get in touch with the feelings. Jot down some of the feelings that emerge in the space below.

REFLECTION

- How would you be feeling?
- Where in your body would you experience these feelings?
- Would you always feel the same way, or would your feelings change?
- What would it be like to feel this way?
- How would the way you feel influence your self-beliefs and actions in the world?

My views and opinions

Living with anorexia and it becoming an integral part of your identity can lead to you losing touch with your authentic views and opinions on key issues and the wider world.

Think about the people you admire; are they people with **views** and **opinions**?

- *How do people form their views and opinions?*

Add some of your own ideas to the examples below.
Examples:

- Reading the newspaper.
- Discussing with others we like, admire or respect.

-

-

-

- One way of exploring and developing your views and opinions is to buy a newspaper or watch the television and have a think about a topic or issue that captures you.

  Pick an article in the newspaper or from the television that most appeals to you or interests you, and bring it to the next session with your therapist for discussion.

  Consider the following:

  - What drew you to this article?
  - What different opinions could come from this article?

  There may be many different viewpoints.

  - What is your standpoint on the issues it raises?
  - What thoughts and feelings does it raise for you?
  - What factors influence your opinions and views?
  - Are these linked to your core values?

Try the following to get in touch with your passions:

- Have a go at brainstorming – 'the things I used to love'. Get back in touch with your passions by designing a collage of all those things you used to love.
- Have a go at brainstorming – 'the things and relationships that used to make me smile'. Make a collage of smile triggers!
- Make a 'love-ability box' – a decorated box wherein you place reminders of how loveable you are! This might include postcards from friends, messages left for you, photos of good times and certificates.
- The things I've never tried to but have always secretly wanted to do if money, time, responsibilities and other constraints were not there.
- Think about your dream job. Imagine you had started work at this dream job. Write a letter to a friend describing your typical week, how you are feeling, what you are doing and how you manage 'off days'.
- Make a list of hobbies you've been drawn to but have been too scared or unwell to begin. Make a resolution to start one this week.

REFLECTION

- What do the above tell you about the longings of your healthy flourishing self?
- What steps can you take to bring these important elements back into your life?

Road testing the new me!

Now really pull together and hold in mind an image of your healthy flourishing self!

Who will allow me to develop?

It is worth bearing in mind that, in the first instance, other people may be a bit resistant to your new ways of being. You see, even though they may well recognise your struggles and want the best for you, it is a fact of human nature that most people like familiarity and consistency. Therefore, they might feel more comfortable with your old ways of being (even though they are harmful) and resistant to your new ways of being. So, consider the following:

- Who do I feel most safe with to explore my new ways of being?
- Who is confident enough in themselves to allow me to grow and blossom?
- Who has been my partner on my road to recovery and has supported my progression toward wellness?
- Who appreciates that some of my ways of being have held me back and has encouraged me to make positive, healthy changes?
- Who is creative and flexible enough to allow me to be just who I am today?

Use the preceding questions to think of people you feel safe enough with to explore these new parts of yourself. It may even be someone new! It is advisable while you explore new ways of being that you:

- Keep a distance from people who are unwell themselves. It may be too threatening for them to see you blossom.
- Work *with* your partner and family and explain that you are trying to make changes and would value their support.
- Keep at it. Old patterns are hard to break, but if you persist the rewards can be enormous.

For the next day, have a go at living and being guided by your healthy flourishing self. Try to think, act and feel as this version of yourself.

This is how Jamie, one of our patients, found trying this out:

For a week, I stopped letting my anxieties and perceptions of criticism worm away at me. I stayed confident in that I was helping others to the best of my abilities and embraced that it was OK to be different. I dared to try out new activities. In stressful situations, I remained calm, was able to practice bigger picture thinking and laughed off the worries. All in all, I stayed smiling and found myself enjoying life more and getting so much more out of it. Letting go of some of my rigid safety behaviours and viewing things with a different perspective had made me happier and had also had a positive influence in my relationships with others. This experiment taught me the important lesson that there is more than one way to live life and I could choose what kind of life that would be.

- *Remember your **posture*** – Be mindful of how your flourishing self would be standing and walking.
- *Think in terms of **acting as if you are your flourishing self*** – At first this may feel clumsy but it will come to feel more familiar and rewarding if you stick with it.
- *Keep reminding yourself of your **guiding principles*** – perhaps jot them down on a card to keep in your pocket.
- *Just **play** with the new ways of being* – Let yourself be guided by the new values and self-beliefs that you hold.
- **Dare** to try out new activities and interact with people *as if* you are your flourishing self.
- *Listen to your feelings* – listen carefully and try to reconnect with your gut feelings.

REFLECTION

- What did you do differently that day?
- How were you feeling? Where in your body did you experience these feelings?
- Did you notice anything about your relationships? How did people treat you?
- What surprised you? What shocked you?
- What was easier than you thought about adopting this new way of being, and what was more difficult?
- What can you do to help bring this new ideal self even more alive?

LETTER-WRITING TASK

MY FLOURISHING SELF IN THE FUTURE

Have a go at writing a letter to a friend five years in the future when your healthy self is really flourishing and in the driver's seat.
Think about:

- What would you be doing?
- What relationships would be central in your life?
- What job would you be doing?
- How would you fill your spare time?
- Importantly, how would you be feeling? Remember to consider that there may be ups and downs.

The case of Clarissa

Clarissa found it almost impossible to think of a flourishing self. She saw her non-anorexic self as bland, boring and 'vanilla'. When she and her therapist drew up her formulation, she found it very difficult to think of any strengths she had. In her childhood she had always felt over-shadowed by her older brother who was amusing, talented and brilliant at sports, captivating her parents' attention. Clarissa had a responsible job in an industry where people who were eccentric, witty or loud were valued. With the help of her therapist she realised that she was an accomplished all-rounder, with diverse hobbies and interests, who quietly, flexibly and effectively got on with many challenges at work and who was valued as a caring, empathic and loyal friend. She also began to realise that she had devalued these strengths as insignificant, criticising herself for not having one 'unique selling point' that defined her. Two things helped her move on – first she realised that she hadn't updated her image of her dazzling brother. As an adult he was a lot less dazzling and seemed much more ordinary, with ordinary struggles in relationships and work. Second, she went to an inspiring talk by a woman leader in her industry who talked openly and movingly about her own difficulties in finding her feet as a younger person and who, just like Clarissa, had under-estimated herself and her own potential because she was an all-rounder. This older woman who had been very successful in her career talked about how helpful her all-rounder strengths had been in building her professional life and coping with the many challenges she had faced. After hearing this talk, Clarissa realised how critical she had been of herself on a daily basis. She began to work on being more self-compassionate and enjoyed this. To practice getting into her healthy flourishing self, Clarissa imagined taking on the persona of the woman leader she admired for a week. She realised that doing this made her feel much more accepting of herself, but also more confident and able to speak up for herself, especially at work.

Chapter 10

The virtuous flower of recovery from anorexia

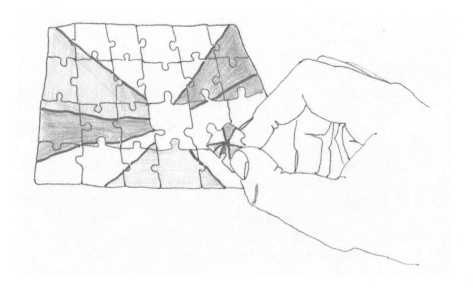

One of our patients, Miriam, asked us: *it's all very well getting a bit better, but how do I keep it up, how do I cope when I have a bad day, what if I forget everything I thought I had learned?*

Betsy, who had been through a few phases of wellness followed by periods of struggle with anorexia described trying to stay well as like *being in one of those phases of grief where just as you have a difficult day you find that everyone who used to support you has disappeared off because they think you should be well now.*

You will have spent lots of time during your recovery process learning about the 'vicious flower' of factors (or petals) that maintained your anorexia. We hope this process has been helpful for you and that you have discovered ways to break some of these unhelpful cycles while also exploring new ways of being that are more fitting with a healthier, happier, more fulfilling life.

Take a look at the following figure (page 208). Again it looks like a flower, but this time rather than being a 'vicious flower' it is a 'virtuous flower', as each petal describes a factor that keeps you free from anorexia and fosters a happy and healthy future. Again we have grouped the petals according to themes and each theme represents positive ways of thinking, behaving and relating.

To think about what positive changes you have put in place please consider the following factors:

- Look back at Chapter 9, 'Identity': think about your healthy flourishing self, perhaps parts that got squashed by anorexia or think about new parts of your identity that have become increasingly apparent as the stranglehold of anorexia has lessened. It is really important that these parts of yourself get nutrients and nurturance across these next weeks and months so that they can really flourish and reach their potential.
- Look back at Chapter 8, 'Exploring Thinking Styles': you may have been practicing new styles of engaging with the world, such as trying to be more flexible in your day-to-day behaviours and in your relationship with food and exercise. Also, do you have new ways of being that enable you to hold onto a 'bigger picture' vision of your future?
- Look back at Chapter 7, 'The Emotional and Social Mind': how has your relationship with your emotions changed? How will you listen to and nurture your emotional self? Have a think about what you can put in place to make sure you check in with and validate any emotions that arise. How will you be more compassionate to yourself, especially when things are not going smoothly?
- What steps have you taken to broaden your social world? What long-lost relationships have you rekindled? Do you have new hobbies, new individuals and groups that are valuable to you? Are you thinking about returning to work? How will you make time for these important connections in your daily life?
- Look back at Chapter 3, 'No (Wo)man is an Island – Working with Support': gathering the right type of support will be invaluable in your recovery process. Who in your world offers the kind of support for you that lets you flourish? What will you need to do to ensure you can access this support? How can you tell them what you need?
- Make a note of any other factors that will be important in keeping well. For example, when you originally worked on the vicious flower of anorexia, were there any strengths that you listed that might help you fight the anorexia? These very same strengths might now come in usefully in maintaining your gains and recovery.

TOP TIP

- Look back over the chapters of this book and try to be specific about all of the positive changes you have made that help you to keep well, no matter how small they are. Every little bit helps.
- Now, have a go at completing some of the petal cycles to highlight factors (these may be new ways of thinking, behaving, feeling or relating) that will help keep your future virtuous and flourishing in all respects!

Virtuous flower of health and happiness

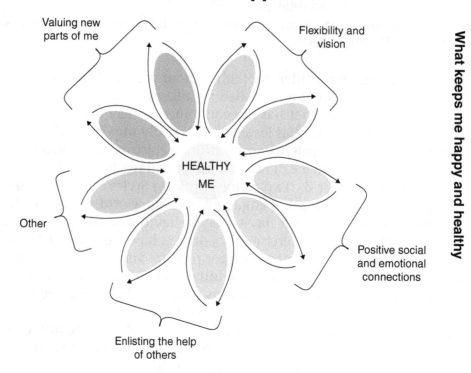

Bella's virtuous flower

Bella had a very busy job as an assistant to two senior people in her company. Unfortunately, her bosses did not talk much to each other. Both made multiple demands on her, requiring their work to be treated as a priority, without considering the other part of her job. When her anorexia was at its worst, she would grit her teeth and work without breaks into the night to finish important deadlines so as to please both bosses. During these times she would be so stressed that she had absolutely no wish to eat. She would neglect seeing any of her friends and avoided her family to escape concerned looks or questions about her health. At work, she would not talk to her bosses or any colleagues about her difficulty managing, because she did not want to be seen as not coping or weak. Bella often felt numb and overwhelmed. She was often at the point of tears, and desperately tried not to get upset. 'I thought showing that I was upset would just make me seem pathetic. So I just pushed upsetting thoughts away as best as I could. I felt utterly alone'.

Bella did well in treatment. Her anorexia has much improved and she now manages to nourish herself properly on a daily basis. In parallel, she decided that to stay well she needed to make important changes in her life. As part of this and with the support of her therapist, she arranged a meeting with both her bosses and a joint plan was worked out that included regular joint reviews of her workload and what to prioritise. Below are Bella's thoughts about the petals of her virtuous flower (i.e. the things she has begun to do more off to stay well).

Flexibility and vision: Now even if I am busy I always take my lunch break, usually going to the staff canteen, sitting with colleagues or, if the weather is good, we have our lunch in the local park. It makes such a big difference to how I feel, having a good break with chatting, laughing and food, giving myself much needed emotional and physical sustenance! I have surprised myself by discovering that I have actually become much more efficient that way, I usually manage to finish my work on time now, rather than dwelling over tasks endlessly. I usually go out with my friends at least a couple of times a week. I have also negotiated with my bosses that I can work from home one day a week so I can concentrate on important things without interruption. Every morning I spend a few minutes doing a WOOP (see Chapter 6) for the day, as this is a way of focusing on what matters to me, and keeping in mind the bigger picture. My vision for myself is to have pride in my work and a life outside it.

Positive emotional and social connections: I talk much more to my mum these days and our relationship is much closer as a result. If something upsets me and gives me strong feelings, I now pause and try to think about what the emotion is trying to tell me, rather than just ploughing on as I would have done previously, and pretending that I am alright. When something upsets me, I talk to one or two close friends who are always good at either helping me get things into perspective or thinking about potential solutions. I love playing the flute and I have gone back to taking classes and have joined a music appreciation group. It is so much fun.

Enlisting the help of others: I don't feel I need to be superwoman anymore and sort out everything by myself. I have become much better at showing people when I struggle, and it has been a wonderful surprise to me at how willing friends and family have been to help me when I have asked. When I recently moved house, the whole gang pitched up to help with this.

Valuing new parts of me: I have become much more assertive and I can forgive myself when I make a mistake or don't do things perfectly.

Savouring moments and cherishing life's positives

To build, nurture and strengthen all petals of your virtuous flower, here is another thing you may want to do. Try to spend a few minutes at the end of each day to take stock. Note down in a diary three things that happened on the day that you have enjoyed or are grateful for and three things that you have done well.

Think of interactions with people, activities or places that you enjoyed. Think about small things and brief moments and notice and capture them (e.g. feeling the warm sun on your neck as you are reading a book by the window; hearing a child sing in the street; the joy in your granny's voice when you call her; the kindness you gave to a stranger or they gave to you). As you note these things down try to reconnect with the positive emotions that they elicited in you at the time (i.e. earlier in the day). This may be quite difficult at first, but over time you will get better at this, and it will build up a treasure trove of positive moments to look back over when times are a bit hard.

When thinking about things that you have done well, really make an effort to be pleased and proud of yourself. In what respects have you been the unsung hero today? Think about things that you would normally overlook and not give yourself credit for (e.g. trying something new or different in relation to what, when and how you eat; trying something new or different in relation to other areas of your life; alternatively praise yourself for simply carrying on with something and acknowledge how brave that is and how hard it can be).

Being realistic

In order to enable your virtuous flower to thrive and flourish, you will need to keep a watchful eye on your anorexia. Overcoming anorexia is hard work. Perhaps you have made considerable progress with your weight and eating and other areas, but inside you still feel rather shaky. Below we have listed a number of the difficult thoughts, feelings and behaviours that people with AN often tell us they experience in their journey to recovery. Look through the checklist, find those items that apply to you and get some tips for how to deal with them.

Problem area		Tick if this applies to you ✔	Tips for how to stay realistic
Thoughts			
Anorexic thoughts:	'I mustn't eat too much or I'll get fat.' 'I want to lose weight.' 'I am fat. I hate it.'		These thoughts are a normal part of getting better. They wax and wane. Often when they are particularly strong this shows that other stresses need to be thought about, for example worries about an impending exam or trouble with a partner.
Unhelpful thoughts about the illness or stage of recovery:	'I am only one small step away from getting ill again.' 'I should be better now.' 'I shouldn't be feeling like this anymore. It should have got easier.' 'I can't stand it anymore.' 'I will never get better.'		It is very hard work to get better and often feels like one step forward, two steps back. Try to see the bigger picture; think of how far you have come, and think of where you want to go. Remember the things you have achieved rather than dwelling on the things you haven't.

Problem area		Tick if this applies to you ✔	Tips for how to stay realistic
Thoughts about others' response:	'They think I look fat.' 'Others don't notice the effort I make' 'Others expect me to cope – but I am not ready' 'All they are interested in is my weight' 'I am fed up with being constantly quizzed about what I have eaten. I am not going to say anything!'		You may still be wrong-footed by innocent and well-meant comments about your appearance or weight. Try to focus on people's intentions rather than what they said. Yes, close others may underestimate the amount of effort that you had and still have to put into your recovery. Is there a way you can let them know how you are feeling and how they can best support you? Make sure there is time to do nice things together. Close others may be as frightened as you are about the possibility of a setback. Negotiate when and how they can ask you for feedback.

Feelings

Feelings	Tense, anxious, vigilant, irritable, moody, fed up		Can you find a way to relax? Do hugs, cuddles or a back rub help? How about going for a walk? Doing something else?

Physical sensations and drives

Cravings	Cravings for food		Can you ask a close other to help you manage these feelings by keeping you company during difficult times, e.g. often straight after a meal cravings are more intense.
Physical sensations/ drives	Increased energy requirements during first 6 months of weight recovery		You need to be aware of this and perhaps discuss with your therapist how best to manage this.

Behaviour

Food and eating behaviour	Bingeing or Following rigid eating plan Limiting variety of foods Eating bland safe foods		Binges may be an expression of increased energy requirements during the first few months after achieving a healthier weight. You need to be aware of this and if needed discuss with your therapist how best to manage this. Be mindful that the preferred anorexic diet (↑ carbohydrates, ↓ fat, ↓ protein) wastes energy and makes it harder to maintain weight or put on weight.
Seeking reassurance	Constantly asking for reassurance regarding food or weight		The effects of reassurance tend to wear off if this is given repeatedly. If this is a problem, talk to your therapist on how best to manage this.

Use this chart as a basis for discussion with close others for how to build on the changes you have made and how to get further ahead.

Remember the 'drip, drip' effect of anorexia, so catch it early!

Individuals who recover from anorexia tell us that in the medium term recovery needs to be a conscious process, something that you actively hold in mind and work hard to promote. As well as holding in mind your virtuous flower of recovery, individuals who recover tell us that being aware of their personal relapse indicators (i.e. signs and symptoms suggesting that things are slipping), and having a way of dealing with these all mapped out in advance, can be invaluable in keeping well, especially when life starts to get challenging again.

An example may make this clearer.

CASE EXAMPLE

SALLY'S TRAFFIC LIGHT RELAPSE PREVENTION PLAN

In order to keep an eye on how the early weeks and months of recovery were going, Sally used a traffic light system to monitor her key signs of relapse and to plan healthy and appropriate responses that matched the degree of relapse. Here is Sally's traffic light relapse prevention plan (see below) which she developed with the therapist she worked with. She shared it with her dad and boyfriend and eventually with her GP. At the end of each *week* Sally ticked the traffic light colour appropriate for each of her key signs of relapse. Each week her GP asked Sally to summarise the categories within the green zone, those in amber and any in red. This helped the GP congratulate Sally on areas she was coping well with and guide Sally back on track particularly where she was having some red zone struggles.

Traffic light relapse prevention plan

As one of our patients said: *My traffic light plan was really helpful in keeping me on track. My anorexia had this way of making me kind of 'not notice' when I was cutting back on food, or isolating myself, but by keeping a track in this way I can spot things and catch myself early.*

Another of our patients points out: *The traffic light plan is only worthwhile if you are truly honest with yourself. So, if you are not eating enough or if you are exercising too much,* **be honest** *and true to yourself, note it down and ask for help . . . do this early to stop loads of heartache later on.*

My relapse signs	Green week	Amber week	Healthy response: Tell mum this has been an amber week and that I need support.	Red week	Healthy response: Tell mum this has been a red week and that I need support.
Weight loss	Weight maintained or gained.	Weight loss of up to 0.5 kg.	Add in a small snack between breakfast and lunch to my meal plan.	Weight loss of up to 1 kg.	Add in a small snack between breakfast and lunch and lunch and tea and ask mum to sit with me at mealtimes.
Cutting out foods	Eating my usual range of foods or having tried some new foods.	More than one meal or snack reduced or food type eliminated.	Challenge myself to add back in the meal or food-type.	Cutting back on carbohydrates or cutting out meals.	Challenge myself to add back in the meal or foods eliminated. Maybe do this gradually over the next week.
Anorexic thinking	Fighting this and winning with the support of my loved ones.	Approx. 50% increase in the frequency or intensity of my anorexic voice.	Use my thought records again.	Experiencing my anorexic voice as bullying, preoccupying and overwhelming.	Use my distraction techniques advised by my therapist and use thought records.
Feeling cold	Feeling no more cold than usual or no more than others around me.	Starting to notice I am a little more cold and am wearing more layers.	Tell myself this will pass as I gain weight to the healthy range.	Feeling preoccupied by the cold.	Challenge myself to get back to my meal plan so that I can gain weight and feel warmer.
Exercise creeping up	Exercising for no more than 20 minutes three times a week.	Walking everywhere. Having thoughts in my head that I am 'lazy' when I sit still.	Ask for mum's help to set healthy limits on my walking to no more than 20 minutes three times a week. Use my thought diary to challenge anorexic thinking.	Feeling overwhelmed by thoughts I am 'lazy' and 'out of control'. Exercise creeping up each day.	Ask mum if she will walk with me for 20 minutes three times a week to help set a limit. Use distraction such as drawing and keeping my thoughts diary when urge is strong.
Isolating myself from friends and family	Drawing on mum and friends for support when I need it. Spending some pleasure time with loved ones.	Still seeing family but isolating from friends, haven't seen my friends this week.	Write down my key fears this week and share them with my mum and support therapist.	Isolating and keeping secrets from friends and family. Anorexia feeling more important than relationships.	Write down my key fears and share them with my mum and support therapist.
Feeling 'flat' and 'cut off'	Feeling this way less than 30% of the time.	Feeling this way less than 50% of the time.	Do at least one activity purely for pleasure this week.	Feeling this way more than 50% of the time.	Do at least one activity purely for pleasure this week.

Keeping one step ahead

TASK

With the help of a supportive other complete the traffic light table at the end of this chapter to high-light your key signs of relapse using examples that are personal, concrete and specific. Also, next to each indicator please highlight a healthy response(s) to such a setback. Always hold in mind, that getting well from anorexia is a work in progress. Setbacks are certainly not a sign that you are failing but they can certainly pick up speed if not caught early. So, think of setbacks as opportunities to prove that you value your future healthy self and that your drive to be well and to get more from life is stronger than your drive for anorexia. This traffic light system should help you keep one step ahead of your anorexia.

Dealing with setbacks

If you are seeing a therapist or GP regularly, we would encourage you to review your traffic light relapse prevention plan with your therapist or GP on a weekly basis. If you are not meeting with a health professional on a regular basis, we would urge you to share your plan with a support-ive other on a weekly basis. This is so that a setback remains just a set-back and does not develop into relapse. We urge you to think of setbacks as opportunities to empower yourself with new ways of coping and not as a catastrophe.

TOP TIP

- Remember: A setback is a **slight** deterioration in a person who has previously made good progress on their way to recovery. Research in other disorders has shown that people's attitudes to a setback critically determine how well they cope with it and whether a setback turns into full-blown relapse. A good idea is to plan in advance what constitutes a slight setback (**be concrete and specific**) and how you will respond to this in a timely and reasoned manner. **It is also very important to have good support from the people around you**.

Time to reflect

Checklist: my immediate responses

Imagine yourself in the following situation:

You are doing quite well but for the past four weeks have been within the amber zone in terms of weight and mood such that you lose half a stone in the run-up to an exam.

Or

You have just reached a healthy weight and you are beginning to relax a bit when following a viral infection you lose half a stone.

TASK

First, check your attitudes to this setback. Please tick any that apply:

A setback would be a major disaster. I couldn't cope.

Setbacks are only to be expected. I'll cope with it.

It is all my fault. I should have been more watchful and prevented this from happening.

A setback is the first step down the slippery slope.

A setback can be overcome.

How could I let this happen? I struggled so hard to get back to a reasonable weight.

A setback is best ignored. Perhaps things will just get better again.

A setback will invariably lead to full-blown relapse.

I've blown it. Here I go again.

A setback is an important learning opportunity.

Now have a read of some balanced, compassionate responses to these setbacks below. People who go on to recover tells us that they have many setbacks along the way. Iesha had been doing very well in her recovery when out of the blue she lost her beloved Nan and found herself drawing on restriction to manage the painful feelings of loss. She had a red week according to her traffic light plan for two weeks running. She shared this with her best friend who supported Iesha to gradually increase her portion sizes and vitally, to talk about how she was feeling. In fact Iesha rewrote the letter 'what others aren't seeing and hearing', and through this was able to communicate her depth of suffering to others and importantly to herself. Once she had nourished her emotional self with some self-compassionate talk, she had an amber week and then a few green weeks. Luckily Iesha knew not to catastrophise this setback. It was all part of her process of recovery.

'A setback would be a major disaster. I couldn't cope'.
This is a very catastrophic view of a setback. This is likely to lead to a sense of panic, which may cloud your ability to keep things in perspective and think rationally about what is best to do.

'Lapses are only to be expected. We'll cope with it'.
Congratulations on being so realistic – you are absolutely right. Lapses are a typical part of recovery. Truly getting better means that you have to learn to be flexibly in control of your behaviour, which means that if you have veered off too far in one direction you can correct the overall course.

'It is all my fault. I should have been more watchful and prevented this from happening'.
There may be all sorts of different factors that lead to a setback. The one black and white statement that is correct here is that a setback is never down to just one person or one situation. A setback is nobody's fault. Blaming yourself is only going to make you feel bad and guilty.

'A setback is the first step down the slippery slope'.
This is a rather catastrophic view of a setback that is likely to lead to a sense of panic, which may cloud your ability to keep things in perspective and think rationally about what is best to do.

'A setback can be overcome'.
Having a realistic, positive 'can do' attitude will be very helpful in overcoming your setback.

'How could I let this happen? I struggled so hard to get back to a reasonable weight'.
Blaming yourself is unlikely to be helpful in helping me overcome the setback.

'A setback is best ignored. Perhaps things will just get better again'.
There are different types of ignoring, passive and active. Passive ignoring is often fear-driven and involves coping strategies such as putting your head in the sand, detaching from what is happening or simply hoping that things will turn out alright. This is unlikely to be helpful. Active ignoring may be a sign that your motivation to stay well is dwindling. It is probably more helpful for you to talk openly about this with your support therapist and loved ones.

'I've blown it. Here I go again'.
A setback is just that, it's a blip. Criticising yourself is unlikely to be helpful in overcoming it. Self-directed anger and frustration may actually worsen things.

'A setback will invariably lead to full-blown relapse'.
This is a rather catastrophic view of a setback. This is likely to lead to a sense of panic, which may cloud your ability to keep things in perspective and think rationally about what is best to do.

'A setback is an important learning opportunity'.
You are absolutely right. There is plenty of research evidence to suggest that having lapses is helpful for learning how to stay well. In fact some therapists prescribe a 'planned setback' to their patients to give them this learning opportunity.

TOP TIP

- If you are doing well currently, write a wise and compassionate letter to your future self (thinking of a time when you might once again be struggling) and giving yourself advice on how you might cope with overcoming the setback. Really get into the spirit of it and what it would feel like, what you could say to yourself, what you would want to remind yourself of, what people might be of help and what practical steps you'd advise yourself to take under the circumstances.

SUMMARY

OK, now you're all set to start to look after yourself in the future:

- You have mapped out your 'virtuous flower' of factors that will keep you healthy and happy.
- You have sketched out your traffic light table of personal signs of relapse and have highlighted healthy responses to these setbacks. You and your therapist will monitor these.
- You have shared your traffic light table of personal signs of relapse with your loved ones and they are ready to support you. You have also shared your traffic light monitoring system with the professionals who will be more directly monitoring your physical health, such as, your GP.
- You are prepared for setbacks and ready to view them as opportunities to learn and to prove to yourself and your loved ones that your drive to be well is stronger than your drive to be unwell and back in hospital.
- You are ready to try and tolerate (with a lot of guidance, support and self-soothing) the fear, frustration and sense of profound uncertainty and 'not knowing' that is likely to come and go as you try to break free from the cycles that keep you stuck and unwell. Try to keep a longer-term perspective in mind and ask for help when you need it.
- You are ready to be kind and forgiving to yourself but you are also ready to be brave and fully committed to the programme. Good luck!

Inspire yourself

Mottos for a bigger life!

Finally we would love for you to go away with some key messages to hold in mind that drive your life in the direction you would like to take it. A motto can be helpful as a shorthand or reminder of the key messages and new ways of thinking, feeling or behaving that you have learned over the course of this workbook. It may help to reinforce and keep a focus on what you have learned in therapy and what you may still want/need to practice in order to have a bigger life.

What is a motto?

A **motto** is a **phrase** or a short list of **words** that describes the motivation or intention of a person, social group, or organisation. Many countries, cities, universities, and other institutions have mottos, as do families with coats of arms.

For example:

Apple Computers: **'Think different'**
Arsenal Football Club: **'Victory comes from Harmony'**
Boy Scouts: **'Be prepared'**
Nike: **'Just do it'**

Clever advertisers present their products with mottos that are likely to appeal to their target population:

'Because I'm worth it' or
'Vorsprung durch Technik' (Advance through technology).

Individuals, too, have mottos. The motto of the Roman statesman and philosopher Marcus Aurelius, **'Carpe diem'**, has become world famous and has a lot to offer even 2,000 years later. This can be translated as **'seize the day'**, **'enjoy the day'** or **'live every day as if it were your last'**.

For ideas try searching for 'motto' in an online encyclopaedia such as www.wikipedia.org

What would be a good motto for you?

Here is a list of mottos some of our patients thought would be useful for them.

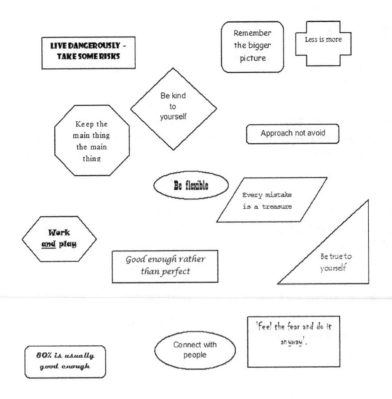

TOP TIP

- Positive mottos work better than negatives, so rather than 'Don't procrastinate', use something like 'Go for it, girl'.
- These mottos are not meant to last you forever. Have a motto of the day, week or month. Review your motto after a period of time, and if it has outlived its usefulness, switch to another one.

Choose one of the mottos from the list or make up your own and add them to the following shapes if you wish. Find something that has meaning for you and sums up what you want your life to be like. Think about an image or theme tune that might go with your motto. This is about having a vision and strengthening your bigger picture thinking.

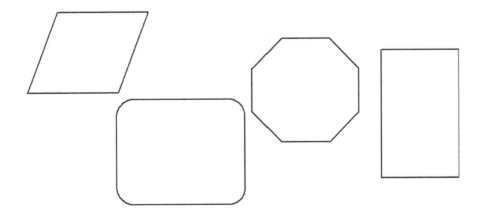

Moving forwards

This is the end of our workbook aimed to help guide you towards recovery from anorexia. The ideas have come from listening closely to those who sufferer with anorexia, those who care for someone with anorexia, those who recover from anorexia and from the many therapists who care deeply about the suffering that anorexia can cause, but who also believe in and have witnessed full recovery from anorexia. We hope that reading this book has as a minimum sparked something within you that helps you see that you deserve more from life than what anorexia will allow. We hope that some of the exercises have resonated with you and have truly increased your options for the way in which you wish to live your life. Most of all we hope that you dare to listen to any longings within you (however faint right now) for a fuller richer life.

We leave you with some blank pages for you to write in – perhaps you may wish to use them for poems, drawings, stories, inspirational sayings, diary notes, or notes marking some of your achievements as you progress toward a more flexible life.

Worksheets for supporters

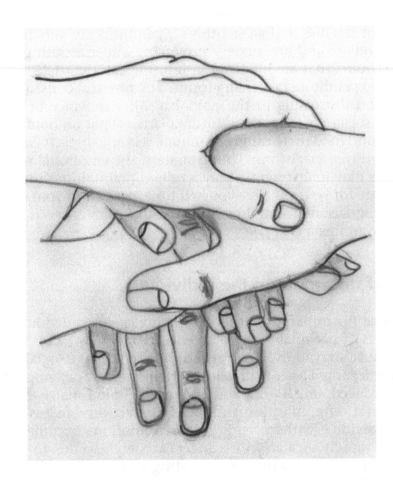

We have written these worksheets for partners, family members and others who are close to someone with anorexia, as we know that you will perhaps be both confused and concerned by the illness and you may value some guidance and help yourself.

Anorexia has a profound impact on other people, both through the direct effect of the symptoms and indirectly by changing the person you know and love. It can seem as though your loved one has been taken over by an 'anorexic minx' who sits resolutely on their shoulder feeding them misinformation. What you may not realise is that your reactions to this anorexic minx can change the course the illness takes. We have tried in these notes to distil some of the wisdom from experienced clinicians, recovered patients and other carers to help steer you through what can seem like a stormy sea. We are providing an outline of what has been found to be helpful or harmful and how you can best provide support and guidance through the many traps created by the anorexic minx.

It may be that you have already found the answers and you are confident that the approach you are taking is working for you. However, if you have some doubts, then please read on.

The impact of anorexia on the family

Eating disorder symptoms can have profound social and emotional ramifications for families and close others. Symptoms are variable in their form and impact and are anxiety provoking and frustrating. The person's behaviours that are involved in limiting calorie intake or increasing calorie expenditure take many forms. The physical consequences are alarming and distressing to the onlooker. All semblance of normality disappears, social life evaporates, future plans are put on hold and interactions around food increasingly dominate relationships. It can feel akin to living within a maelstrom. Unfortunately, the emotional response of close others may inadvertently play a role in maintaining the problem. How you care for yourself, give yourself time away from your caring role to the 'Eating Disorder individual' (**Edi**) and reflect on your behaviour towards the anorexia is key.

The impact of anorexia on the individual

Brain starvation impacts on the core being of an individual causing some aspects of personality to be accentuated or new facets to emerge. This is because starvation impairs the ability to manage social and emotional functioning. Facial expressions of emotion, for example to pleasure, are reduced and the individual appears emotionally 'bland', cut off or frozen. Communication and social interactions are less rewarding and the individual withdraws. Regulating emotions becomes difficult. Frustration rapidly escalates into anger. Anxiety ascends to dread and fear becomes terror, sometimes manifesting as a panic attack. For others the core issue is too much inhibition of emotions. An individual can be reliant on their anorexia to numb unpleasant emotions. Stress levels are high and there is an increased sensitivity to threat. Both body and brain can become locked in a fight, flight or freeze type of response, leaving Edi exhausted and unable to see a way ahead.

The cognitive resources that humans use to make complex decisions and to understand the perspectives of other people are depleted and individuals become increasingly isolated which sets in train further problems in mood and allows the eating disorder to take a greater hold and the behaviours to become ritualised and run on autopilot. Attention becomes focused on the minutiae of the moment, particularly relating to food and weight and it is hard for the individual to see the bigger picture of life beyond this narrow vantage point.

For you, the person that you have known and loved appears to be lost or transformed because of these deficits in complex aspects of brain function. If you are a parent you grieve for the loss of your child. If the person with the illness is your partner, you will have lost the source of solace and comfort that intimate relationships provide. You may feel like the possibility of normality ever returning is but a faint dot on the horizon. However, recovery from anorexia is possible no matter how many years ago the illness has taken hold.

What causes anorexia?

Causal chains

A common concern is to try to pinpoint the root cause or timing of the problem, however the illness remains an enigma. We are gradually getting closer to a coherent explanation of anorexia, involving the interplay of several factors, each of which contributes small effects. Added together, these can build momentum over the course of time. We also know there are different forms of anorexia. So who is at risk?

- Individuals who are more sensitive to punishment or threat are at risk. There may be many causes of this excess sensitivity. They can be genetic or related to difficulties experienced while in the womb or during early life.
- Another trait that endows risk is an enhanced ability to perceive and analyse detail. This may be associated with a tendency to be focused and somewhat inflexible.
- Stress (minor or major) can trigger onset, especially if it occurs during adolescence. Restricting eating is perceived to be of benefit.

A different set of factors may contribute to helping anorexia take a hold over the person's life. Restricting eating may be perceived by Edi to be a way of dampening down difficult emotions and anxieties. The emotional numbness and child-like state which results from being at a low weight can seem a safer place to be. The perceived gains from anorexia vary between individuals.

Many questions remain and misunderstandings abound. What is becoming clear is that it may not be possible to reverse this causal chain. This is not as bad as it may first sounds. We know that treatment can be very effective if it focuses on factors that cause the illness to persist rather than those that have caused it.

Perpetuating processes

Secondary consequences of anorexia produce problems that make recovery difficult. We have alluded to these in the preceding section. For example, the brain usually runs on 200–300 calories a day. The restricting nature of anorexia deprives the brain of nutrition. Function is impaired leading to the transformation in personality described earlier. Furthermore, the illness often strikes at a critical phase of brain maturation when neural connections are being consolidated into the adult form. The loss of neuronal growth and hormonal factors caused by starvation arrests this maturation process. The brain shrinks and cognitive, perceptual and emotional functioning is impaired. Also the appetite control system can become severely deregulated.

What it all means for you

First, you must banish the common assumption that somehow you have done something to cause the problem or that you are in some way to blame for the anorexia. Guilt is not only misapplied but can trap you into responding with unhelpful behaviours. Parents, partners and close others can be the solution, not part of the problem. Remember you are a resource, a bridge to social connection. Anorexia can and does put tremendous demands on the coping abilities of family members. Scheduling time out to relax and recharge from your caring role is key.

It can be helpful to look at what you can do to interrupt any of the vicious circles that are maintaining the anorexia. In the following section we illustrate some of these 'traps'. Breaking through these traps will not be easy. However, we never fail to be impressed with how quickly and effectively carers pick up the psychological principles that professionals take six or more years to master. Often family members have the same strengths in analysis and persistence as the individual with anorexia and these can be used to good effect. The more heads that are used in this process, the better. We cannot emphasise enough the importance of a consistent joint approach.

How you can adapt family life around the illness

It is a natural human response to care for someone who is sick and to somewhat spoil them. For short-term viral illnesses, this helps recovery. However, for longer-term emotional problems, the reverse can be true. We pose some questions about processes that commonly occur and suggest why they can be harmful.

Questions: Does the individual with an Eating Disorder (Edi) dictate to you about what, when and how you eat? Are you bullied about when and how you can use the kitchen and/or bathroom? Perhaps you are controlled by Edi about what, when and how you shop? Or about when and how mealtimes are arranged? Or about portions or ingredients?

The downside of walking on eggshells and submitting to the control of the 'anorexic minx' is that anorexia bullying is rewarded. It is gratifying to have people obeying our commands. A trap is sprung.

> *Questions: Are you covering up or turning a blind eye to the negative consequences of Edi behaviour: clearing up mess, dealing with bathroom problems, buying more food, cooking a meal that you know is nutritionally inadequate? Perhaps you are turning a blind eye to anti-social behaviour, such as hoarding, stealing or addictions?*

Ignoring or covering up unpleasant aspects of the eating disorder prevents learning about negative consequences and then working on and encouraging change in Edi.

> *Questions: Perhaps you have been giving constant reassurance to questions such as 'Will I get fat by eating this?' Or have you been sucked into obsessional rituals or compulsive concerns?*

The problem with providing reassurance on tap or finding ways of avoiding anxiety in Edi is that you prevent Edi developing effective emotional regulation. You become their shield against the world. Edi will become dependent on you to feel safe, make decisions on their behalf and may then resent being so trapped. Try to encourage flexibility and growth of independent thinking in Edi. Remember the saying: 'What you practise, you become'.

Your reaction to the illness

Eating disorder symptoms and their consequences, such as changes in personality and deterioration in physical health may lead you, as a carer, to react in particular ways. It is understandable that responses can be the source of hostile or critical confrontations occurring in both professional and family settings. Unfortunately, the result may be that Edi feels increasingly alienated and stigmatised, retreating further into their eating disorder behaviour.

Animal metaphors (jellyfish, ostrich, kangaroo, rhinoceros, terrier) help to explain how these instinctive reactions can be unhelpful. A veritable menagerie emerges as we metamorphose from one animal state to another in a desperate attempt to remedy the situation. Each animal analogy may be your default way of coping with stress, or part of your natural temperament, for example, acting in an over-protective, logical, overtly emotional or avoidant manner. In order to change these responses, you may have to challenge yourself and experiment with trying out new responses which do not feel natural or spontaneous. Don't worry if you do not succeed at first. Try and remember to keep looking to the bigger picture. You need to make plans to avoid falling into these traps. Remember, 'if you fail to plan, you plan to fail', so put in time and effort and get support yourself in order to regulate some of your own emotionally driven behaviours. This will not be easy, so remember 'every mistake is a treasure', which gives you more information to learn from.

The jellyfish: too much emotion and too little control

Some carers may be unable to regulate their own intense emotional responses to the anorexia. Their distress and anger is transparent to all. In this sea of emotion it is hard to steer a clear path. Also, like a jellyfish overt anger and anxiety can exert a poisonous sting with the same emotions being mirrored in Edi. Unfortunately, this serves to strengthen the anorexic hold. The downside is that these 'sad and mad' emotions escalate, causing tears, tempers, sleepless nights and exhaustion in all parties.

It can be hard to regulate your emotional reaction if you hold some false interpretations about the anorexia, i.e. have high levels of self-blame or perfectionist expectations about your role as a parent. It is also hard to regulate emotions when you are tired, tense and stressed. Ask yourself the following questions in two ways, as yourself and as if you are a kind, compassionate friend looking on at yourself.

- Reflect on your jellyfish tendencies. How do they make you feel?
- What are the effects of these responses on yourself? On others?
- How important is it that you work on your 'jellyfish' responses?
- If you were advising a friend with the same problem, what would your advice be? How would you help them take the step to change their jellyfish behaviour?
- What beliefs do you need to work on in order for this change to happen?
- How can you protect yourself from getting total emotional burnout?
- Brainstorm scheduling some fun into your life and ways to nurture yourself. This may be through a hobby, seeing friends or taking a walk while listening to music. Try writing your ideas down and then timetable this relax and recharge time into each day. Another plus side to this approach is Edi will learn to find ways of coping when you are away.
- The fact that you are reading these worksheets shows that you are open to new ideas. Well done!

TOP TIP

- If your emotional reaction is taking over, this will be mirrored and exaggerated by Edi. So rather like the safety advice in an aircraft, where in case of an emergency you are advised to put your own life jacket or oxygen mask on first, do look after your own stress first.

- If you role model self-care and compassion, this will help Edi think about their own self-care as a first step towards change. If possible, try to work on coming up with ideas on how **you** can achieve some 'me' time. Remember the importance of your own wellbeing in both your physical and mental health. Well done for considering taking the first step.

The ostrich: avoidance of emotion

The ostrich finds it hard to cope with the volcanic situation which often arises when trying to tackle the difficult problem of anorexia. Emotions and the complexities of human behaviour are too chaotic and confusing. The ostrich literally prefers to put his head down into the sand. This is something he knows he confidently can do, avoiding what seems too hard. The downside is that Edi may misinterpret this approach, seeing you as uncaring and ending up feeling unloved. Self-esteem is sapped away. Additionally, the concealment of emotions sets an unhelpful example for Edi to follow. Setting an example of emotional honesty and spreading the concept that having emotions is normal and acceptable human behaviour, will aid Edi in coming to terms with their own difficulties with emotional expression. Living with others who can and are able to convey their feelings with words will aid Edi in changing their only way of articulating their own emotions (i.e. through food).

Ask yourself the following questions and answer these questions as if you are a kind compassionate friend looking on.

- Reflect on your ostrich tendencies. Have they succeeded in helping you and those you love feel safe and secure?
- Could you take steps to become less of an ostrich?
- Who can support you in experimenting with new responses and help you reflect on how you are doing in this non-ostrich role?
- What would you want this person to do/say? A list of suggestions is often useful.
- What do you think about involving others in helping you make changes?
- How do you feel about making these changes? Are you ready to take the baton and run with it?

TOP TIP

- Change can be difficult and uncomfortable. It may be worthwhile engaging the help of a supportive family member/friend to support you in your quest. Think about your own self-esteem and how role modelling confidence in facing rather than avoiding difficulties might help Edi experiment with changing their own behaviour. The fact you are reading this sheet and considering these questions is already a huge step. Well done!

The kangaroo: trying to make everything right

The kangaroo does everything to protect by taking over all aspects of Edi's life. They treat the sufferer with kid gloves, letting them jump into the kangaroo pouch in an effort to avoid any upset or stress. The downside of this type of caring is that Edi fails to learn how to approach and master life's challenges. Edi finds she/he only feels safe living in this limbo land suspended in a child-like role unable to visualise taking on the world in all its colour or the mantle of adulthood.

Ask yourself the following questions and also answer these questions as if you are a kind compassionate friend looking on.

- Reflect on your kangaroo responses. How are they working for you?
- What difficulties are you encountering? Give an example of what is not working for you.
- What aspects of your kangaroo behaviour can you experiment with?
- How important is it for you to address some of your kangaroo responses?
- Think back to one of your kangaroo behaviours in recent weeks. How can you change that behaviour a little? What would be the first step?

TOP TIP

- Change is tough: remember to congratulate yourself after having attempted the change! Taking safe risks is a key aspect of change. You may need to make the change with baby steps.
- Role modelling respect and confidence in the innate wisdom of Edi will help build her shattered self-esteem.

The rhinoceros: it uses force to win the day

Fuelled by stress, exhaustion and frustration, or simply one's own temperament, the rhino attempts to persuade and convince by argument and confrontation. The downside is that even when Edi does obey, confidence to do so without assistance is not developed. In fact, the more likely response to a rhino 'in a china shop' is to argue back with a strong anorexic voice. Unfortunately, the more the anorexic minx retaliates, the more the anorexia identity is consolidated and embedded.

Ask yourself the following questions and answer these questions as if you are a kind compassionate friend looking on.

- Reflect on your rhinoceros responses. Are they working for you?
- What difficulties are you encountering?
- How can you avoid these obstacles?
- What might be the repercussions of changing your rhino response, both positive and negative?

- Whilst contracts work in a 'crisis situation', try to motivate and encourage Edi to grow their own garden of independent thinking by letting them make decisions and come up with innovative solutions.
- What can you do for yourself to lower your anxiety, stress or anger levels?
Set a goal for yourself with regards to this. How do you think this will make you feel?

TOP TIP

- Remember that the more you argue for change, the more it gives Edi the opportunity to argue for no change. This allows anorexia to embed itself more deeply. A key skill is allowing Edi the opportunity to present her/his own arguments as to why change is needed.

The terrier: it uses persistence (often criticism)

The terrier persistently criticises, cajoles, nags and tries to wear out the anorexic minx. The downside of this terrier type behaviour is that either Edi tunes out to what they perceive as irritating white noise, or it serves to sap morale so Edi loses the inner resource to face the rich tapestry of life without an anorexic identity.

Look at the following questions and answer them from the perspective of a kind compassionate friend looking on.

- Reflect on your terrier tendencies. How do they make you and the family feel? Are they working and helping Edi feel safe enough to leave AN?
- What are the effects of this terrier response on yourself? And on others?
- How important is it that you work on your 'terrier' type behaviour?
- If you were advising a friend with the same problem, what would your advice be?
- How can you develop more rewarding communication? A key skill is trying to listen to what Edi might be struggling to say.
- What beliefs do you need to work on in order for this change to happen?
- How can you take steps to be an active listener?
- The fact that you are reading these worksheets shows that you are open to new ideas. Well done! What specifically can you do now to get started with these different patterns of responding?

TOP TIP

- The anorexia itself is rather like a terrier constantly criticising Edi, saying she/he is not good enough and needs to try harder.
- Role modelling active listening and reflection with compassion and sensitivity with the positive will help Edi take this stance with her anorexic voice.

Inspirational animals

Of all the animals in the animal kingdom, we want you to aspire to be a dolphin, for its wisdom and hands-off form of support; and a St Bernard dog, for warmth and compassion in the face of danger.

The dolphin: just enough caring and control

An optimal way of helping someone with an eating disorder is to gently nudge them along. Imagine your daughter/son is at sea. The anorexic identity is their life vest. They are unwilling to give up the safety of this life vest while living in the frozen wasteland of anorexia. You are the dolphin, nudging them to safety, at times swimming ahead, leading the way, showing them new vistas, at other times swimming alongside with encouragement, or even quietly swimming behind.

The St Bernard: just enough compassion and consistency

Another optimal caring response is one of calmness, warmth and compassion. This involves accepting and processing the pain resulting from what is lost through anorexia and developing reserves of kindness, gentleness and love. The St Bernard instils hope in Edi they can change, that there is a future full of possibility beyond the eating disorder. The St Bernard responds consistently. He is unfailing, reliable and dependable in all circumstances. He has a good antenna attuned to the welfare and safety of those who are lost: calm, warm and nurturing.

TOP TIP

- Another metaphor that carers have found helpful is to think of how a herd of elephants cares for its young. Everyone in the herd contributes in some way. Do not fall into the trap of getting isolated yourself. Enlarge your team as much as possible but make sure you have a shared strategy. The eating disorder can easily 'divide and rule'. Ensure that you have a collaborative approach with respect and mutual support for each other.

These first steps you have taken to wisely manage your own emotional reactions and get support, not only help you but they show by example the type of things that the individual herself may need to do to recover. Next you may be in a better position to provide a nudging type of support.

How to be an effective mentor to support change

The following ideas are derived from established psychological principles about ways of helping people change. The process involves gentle guidance and compassionate coaching. Some of the suggestions focus on what you, as a carer, can do to maintain a helpful stance when faced with the challenges of the anorexic minx. Some other suggestions focus on how you can support Edi to come up with their own strategies for change.

- Helping someone to change is not easy. Nagging (terrier), imposing change (rhino), or doing it for them (kangaroo) by making suggestions or commands about what to eat hinders change if someone has mixed feelings. It may push them in the opposite direction.
- Rather it helps to have a positive outlook in mind (think of the smiling face of a dolphin). Write a letter or notes and keep a log about their positive attributes, things that make you love them, things that make them special and make you smile to capture and relish positive moments. Look to the past to find positive moments; perhaps find photos to hold that memory in mind.
- Edi may be more comfortable and able to talk about change in certain settings/situations. For example, if the family home is currently a place of conflict, somewhere neutral (a park bench, somewhere outside) may evoke more confidence or readiness in Edi to consider talk about change.
- Emotions can be difficult for Edi to express or regulate when in 'flight, fight or freeze mode'. You may be able to label the emotion (one of the first steps in regulating emotions) and validate the experience by using your empathy and emotional wisdom. This actively demonstrates that emotions can be understood and managed rather than avoided.
- Be alert for any glimmers of change, or talk about change. Pay special attention to these 'windows of opportunity' increases the odds that more change will happen. Keep motivating Edi. Recovering from an eating disorder is a journey, not a destination.
- Have conversations where you gently encourage Edi to talk about what they can do to help facilitate a change in their behaviour. The best approach is to elicit from Edi their own strategies. The following questions may help. What can they visualise themselves doing in the future? What advice would they give a friend in a similar situation? Have they read about strategies that have worked for other people? Suggest drawing two ruler scales. Label one scale 'readiness or confidence to change' and the second scale 'ability to see a change through'. Ask Edi what score they would give themselves out of 10 on each of these scales. Then ask Edi what would help them have a higher score? Can you help them achieve this higher score? Could Edi imagine making a small change today? Revisiting and revising these motivation scales can be a helpful way of reviewing progress and keeping the momentum towards recovery going.
- Remember anorexia is not just about food. Change involves becoming more flexible and able to see the bigger picture. It involves becoming more mindful about emotional factors. It also means being able

to see things from many perspectives. It involves reconnecting with other people. So be on the lookout for a desire to engage with these behaviours and then start to make plans with baby steps about how to start the approach. Making plans in great detail as if designing a storyboard, visualising each step is both useful and plays to the strengths of 'super-organiser' individuals.

- Encourage Edi to write down plans and goals helps them to step back from the confusion of mixed feelings. Additionally, noting down their aspirations and future ambitions will help them at a time when the bigger picture is lost and their world has narrowed to eating, food, weight and calories.

Pearls of wisdom

Nobody gets it right all of the time. In challenging times it is important to remember the adage, 'every mistake is a treasure'; and as Martin Luther King Jr. said, 'You don't have to see the whole staircase – just take the first step'.

Further reading

Treasure, J., Smith, G., & Crane, A. (2017). *Skills-Based Learning for Caring for a Loved One with an Eating Disorder* (2nd edition). London and New York: Routledge.

Langley, J., Todd, Gill, & Treasure, J. (expected 2018). *Training Manual for Skills- Based Caring for a Loved One with an Eating Disorder*.

Treasure, J. & Alexander, J. (2013). *Anorexia Nervosa: A Recovery Guide for Sufferers, Families and Friends* (2nd edition). London and New York: Routledge.

National Institute for Health and Care Excellence. Eating disorders: recognition and treatment. 23rd of May 2017. nice.org.uk/guidance/ng69.

www.b-eat.co.uk/?gclid=CMbPntP0gNQCFW4R0wodINkPeg.

Writing in therapy

Introduction

Over the course of your therapy your therapist will ask you to do a number of written experiments. Here we explain why we think this is helpful for people with anorexia.

If the idea of writing things down worries you in any way, please discuss your concerns with your therapist. This approach may not suit everyone.

Why use writing in anorexia?

1   Many people with anorexia nervosa are rather shy and private people who find it hard to talk frankly about topics of a personal nature. You may find it hard to trust other people, including your therapist, with your innermost thoughts and feelings. People with anorexia also often have very high standards for themselves and think that to express more difficult and perhaps somewhat negative thoughts and feelings about other people, is somehow disloyal. **Writing, rather than talking about these issues, may be easier – at least that is what a lot of our patients tell us**.

2   Moreover, when you write about somebody or something that is troubling you, you go on a journey of discovery by yourself and you can involve your therapist as much or as little as you want. The **writing experiments which we will introduce you to will teach you skills** which you can apply to any tricky situation later in your life where you are confused, unable to work out your thoughts and feelings and/or find it hard to talk to someone else.

3   Lastly, people with anorexia often are very exceptionally good at being focused and precise and pay a lot of attention to detail. What they sometimes lack is the ability to switch perspective and to see the bigger picture. You may ask – why does this matter? With any life problem, but especially with interactions between people to be able to look at the issues from different perspectives can help a great

deal in understanding things, coming to terms with upsetting things, finding new meanings and new solutions. To be able to see the bigger picture rather than to be stuck in a morass of small detail can also be really helpful in finding more creative, bold solutions to entrenched difficulties. **Writing can** be a great help with this and can **make your thinking style more flexible and help you to see the 'bigger picture' in life**.

The scientific basis of expressive writing

A number of different researchers have studied the effects of writing.

One of them, James Pennebaker, a psychologist from the United States, has done research studies where he has asked people to write about current or past stresses, traumas or difficulties in their life. All his studies have included comparison groups of people who were given a plausible control task, which involved writing about something non-emotional (such as writing about how they managed their time). Time and again, Dr Pennebaker has shown that the **people who were asked to write about some of the past or present difficulties in their life do better than those given a control task**. Other researchers in this area have shown that you do not necessarily need to write about upsetting or traumatic areas of your life, but that instead to focus on positive aspects of your life and future can also be very beneficial.

The effects of this writing are widespread.

For example, there are positive **effects on the immune system** and on other indicators of improved physical health and there is a **reduction in stress levels**. There have also been a number of long-term psychological benefits such as **improvements in mood**. Lastly, in a number of studies, people have been found to do **better at school or work** and got on better with other people.

What are the effective ingredients of writing?

- **Being open and honest**: The more you are open and honest with yourself during writing, talking about positive and negative thoughts and feelings, the more you are likely to experience benefits from writing.
- **Don't write to please or impress others**: Writing should not be done to please a reader. So if you are an English graduate or a journalist and are writing with an eye on an audience, this is less likely to be helpful.
- **It is fine to keep a secret**: Writing has been found to be helpful, whether it was shared with other people or not. So if you want to keep some of your writing a secret, that is fine. The important thing is to be honest with yourself.

- **Switching perspective**: This seems to be really important. So if you are writing about something and you see it entirely from your own perspective, to become able to see if from other people's perspective too is the helpful 'ingredient'. Alternatively, if you are just used to thinking about something that has happened to you from the perspective of other people, but not about your own wishes, needs, thoughts and feelings, then to become aware of these will be helpful. Some of the writing experiments we will ask you to do have been designed specifically to help you switch perspective.
- **Constructing a coherent story**: Sometimes people are very confused about some of their relationships or something that has happened to them. Writing about a particular topic, especially if done repeatedly, can often help the person understand what is going on much better, find a meaning in what has happened and this is helpful.

Some potential concerns about expressive writing

These are minor concerns but they need to be mentioned nonetheless.

- **Getting emotional after writing**: When people write about something that was very upsetting for them, it can make them rather emotional straight afterwards. However, this usually settles down quite quickly, and the longer-term effect of writing is that it improves mood. If you plan what to write about together with your therapist, you will minimise the risk of getting overly upset by a writing task.
- **Unwanted readers**: The second concern is that someone around you may read what you have written and that this may cause upset to both of you. If this is a risk, do your writing and destroy what you have written afterwards. You do not need to keep what you have written for it to be beneficial.

What to write

Dr Pennebaker showed that writing about anything that is emotionally significant to a person can be helpful, whether this is something from the past or the present, especially if it is about things that you haven't been able to share much with other people. Your therapist will work with you to decide on writing experiments that you might find interesting and helpful. If while you are writing you find yourself going off into a different topic that seems important, just go with the flow. The important thing is that you keep writing about things that are significant and meaningful to you. If you find yourself getting bored or veering off into mundane descriptions of everyday life, switch topics.

Does it matter if there are mistakes or errors in my writing?

No it doesn't. We do not want you to produce A Grade essays. The more raw and heartfelt what you write is, the more likely it is that you are touching on important thoughts and feelings. Research has also shown that writing by hand may be more beneficial than writing something on the computer. This is mainly because for most people, it requires additional mental energy to type. If you are very proficient at typing, doing your writing on the computer should be fine.

I don't feel ready to write about certain things in my life

If you are not ready to write about something, don't write about it. Only write about things that you are happy to think about more deeply.

Practical aspects of writing

Writing is meant to be part of a healing process and therefore to create a healing environment for yourself is important. Some people may want to write at home in a particular place, perhaps listening to a particular piece of music at the time that allows them to be calm and focussed. Others find that writing at home they are likely to get disrupted, and perhaps going to a public library or in the summer to sit in the park may be a more helpful environment.

After the writing put your papers in a safe place, have a cup of tea, a bath, listen to music, get some fresh air, whatever you feel is helpful to soothe yourself. Engaging in a writing experiment may stir up emotions. This can sometimes mean that you may feel worse at first before you start feeling better. So do look after yourself in this process to get safely to the other side. Be curious about the nature of the emotions. What is it that you are feeling? What does that tell you? If you become too distressed to continue writing, please stop and gather yourself with the preceding techniques and go back to it when you feel able to do so. If you are not able to, leave it and discuss it with your therapist in the coming session.

Further reading

James W. Pennebaker (2004). *Writing to Heal: A Guided Journal for Recovering from Trauma and Emotional Upheaval*. Oakland, CA, USA: New Harbinger Publications.

Writing experiment sheet

PLANNING THE EXPERIMENT:

> **Insert description of experiment:**

SOME POINTS/ QUESTIONS TO COVER:

- **How ready are you to do this writing experiment?**

1	2	3	4	5	6	7	8	9	10

- **How confident are you that you can do this writing experiment?**

1	2	3	4	5	6	7	8	9	10

- **I predict the outcome of doing the experiment to be**............

  ....

- **Obstacles that might get in the way of me completing the experiment**..

  ....

- **How I might overcome the obstacles** ....

....
(Use what you have learned in Chapter 6, and make a WOOP to help you here.)

- **I will make time on** ....**(insert date and time) to do the experiment**

- **I will conduct the experiment in** ....

........................**(where)**

REFLECTION

Immediately after completing your writing experiment, rate the following on a scale of 0 to 10.

- To what degree did you express your deepest thoughts and feelings?

- To what degree do you currently feel sad or upset?

- To what degree do you currently feel happy?

- To what degree was today's writing valuable and meaningful for you?

Now spend a few minutes (not more than three or four) writing down how your writing went today.

What did you learn?

Emotions diary

Recognising and putting my feelings into words, learning what I need and how to soothe myself.

Trigger	Thoughts and images	My experience:	What words can I put to my	Self-soothing
• Where am I? • Who am I with? • What am I doing?	• What am I thinking? • What image comes to mind?	Consider any/all of the following that most help you connect with your experience: • Where in my body do I sense the feelings (e.g. head, chest, stomach)? • What texture sums up the feeling? • What colour or temperature depicts the feeling?	feelings? e.g. Anxious, scared, tired, happy, low, worried, annoyed, excited, hopeful. How intense is this feeling? (0–100)	• What do I need right now? • How can I respond to this? e.g. asking for support, listening to music, writing down my feelings, crying, hugging a comforting object or just allowing myself the space to feel this way.

Traffic light relapse prevention plan

My relapse signs	Green week	Amber week	Healthy response	Red week	Healthy response

Index

Note: Page numbers in *italics* indicate figures and in **bold** indicate tables on the corresponding pages.